International Communications

International Communications

A Media Literacy Approach

Art Silverblatt and Nikolai Zlobin

M.E.Sharpe
Armonk, New York
London, England

Library of Congress Cataloging-in-Publication Data

Silverblatt, Art.
International communications : a media literacy approach / Art Silverblatt and
Nikolai Zlobin.
   p. cm.
Includes bibliographical references and index.
ISBN 0-7656-0974-6 (cloth: alk. paper) — ISBN 0-7656-0975-4 (pbk.: alk. paper)
   1. Communication, International. 2. Mass media criticism. I. Zlobin, Nikolai, 1957–
II. Title.

P96.I5S55 2004
302.2—dc22

2003061437

Printed in the United States of America

The paper used in this publication meets the minimum requirements of
American National Standard for Information Sciences
Permanence of Paper for Printed Library Materials,
ANSI Z 39.48-1984.

BM (c)   10   9   8   7   6   5   4   3   2   1
BM (p)   10   9   8   7   6   5   4   3   2   1

To Jack
And to the media literacy students at Webster University,
who have taught me so much

—Art

To Klara

—Nikolai

Contents

II. Comparative Analysis: National Media Systems

III. Applications of International Media Communications

Figures, Photos, and Tables

Figures

Photos

Tables

Preface

International communications textbooks generally are modeled after introduction to mass communications texts, which provide extensive information on the histories and characteristics of media systems around the world. This text comes from the tradition of media literacy, which, in addition to the above, focuses on the critical analysis of international communications.

At the same time, this book expands the scope of media literacy by extending the principles of media literacy to the study of international communications.

Organization of the Text

The introduction consists of an overview of international communications, as well as a discussion of the definition and principles of media literacy.

Part I presents approaches to the study of international communications. The text builds on the methodological framework outlined in *Media Literacy: Keys to Interpreting Media Messages,* by Art Silverblatt (2001). While the *Media Literacy* text focused on ways to make sense of American media, in this text, the methodological framework is applied to international communications.

Although a familiarity with *Media Literacy* is helpful, the presentation of the media literacy concepts in this text should provide you with the necessary theoretical tools for the analysis of international communications. For those who are already familiar with the concepts, the brief discussion in this text should act as a helpful review.

Part II focuses on national media systems. Chapter 6 presents a set of criteria that help students identify the characteristics of national media systems. This information is invaluable in assessing media content from these countries. Chapter 7 consists of a series of case studies from media professionals around the world, who describe the media systems in their countries using the criteria defined in the chapter.

Part III considers various applications of international media literacy. Chapter 8 applies the strategies of media literacy to a major form of global communications: advertising. Chapter 9 contains examples of media literacy analysis by students. These applications should be useful for students interested in seeing how the concepts outlined in the text can be applied to analysis of media content.

Each chapter is divided into two parts. The first section outlines the basic principles of the chapter. This is followed by a section focusing on lines of inquiry, which offers specific approaches to the analysis of international media presentations.

Definition of Terms

Defining the following terms will clarify the information presented in the text:

- *Media:* A channel of mass communication that enables a media communicator to convey information to a mass audience separated in time and space from the media communicator. The major channels of mass media are print, photography, radio, film, television, and the Internet. Other, less obvious forms of media include billboards, video games, designer clothing labels, and product packaging.
- *Media presentation:* A specific media program (e.g., newspaper, magazine article, film, or Web page). Also referred to as *production, programming, text,* and *content.*
- *National media presentation:* Programming that is produced in a particular country. Examples would include films made in India or a newspaper published in Pakistan. Also referred to as *domestic media presentation* or *local media presentation.*
- *Media communicator:* The person (or organization) responsible for constructing and disseminating information through the channels of mass communication. Examples include newspaper reporters, film directors, and Time Warner. Also referred to as *producer.*
- *Media messages:* The underlying themes or ideas contained in a media presentation.

Acknowledgments

We would like to acknowledge the following media scholars who contributed monographs describing media systems in their countries: Juyan Zhang, Shahira S. Fahmy, Dharma N. Adhikari, Berle Francis, Takashi Yasuda, Natalia Angheli, Geoff Lealand, Aleksander Grigoryev, and Maretha de Waal.

Many thanks to Monica Wallin, Melissa Waugh, Patsy Zettler, and Steven Schoen for allowing us to include their excellent examples of media literacy analysis in the book.

We would also like to thank the following international students attending Webster University who provided invaluable input on culture-specific nonverbal behaviors: Sandra Basso (Croatia), Miguel Basso (Portugal), Juan Hernandez (Mexico), E.M. (Bosnia), and N.S. (Pakistan/America).

We are also grateful to Lee Kuehner for his outstanding work as photographer during the project.

Niels Aaboe, editor at M.E. Sharpe, has been extremely helpful in the production of the book.

And finally, special thanks go to Anne Bader, research assistant, for her remarkable persistence, professionalism, and ingenuity.

International Communications

1

Introduction

International Media Literacy

The world has moved into an unprecedented stage of human development—the era of global communications. In the past, national boundaries have impeded our ability to imagine communities beyond our
borders. Benedict Anderson declares:

> The nation is imagined as limited because even the largest of them, en-
> compassing perhaps a billion living human beings, has finite, if elastic
> boundaries, beyond which lie other nations. No nation imagines itself
> coterminous with mankind. The most messianic nationalists do not dream
> of a day when all the members of the human race will join their nation in
> the way that it was possible, in certain epochs, for, say, Christians to dream
> of a wholly Christian planet.
>   . . . It is imagined as a community, because, regardless of the actual
> inequality and exploitation that may prevail in each, the nation is al-
> ways conceived as a deep, horizontal comradeship. Ultimately it is this
> fraternity that makes it possible, over the past two centuries, for so many
> millions of people, not so much to kill, as willingly to die for such lim-
> ited imaginings.[1]

However, innovations in media technology such as the Internet and communications satellites have obliterated these traditional borders. As
United Nations secretary-general Kofi Annan observes, "Today's real
borders are not between nations, but between powerful and powerless,
free and fettered, privileged and humiliated."[2] Thanks to media technology, people are now engaged in daily conversations across the globe.
For instance, during 2000, an estimated 400 million people communicated and conducted business online. These channels of mass communication have the potential to bring people together who share common
beliefs, attitudes, backgrounds, and experiences. To illustrate, media
technology empowers political activists to organize at levels once avail-

3

able only to governments. In October 2002, individuals opposed to the impending U.S.-led invasion of Iraq built an antiwar coalition throughout the world by exchanging the following message via e-mail:

> Stand for Peace.
> War is NOT the Answer.
> Today we are at a point of imbalance in the world and are moving toward what may be the beginning of a THIRD WORLD WAR. If you are against this possibility, the UN is gathering signatures in an effort to avoid a tragic world event. Please COPY (rather than Forward) this e-mail in a new message, sign at the end of the list, and send it to all the people whom you know.
> If you receive this list with more than 500 names signed, please send a copy of the message to: unicwash@unicwash.org
> Even if you decide not to sign, please consider forwarding the petition on instead of eliminating it.

This message crisscrossed the globe. One of the threads originated in France and found its way to sympathizers in Switzerland, Scotland, Sweden, Finland, New Zealand, England, Ecuador, Hong Kong, South Africa, Spain, Argentina, Chile, Mexico, Belgium, the Netherlands, Denmark, Germany, and a number of cities throughout the United States. This form of "virtual social activism" played a significant role in the rise of the international antiwar movement.

In addition, small revolutions occur every day around the world, thanks to the media. To illustrate, in the remote town of Robatkarim, Iran, students instituted an environment project on the Internet, researching information and programs that convinced their parents and their school to start a trash recycling program.

International media have even emerged as a factor in the geopolitical arena. In November 2001, the United States captured members of the Taliban in Afghanistan and took them to Guántanamo Bay, Cuba. Initially, there was little critical discussion on the part of the American press regarding the treatment of the prisoners. However, photographs showing the prisoners locked in six- by eight-foot open-air, chain-link cages were published by the British press. These photos launched a global campaign to pressure the U.S. government to grant the prisoners basic amenities, as stipulated by the Geneva Accords. Finally, the United States modified its policy, granting the captives status as prisoners of war and distributing copies of the Koran among them.

A number of private organizations also furnish information to countries that face government restrictions on information. As an example, Washington ProFile (WPF) is a Russian-language agency that furnishes news and analysis to Russian speakers around the world. It features exclusive material, including news, statistics, and interviews from the United States; a fully searchable archive; and a subscriber database of over 30,000 media outlets and individuals. Information from WPF is read by millions of people across the former Soviet Union, including leading research organizations, ministries, military personnel, and political leaders.

However, universal *access* to the media should not be confused with media literacy. Media literacy is a critical thinking skill that is applied to the source of most of our information—the channels of mass communication. This discipline provides strategies that enable you to analyze and discuss the information being conveyed over the global channels of mass communication. Media-literate individuals have learned to develop a critical distance from the information they receive through the media, so that they are in a position to make independent judgments about: (1) what programming they choose to watch, read, or hear, and (2) how to interpret the information that they receive through the channels of mass communication.

Thomas Friedman provides a striking example of the need to develop a critical approach to media messages:

> An Indonesian working for the U.S. Embassy in Jakarta, who had just visited the Islamic fundamentalist stronghold of Jogjakarta, told me this story: "For the first time I saw signs on the streets there saying things like, 'The only solution to the Arab-Israel conflict is jihad if you are true Muslim, register yourself to be a volunteer.' I heard people saying, 'We have to do something, otherwise the Christians or Jews will kill us.' When we talked to people to find out where [they got these ideas], they said from the Internet. They took for granted that anything they learned from the Internet is true. They believed in a Jewish conspiracy and that 4,000 Jews were warned not to come to work at the World Trade Center [on September 11]. It was on the Internet."
>
> At its best, the Internet can educate more people faster than any media tool we've ever had. At its worst, it can make people dumber faster than any media tool we've ever had. The lie that 4,000 Jews were warned not to go into the World Trade Center on September 11 was spread entirely

over the Internet and is now thoroughly believed in the Muslim world. Because the Internet has an aura of "technology" surrounding it, the uneducated believe information from it even more. They don't realize that the Internet, at its ugliest, is just an open sewer: an electronic conduit for untreated, unfiltered information.[7]

As applied to international communications, media literacy can be defined as follows:

Understanding the Process of Mass Communication

Media literacy focuses attention on the production, transmission, and interpretation of media messages: who is constructing the message, what the function (or purpose) of the message is, and how the audience interprets the content.

An Awareness of the Impact of the Media on the Individual and Society

The media have revolutionized the ways we think about each other, our world, and ourselves. Media literacy focuses on the global impact of international media systems on the attitudes, values, and behaviors of traditional societies.

The Development of Strategies with Which to Analyze and Discuss Media Messages

Manifest messages are direct and clear to the audience. We generally have little trouble recognizing these messages when we are paying full attention to a media presentation. However, *latent messages* are indirect and beneath the surface and, consequently, escape our immediate attention. Latent messages may reinforce manifest messages or may convey an entirely independent meaning. In addition, *cumulative messages* occur with such frequency over time that they can convey recurring meanings, independent of any individual production with regard to gender roles, violence, definitions of success, and racial and cultural stereotypes. These cumulative messages are reinforced through the countless hours of media programming.

These strategies for analyzing media messages can facilitate the discussion of media content with others—including children, peers, and the people responsible for producing media programming.

An Awareness of Media Content as a Cultural "Text"

A country's media system is in large measure a reflection of its political, economic, and cultural systems. The study of international communications can furnish perspective into the prevailing cultural, historical, political, economic, religious, and legal sensibilities of a country. And conversely, the study of national media systems can provide insight into a country's history, culture, political system, and economic structure.

Understanding the Range of Media Systems Around the World

There are significant differences in the ways that individual countries construct messages and disseminate information through the media. The distinctive characteristics of a nation's media system has an impact on the content of its films, television shows, newspapers, and Web pages it produces. At the same time, international media literacy makes it possible to identify common features in the media systems of different countries.

The Cultivation of an Enhanced Enjoyment, Understanding, and Appreciation of Media Content

Media literacy should not be understood merely as an opportunity to bash the media. A well-produced media presentation can be enormously worthwhile, exposing you to different ideas and cultures. Media literacy should not detract from your enjoyment of programs. Indeed, critical interpretation should enhance your enjoyment and appreciation of media at its best: insightful articles, informative news programs, and uplifting films.

In the Case of International Media Communicators: The Ability to Produce Effective and Responsible Media Messages

In order to be effective in a global arena, media communicators must demonstrate an awareness of the challenges presented by communicating with a global audience. And further, in order to improve the media industry, media communicators must recognize the responsibilities involved in producing pogramming that serves the best interests of the public.

I

Media Literacy
Approaches to
International
Communications

2

Process

Function

The channels of mass communication are, in themselves, neither good nor evil. What determines whether a media message is positive or negative is its *function*, or purpose for sending or receiving a message. For example, the media can introduce people to a range of new ideas. In Tanzania, which has been ravaged by the AIDS epidemic, information about prevention has been incorporated into a popular radio soap opera, *Twende na Wakati* (Let's Go with the Times). This strategy has been so successful that three-fourths of the program listeners have altered their sexual behavior.[1]

But all too often, the channels of international mass communication simply reinforce preexisting opinions and ways of seeing the world. Thomas Friedman explains:

> Just when you might have thought you were all alone with your extreme views, the Internet puts you together with a community of people from around the world who hate all the things and people you do. And you can scrap the BBC and just get your news from those Web sites that reinforce your own stereotypes.[2]

Therefore, identifying the communications function is crucial in deciding how to interpret media content. The *manifest* function of the communication offers the obvious or primary reason of the media presentation. However, there may also be *latent* functions; that is, instances in which the media communicator's intention may not be immediately evident to the audience. To illustrate, the Russian TV show *Naked News* features young, attractive anchorwomen who disrobe while presenting the news of the day. Although the manifest function of this program is to convey information, the not-so-subtle latent function is to attract viewers.

The manifest function can divert the audience's attention from the latent function behind a message. For instance, in 2002, approximately 72 percent of children's Web sites collected personal information, which was then used for commercial purposes.[3] Thus, because the manifest function of a children's game on the Internet is to entertain or educate, children are not aware that its underlying purpose is to generate product sales.

A communication activity may be motivated by many functions, or purposes:

Information

The channels of mass communication can provide valuable information for people throughout the globe. As an example, Quechua-speaking peasants in Ecuador use the Internet to gather valuable crop information.[4]

Expression

In these situations, communicators inform the audience of their frame of mind—what they are thinking at that moment, how they are feeling, or their attitudes toward people and issues.

Description

This function refers to occasions in which the communicator elaborates on general statements or provides concrete examples.

Instruction

This function refers to those occasions in which the purpose is either to inform the audience about a subject with which they are unfamiliar or to furnish additional information about a subject with which they are already acquainted.

Entertainment

Jokes, stories, and gossip divert us from the more serious, pressing matters of the day. Humor is also a social mechanism that brings people together. Sharing laughter is a time-honored way to break down traditional barriers. As a result, speakers often begin their talks with an amusing anecdote in order to make their audience feel comfortable.

Creative Expression

Novelists, painters, and experimental videographers express themselves through their art and share their artistic vision with the audience.

Profit

The emergence of the transnational media industry as a for-profit enterprise has had an enormous impact on the production and dissemination of information throught the media. Increasingly, the drive to maximize profit influences the construction of media messages. Consequently, regardless of the manifest function of a media presentation (e.g., entertainment or information), profit is an important latent function. (For further discussion, see Chapter 3.)

Persuasion

For an example of persuasion in international communications, see the case study on propaganda at the end of this chapter (p. 45). At the same time, the media can also stimulate economic development in a region. For instance, Ecuadoran natives are now able to sell their crafts over the Web.[5]

Media Communicator

The media communicator is the person (or organization) responsible for constructing and disseminating information through the channels of mass communication. The media communicator makes choices that determine what the audience learns about a topic and how the audience interprets the information.

In print journalism, one clear-cut way to identify the point of view of the media communicator is to compare the editorial commentary in international newspapers. For instance, in May 2000, there was a serious military confrontation between India and Pakistan. Editorials from Pakistani and Indian newspapers reflect very different national perspectives on the crisis:

From **The Statesman**, *Peshawar, Pakistan*

The missile tests carried out by Pakistan were unavoidable in the current alarming situation arising from India's unabated aggressive posture and irresponsible threats at the highest level. The powers that have questioned the demonstration of national defense capability by Pakistan when it was most needed conveniently gloss over the feverishly pursued missile development program of the belligerent side.

Since the present crisis erupted in December last year Pakistan has exercised maximum restraint and continues to adhere to this policy, seeking dialogue and discussion with the neighbor to settle differences peacefully. It has responded positively to international counsel for bilateral talks to reduce tension and end the dangerous military confrontation on the borders.

New Delhi has done nothing to control extremist groups responsible for communal hatred and massacres in India. At the same time, it continues to blatantly defy international counsel for negotiations to address the Kashmir dispute. The international community needs to pressure the Indian leadership to see reason, give up the war hysteria and adopt the path of dialogue with Pakistan to address each other's concerns.[6]

From **Hindustan Times,** *New Delhi, India*

Few will be surprised by the disclosure by a U.S. Army spokesman that virtually the entire top leadership of al-Qaida and the Taliban is now in Pakistan. . . . India's External Affairs Minister Jaswant Singh was quite right, therefore, in saying that Pakistan is the new "epicentre" of international terrorism. This may well be the reason why the United States and the international community are currently more than willing to accept India's charges about cross-border terrorism.

Pakistan's dilemma is that it still believes that the jehadis can enable it to wrest Kashmir from India. . . . Kashmir, on the other hand, is part of a democracy and even its separatists are wary of outsiders. It is entirely possible that if calm is restored in the state with the elimination of terror, the logic of democracy will prevail with the holding of (hopefully) free and fair polls. Ironically, Pakistan, too, will go to the polls at about the same time. But it is unclear whether the logic of democracy will be allowed to assert itself there by the military junta with links with the terrorists.[7]

However, the point of view of the media communicator can also be found in the news sections of newspapers, as well as in advertising, entertainment programming, and television news broadcast. Caryn James provides the following example:

After taking a Taliban-guided tour into Southern Afghanistan last week, along with other Western journalists, Simon Ingram wrapped up his four-day experience for *BBC World News*. The cameras showed a crowd of village men in turbans, fists raised in anger as soldiers looked on.

"Within the Taliban stronghold of Kandahar is evidence of the challenge Washington is facing," Mr. Ingram said. He described the men chanting their allegiance to the Taliban and death to America and added, "No sign here that the intensifying American bombardment is achieving its goal." ABC's Dan Harris, who was also on the tour, summed up his experience for *Good Morning America*. He, too, said the villagers were angry at America but emphasized how friendly they were to him. "It's not that they're not bitter about the almost daily U.S. bombings," Mr. Harris said, in a warm and fuzzy tone. "They simply don't blame individual Americans."

The soft American and the stern British tone is typical of these reports, and the difference highlights the value of seeing the world from a broader perspective. If a priority of America's war on terror is holding a global coalition together, it helps to know, without sugarcoating, what the rest of the globe is thinking.[8]

Media content may reflect widely held cultural values and attitudes, as well as the embedded value system of a media communicator. Embedded values may appear in the text through such production techniques as editing decisions, point of view, and connotative words and images. To illustrate, an article by reporter Rick Lyman contains the following passage:

> Many believe that the recent trickle of Hollywood films into Chinese theaters, along with those illegal DVDs, has played a role in spurring yearnings for accelerated change among ordinary Chinese citizens. Images of prosperous, independent Westerners—if not explicitly standing up for their rights, at least dressed in cool style and living it up—might have a fundamental impact on this huge, complex society as it emerges from its *cocoon*.[9] (emphasis added)

The reporter's use of the phrase "in a cocoon" reflects his personal belief that China is an undeveloped country, which is moving from an unfavorable stage of evolution (i.e., traditional Chinese culture) to a superior stage of evolution (Western culture).

A familiarity with the media communicator, then, can add considerable insight into media messages. However, it is not always easy to identify who is the actual media communicator. We generally assume that the person in front of the camera or microphone is responsible for what is being said; however, this person is often simply an actor reading a script prepared by others, who are invisible to the audience. Further, media communicators are often separated both in time and space from their audience, making it more difficult to identify them.

But because media communicators are products of their own experiences, identifying the following demographic characteristics of the media communication can help put their contributions into meaningful perspective.

Nationality. For instance, during the 2002 Olympics the U.S. media primarily focused on their own competitors, covering events in which American athletes were regarded as favorites to win. In similar fashion, the Canadian media devoted considerable attention to a controversy in which the gold medal in figure skating was awarded to a Russian team rather than the Canadian entry. In both cases, the media underplayed the significance of the overall winners and losers and the notable accomplishments of athletes from other nations in order to cover their own athletes.

Level of expertise. Anyone who produces a media program or appears in a media presentation is instantly accorded the status of expert. But is this person truly qualified to speak authoritatively on the subject? The criteria for being considered an expert may vary in different countries. In Iran, clerics are automatically conferred with expert status, while in the United States celebrities often serve as spokespeople to promote particular causes or products. Moreover, experts may offer opinions on a wide range of topics outside their area of specialty. Consequently, it is important to consider whether the expert's contribution falls within his or her range of expertise.

Affiliation. Newspapers, television programs, and Internet sites often have political agendas and editorial policies that affect how they present information. In addition, media operations are often dependent on sources of funding (e.g., advertisers or the government) which can also influence how they present information. An article or television program may cite the sponsoring organization; however, there is rarely any accompanying information that provides information on who funds this organization, its mission, or ideology.

The challenge of identifying the media communicator is compounded in the arena of global communications. The sheer number of reporters, editors, filmmakers, and Webmasters makes it impossible to be familiar with all of their backgrounds, credentials, and orientations, as well as an acquaintance with the educational institutions where a foreign media communicator received his/her training.

Identifying Sources

Journalists frequently rely on sources—experts who provide analysis, clarification, or background on a subject. The same sources often appear repeatedly in the media. For instance, the lineup for the American Sunday morning television news shows on April 6, 2003, featured a familiar set of faces:

* *Meet the Press* (NBC): Deputy Defense Secretary Paul Wolfowitz and General Peter Pace, vice chairman, Joint Chiefs of Staff. 8 A.M.
* *Fox News Sunday:* Deputy Defense Secretary Paul Wolfowitz and Kanan Makiya, Iraqi National Congress. 9 A.M.
* *Face the Nation* (CBS): Deputy Defense Secretary Paul Wolfowitz. 9:30 A.M.
* *This Week* (ABC): General Peter Pace, vice chairman, Joint Chiefs of Staff, and Senators John Warner (R-VA) and Joseph Biden (D-DE) 10 A.M.
* *Late Edition* (CNN): General Peter Pace, vice chairman, Joint Chiefs of Staff, and Senators John Warner (R-VA) and Carl Levin (D-MI) 11 A.M.

Understanding *motive* is critical to putting a source's contributions into perspective: why has this source chosen to present information? For some politicians, appearing as a source is a way to gain public visibility and legitimacy, which can be helpful for campaigning and fund raising. In countries such as Russia, sources are sometimes paid for information. For example, in 2000, there were two underwater explosions on the submarine *Kursk.* Journalists were unable to obtain an official list of the crew members who died in the tragedy. However, reporters from *Komsomolskaya Pravda* bribed a navy officer for the names, in the amount of $300, and the paper published the list of names the next day.

The use of *anonymous sources* further complicates the identification of the media communicator. Using unnamed sources gives reporters wider access to information, while enabling informed individuals to supply information without fear of recrimination. In some countries, the media use anonymous sources routinely. For instance, correspondents for British TV news programs are not required to cite sources for their information.

In the United States, there is no constitutional protection or federal shield law that protects journalists from being forced to reveal their confidential sources. According to Don Corrigan, individual states can enact shield laws. "Thirty-one states have done so, but the laws are hard to enforce, and judges frequently ignore them when they do exist."[10] David H. Donaldson Jr. declares, "Until the reporter's qualified privilege is clearly recognized as a constitutional privilege . . . , the only protection that journalists have for their information and their relationship with their sources is their willingness . . . to fight the subpoenas and to go to jail to back up their promise of confidentiality."[11]

In 2002, a Texas writer was incarcerated for five months for defying a court order to provide notes and files to help police in a murder investigation. In the same year, a U.S. attorney's office notified the Associated Press (AP) that it had secured telephone records of an AP reporter to determine his source in a case involving leaked confidential Justice Department information.

However, the use of anonymous sources also makes it impossible for the reader to determine the credibility, affiliation, and motive of the person providing essential information. To illustrate, in April 2002, Crown Prince Abdullah of Saudi Arabia met with U.S. president George W. Bush to discuss the Middle East crisis. In an article published before the meeting, *New York Times* reporter Patrick Tyler wrote that "a person close to the crown prince" who was "familiar with the Saudi's thinking" disclosed that the crown prince planned to warn the president that, unless the United States reconsidered its unqualified support for Israel's military policies, the strategic relationship between their two countries would be threatened.[12] However, when the two leaders met, the warning never materialized.

Without knowing the source, columnist William Safire could only speculate about the possible motives behind this anonymous "misinformation campaign":

> 1. The Saudi source was an uninformed hothead, speaking with no authorization from anyone close to the ruler, deliberately misleading us with no concern about the effect his smoke-blowing would have on his credibility. Highly unlikely.
> 2. The Saudi source was indeed "familiar with" Abdullah's thinking, but that thinking changed radically in the day or two between the time the source spoke to the reporter and the time the Saudi ruler spoke to the president. Also unlikely.
> 3. The Saudi source was acting on Abdullah's direct instructions to panic the president into one-sidedly denouncing the Israelis and treating Yasir Arafat as victim rather than terrorist. In this scenario, Saudi threats to the U.S. economy and military deployment would be issued but not attributed, allowing the crown prince to get the intimidating benefit of a threat he was too sly or squeamish to deliver personally. Possible.

4. The Saudi source was trying to push Abdullah into getting tough with Bush. By putting out semiofficial word that Abdullah was "expected to tell" the president that America's oil supply and troop deployment were in jeopardy, he was putting pressure on the crown prince to issue just those warnings. Likely.[13]

Media communicators may be hampered by their ignorance of the history and culture of the countries with which they are interacting. Craig S. Smith provides the following example:

> Duncan Clark, a consultant based in Beijing, says locally hired secretaries are generally a better first line of defense for multinationals. He recalled that during his days at Morgan Stanley in Hong Kong the firm ordered expensive clocks to give as gifts commemorating the closing of a deal. The firm's local staff caught the mistake: to "give a clock" in Chinese sounds the same as "seeing someone off to his end."[14]

Media producers can avoid unintended errors and improve the effectiveness of their communication by diversifying their staffs from an international perspective. Staff members could either be centralized in one location or spread throughout the globe. Indeed, some companies have begun to hire firms that specialize in checking the language translation, graphics, and cultural nuances of presentations with a global outreach.

Ownership Patterns

The "ultimate" media communicator can be regarded as the entity (individual, government, or corporation) that owns the media production company. The owners make the major decisions (or oversee the decisions) that affect the production and distribution of media messages.

There are four basic types of global media ownership systems, each of which exercises a distinct influence on the construction of media messages: state ownership; public ownership; private ownership; and hybrid ownership.

State Ownership

In authoritarian countries such as China, Cuba, and North Korea, the media industry is controlled by the government. Under this system, television programs, radio shows, films, and newspapers, as well as books and magazines, are produced and distributed under the close supervision of the government.

State-owned media systems make up a sizable proportion of the worldwide media operations. According to the United Nations (UN) *Human Development Report 2002,* 29 percent of the world's largest newspapers are state-owned.[15]

State ownership systems operate on both the national and local level. For example, during the era of the Soviet Union, local newspapers and radio stations were part of a huge propaganda campaign originating in Moscow, giving a local twist to the national party line.

Under this system of ownership, the news information agencies belong to the state. For instance, in China, all news is filtered through the state news agency Xinhua. Even foreign news is channeled through these state news agencies. Surprisingly, a breadth of information can sometimes be found in the newspapers, television, and radio of these countries. Because independent sources of information are not available, stories are difficult to substantiate, which undermines public confidence in the media. But since people do not believe what they read in the papers or watch on television, the state does not have to be entirely scrupulous about the need to suppress information.

Under state ownership, editors, reporters, anchors, and television producers are government employees who are subject to state labor laws and practices. Because the state is the only employer, media communicators are unwilling to jeopardize their positions, knowing that they would be unable to find another job in the field. In addition, media communicators generally are members of the political establishment. For instance, in the former Soviet Union, all employees of the state media were required to be members of a political Communist organization (the Union of Journalists of USSR). This created a potential conflict of interest with regard to their coverage of governmental activities.

State-owned media systems are under no particular pressure to attract high audience ratings or generate advertising revenue through advertising. As a result, "official" state media content is very prescriptive, telling its audience what to think and how to act.

Public Ownership

Under a public system of ownership, the media are owned by the public but operated by the government. In countries such as Sweden, the Netherlands, and Kazakhstan, the revenue required to cover the operating costs of newspapers, television stations, and radio stations is generated through public taxes. Because of the public financing of the media, regulations and policies in many of these countries guarantee a diversity of sources of information. For example, Swedish law stipulates that at least two newspapers must be published in every town. Journalist Aleksander Grigoryev explains, "One newspaper is generally liberal, the second is conservative. In cases in which one of the papers (generally the liberal newspaper) is unprofitable, Swedish law stipulates that the town taxes and donations from the city go to support the struggling paper."[16]

The people responsible for producing media programming (e.g., writers, editors, and technicians) in a public system are civil servants who maintain a degree of autonomy from whatever political administration happens to be in office. Because the money to produce programs (and pay salaries) is generated by public financing, media producers are insulated from market pressures, so they are free to produce thoughtful quality programming. But this system can also promote an environment in which programming reflects only the narrow concerns and interests of the media communicator, ignoring the audience altogether.

Private Ownership

In countries such as the United States, newspapers, magazines, radio stations, film studios, and television stations are privately owned—either by individuals or, increasingly, by large, multinational corporations. Under this market-driven system, the primary purpose, or function, is to generate the maximum possible profit.

Private media ownership can take one of the following forms: local, national, regional, and transnational.

Local ownership. Throughout the world, a significant number of newspapers, television stations, and radio stations are owned by individuals or small, local companies. To illustrate, as of 2003, there are over 3,500 regional and city newspapers in Russia, with a total circulation of over 32 million copies. Twenty new local and regional media publications are registered in Russia every day.[17] Many of these local media companies are family-owned operations. For example, 24 percent of the radio stations across the globe are family-owned.[18]

Local media presentations provide information of interest to their community, such as weddings, highway improvements, and weekly school menus. These media communicators have a stake in their community and often exert considerable influence on public opinion.

Given the huge expenses associated with running a media operation, local media companies are often under enormous pressure to remain financially solvent. These media companies are primarily supported by local advertising. Indeed, newspapers, radio stations, and television networks may depend upon two or three major advertising accounts. Consequently, these media companies can be susceptible to pressure from these companies to include or omit information or to provide favorable news about their sponsors.

Because of their limited resources, local companies are often vulnerable to legal challenges. As a result, newspapers, magazines, and television news programs may be unwilling to run stories that could offend powerful interests for fear of incurring an expensive lawsuit.

Increasingly, local media enterprises are being bought by larger national or transnational companies. This ownership change is reflected in the types of information that the community receives. To illustrate, in 1998 the *St. Louis Riverfront Times,* a local community paper, was bought by the New Times, a national conglomerate based in Phoenix, Arizona. Almost immediately, the newspaper dropped its previous focus on local political issues, becoming exclusively an entertainment periodical.

National media systems. National media companies concentrate on owning media properties within the borders of one country. These wealthy, influential media companies frequently have ties to the political establishment, creating conflicts of interest. For example, at the outset of Gulf War II, Clear Channel, Inc., the largest radio conglomerate in the United States, with 1,200 stations scattered throughout the country, organized and paid for a series of prowar rallies in Cleveland, Atlanta, Philadelphia, and other cities. Clear Channel is a corporation whose vice chairman, Tom Hicks, has financial ties to President George W. Bush.

The most extreme example of conflict of interest is in Italy, where Prime Minister Silvio Berlusconi is the largest media mogul in the country—owning three of the state's seven national television stations, a major film production studio, and a large publishing house. This conflict of interest clearly compromises these media operations' coverage of the prime minister and his administration.

Regional media systems. Regional conglomerates have recently become major players in the global media landscape. To illustrate:

- Bonnier AB, based in Sweden, is the largest media company in Scandinavia, with operations in seventeen countries. Bonnier controls a wide range of media, including newspaper and magazine publishing, radio, television and film production, film theaters, music production, and multimedia services.
- TV Azteca, a Mexican-based television network, has extended its outreach into U.S. markets, including Los Angeles, Austin, and Miami. As of 2002, TV Azteca reaches approximately 53 percent of Latino households in the United States.
- Arab television network al-Jazeera has emerged as a primary source of global news on the Middle East. Al-Jazeera (which means "the Peninsula") was established by Sheikh Hamad bin Khalifa al-Thani of Qatar in October 1996. Al-Jazeera beams its signal free of charge to most countries. In 2003, al-Jazeera claimed a global audience of 35 million Arabic-speaking viewers in more than twenty Arab countries, mostly through private satellite dishes. In 2003, al-Jazeera announced plans to extend its global influence by opening an English-language Web site, distributing English-language news programming by satellite and cable, and launching an Arabic documentary channel.

Regional media operations typically address the common concerns and interests of the audience in the area. These media companies may present a distinct point of view with regard to regional events. For instance, Al-Jazeera has been criticized for presenting a pro-Palestinian bias in its news coverage. Kuwait and Saudi Arabia have complained about al-Jazeera's extensive reporting on the misery of Iraqis living under UN sanctions. Osama bin Laden has released videotaped messages to the public through the network, and the terrorist group al-Qaeda has used the network to release information to the public.

Transnational media conglomerates. A transnational media conglomerate is a nationally based company with diverse holdings (including multiple media companies) and overseas operation in two or more countries. The transnational media conglomerate is part of a larger trend toward global economic consolidation. In 2001, multinational corporations accounted for 20 percent of world production and 70 percent of world trade.

The concentration of ownership in the global media industry has become an extremely troubling trend. As of 2003, nine corporations owned or controlled the majority of media outlets in the world: Time Warner (see Figure 2.1), Disney, Vivendi Universal, Viacom, Sony, the News Corporation, AT&T broadband, General Electric, and Bertelsmann. This ownership model fits F.M. Sherer and D. Ross's definition of an oligopoly:

> Oligopoly refers to an industry characterized by a few mutually interdependent firms, with relatively similar shares, producing either a homogeneous product (a perfect oligopoly) or heterogeneous products (an imperfect oligopoly). Under such a market structure, the industry leader often sets the price.[19]

Media conglomerates own numerous media subsidiaries, including television stations, film studios, music companies, newspapers and magazines, and interactive media providers. To illustrate, four of the five largest book publishing companies in the world are owned by transnational corporations: Random House (Bertelsmann); HarperCollins (News Corporation); Simon & Schuster (Viacom); Little, Brown & Company and Warner Books (Time Warner).[20]

The principal goal, or function, of the transnational media conglomerate is to maximize its profits. At times, the profit imperative undermines other important functions, such as informing or entertaining the audience. Richard A. Gershon maintains that the profit function is not always compatible with the distinctive nature of the product-information: "The Transnational Media Corporations should be treated differently . . . because of their unique ability to influence world opinion. . . . Strategic decision making and the allocation of resources is predicated on economic goals and efficiencies with little regard to national boundaries, interests or priorities."[21]

For subsidiaries of large corporations, the financial bottom line becomes the paramount consideration in the production and distribution of media presentations. Media programming such as films, television programs, and newspapers is expected to generate cash flow for the parent transnational conglomerates. As Rick Lyman and Laura M. Holson explain, "Making the battle for success all the more important is that [film] studios, which [in 2002] have enjoyed record grosses expected to top $9 billion, are being counted on to keep funneling torrential revenues to the

Figure 2.1 Time Warner: Worldwide Holdings in Film, Television, Publishing, and Internet Services

**Warner Bros.
Entertainment**
Warner Bros. Pictures
Warner Bros. Television
The WB Television Network
Kids' WB!
Castle Rock Entertainment
Telepictures Productions
Warner Home Video
Warner Bros. Consumer
  Products
Warner Bros. Cinemas
Warner Bros. Online
Warner Bros. Animation
Looney Tunes
Hanna-Barbera
DC Comics
MAD Magazine

New Line Cinema
New Line Cinema
Fine Line Features
New Line Home Entertainment
New Line International Releasing
New Line New Media
New Line Television
New Line Distribution
New Line Licensing/
  Merchandising
New Line Music
New Line Theatricals

**Turner Broadcasting
System, Inc.**
TBS Superstation
TNT
Cartoon Network
Turner Classic Movies
Turner South
Boomerang
TCM Europe
Cartoon Network Europe
TNT Latin America
TCM & Cartoon Network/Asia
  Pacific
NASCAR.com
PGA.com
Cartoon Network Studios
Atlanta Braves
CNN/ U.S.
CNN Headline News
CNN*fn*
CNN International
CNN en Español
CNN en Español-Mexico
CNNRadio
CNN en Español Radio
CNN Newsource
CNN.com
CNNMoney.com
CNNStudentNews.com
CNN.com.br (Portuguese)
CNN.com International Edition (English)
CNN.de (German)
CNNenEspañol.com (Spanish)
CNNItalia.it (Italian)
CNNArabic.com

CNN.co.jp (Japan)
CNN.com.mx (Mexico)
CNN Airport Network
CNN to Go
CNN Mobile
CNN Deutschland
Asia.CNN.com/Korea

Joint Ventures
Cartoon Network Japan
NBC/Turner NASCAR Races
Viva+
Viva Media
CNN+
CNN Turk
n-tv
Accent Health
Court TV

Home Box Office
HBO
HBO2
HBO Signature
HBO Family
HBO Comedy
HBO Zone
HBO Latino
Cinemax
MoreMAX
ActionMAX
ThrillerMAX
WMAX
@MAX
5StarMAX
OuterMAX
HBO Video

Joint Ventures
HBO Asia
HBO Brazil
HBO Czech
HBO Hungary
HBO India
HBO Olé
HBO Poland
HBO Romania
A&E Mundo
E! Latin America
SET Latin America
WBTV Latin America
The History Channel Latin
  America

Time, Inc.
Time
Sports Illustrated
People
Entertainment Weekly
Fortune
Money
In Style
... and 126 other Magazines
  (U.S. and international)
Time Life, Inc.
Oxmoor House
Leisure Arts
Sunset Books

Southern Living at Home
Media Networks, Inc.
First Moments
Targeted Media, Inc.
Time Inc. Custom Publishing
Synapse Group, Inc.
Time Distribution Services
Time Inc. Home Entertainment
Time Customer Service
Warner Publishing Services
This Old House Ventures, Inc.
Time Inc. Brand Licensing
Life

Joint Ventures
BOOKSPAN
Essence Communications
Partners
European Magazines Limited
Avantages S.A.

America Online, Inc.
AOL
AOL International
CompuServe
ICQ
MapQuest
Moviefone
Netscape
AOL Music
AOL Mobile
AOL Instant Messenger (AIM)
AOL for Broadband

Time Warner Cable
Time Warner Cable
Road Runner
Local News Channels
News 9 Albany (Albany, NY)
New 8 Austin (Austin, TX)
NY1 News (New York, NY)
R News (Rochester, NY)
News 14 Raleigh (Raleigh, NC)

Joint Ventures
News 14 Carolina (Charlotte, NC)
News 24 Houston (Houston, TX)
iNDemand
Kansas City Cable Partners
Texas Cable Partners
Urban Cable Partners

Source: Information in this chart compiled from Time Warner's Web site and other news sources, December, 2003.

beleaguered media conglomerates that own most of them and whose stock prices have dropped by as much as 80 percent this year."[22]

Because of this bottom-line mentality, film studios produce only sequels, spinoffs, and movies with formulaic plots and "bankable" stars. In addition, newspapers, television, and radio stations increasingly rely upon syndicated programs and news services to save the expenses associated with producing their own local programming. Over 2,000 radio and television affiliates in the United States now subscribe to Metro Networks, a reporting service that supplies news, sports, weather, and traffic information. This, of course, further reduces the number of diverse voices available to the public. Another cost-cutting strategy involves carrying the same programming over different media. To illustrate, in 2002, Infinity Radio Network announced plans to carry the audio portion of David Letterman's television talk show on CBS. Both Infinity and CBS are owned by Viacom.

When programming is regarded simply as "product" rather than news, entertainment, or art, the quality of the productions can suffer. In late 2002, NBC Television announced plans to bring back its hit sitcom *Friends* for the 2003 season, even though the producers, writers, and actors had expressed concerns about being able to maintain the quality of the show. However, NBC regarded this "product" as too valuable to give up.

The emergence of transnational media conglomerates affects the production of media content in a number of respects:

Weakening of national culture. A major liability of transnational media conglomerates is the loss of distinctive local culture. Transnational media conglomerates have a distinctly American influence—regardless of their country of origin. For instance, although Bertlesmann is a German-based corporation, in 2001, its largest proportion of its revenue (35 percent) came from its U.S. media subsidiaries, including Bantam, Doubleday Dell, and Random House publishing companies, *Family Circle* and *McCall's* magazines, and Arista and RCA record labels.[23]

In 2001, Jean-Marie Messier, chairman of the French media giant Vivendi Universal, created a stir by declaring, "The Franco-French cultural exception is dead." This remark suggests that the worldview of transnational media programming would inevitably overwhelm the French culture. Alan Riding declares:

[The remark] was largely meaningless to most of the French, but those in the movie industry read it as a threat to their survival. For them, it was a signal that Mr. Messier was declaring war on France's complex system of financing movies through government subsidies, special taxes and mandatory investment by television companies.[24]

Audience members are often comfortable with "cultural hybridity"— that is, they are able to assimilate information produced by both local and global media corporations—so long as the local media system is not overwhelmed by the International Media Programming.[25]

Support of status quo. Transnational media conglomerates are beneficiaries of the existing political and economic systems. Ben Bagdikian declares, "The lords of the global village have their own political agenda. All resist economic changes that do not support their own financial interests."[26] Thus, despite their recent financial woes, the conglomerates that own media companies benefit from global economic consolidation. As a result, although the media oligopoly may call for some refinements within the existing market-driven corporate model, it cannot be counted upon to press for significant changes in the current system.

Further, the owners of transnational media conglomerates are a homogeneous group, with common backgrounds, experiences, and worldviews. Project Censored came up with the following findings:

> The top 11 media corporations in the U.S. form a solid grid of overlapping interests and affiliations. The 155 directors of these 11 media corporations . . . are mostly individuals who inherited wealth, were educated in private preparatory schools and Ivy League universities. . . . They represent private wealth, private education, private clubs, conservative politics and they control the way most Americans get their news.[27]

Indeed, it is not uncommon for these CEOs to serve on the boards of directors of other transnational conglomerates. For instance, Time Warner shares directorships on Fortune 1000 boards with the *Washington Post*, NBC (General Electric), Gannett, Viacom, and the Times Mirror Corporation.[28]

Homogeneity of content. As media conglomerates acquire more media subsidies, the number of different voices is reduced. For example, Clear Channel owns twenty-three of the eighty commercial stations throughout the state of North Dakota. And in Minot, the state's fourth-largest city, with a population nearing 37,000, Clear Channel owns all six commercial stations.

Controlling access to content. Transnational media corporations control both the production and distribution of media content. This merging of content and carrier means that a transnational media conglomerate is able to control all phases of the media industry: production, distribution, and exhibition. For instance, production companies owned by Time Warner include Warner Brothers Films, and Electra Records. And at the same time, subsidiaries such as America Online, HBO television, Turner Broadcasting, and Warner Brothers Network provide a powerful distribution system for the content produced by this transnational media conglomerate.

The merging of content and carrier raises concerns that the programming produced by a transnational media conglomerate will be only carried by its own distribution companies. In 2002, Time Warner announced that the online editions of *Entertainment Weekly, People, Teen People, InStyle, Time for Kids,* and *Sports Illustrated for Kids* (owned by sister companies Warner Brothers, Turner Broadcasting, and Time, Inc.) would appear exclusively on AOL.[29]

But even more serious is the prospect that a transnational media conglomerate will refuse to carry programming that is not produced by the corporation. In May 2000 Time Warner dropped Disney's programs from its cable service in a dispute over how much Time Warner would pay Disney for its cable channels. Channels owned by Disney, including ABC, were pulled from cable systems in 3.5 million homes during sweeps week, affecting the overall ratings share that ABC was able to attract. Time Warner quickly rectified the situation after public outcry; however, this incident underscored the power of a gatekeeper to limit access to content.

Conflicts of interest. Conflicts of interest may arise when a media conglomerate covers stories in which the parent company has an interest. To illustrate, in 2002, General Electric (GE), which owns NBC, one of the world's leading manufacturers of jet engines for military aircraft, was awarded $1.7 billion in contracts from the U.S. Defense Department.[30] General Electric also has a very lucrative business exporting defense equipment internationally. During the second quarter of 2000, GE received more than $600 million in military contracts, including a contract with the Air Force of the Republic of Korea.[31] General Electric's reliance on defense technology as a principle source of revenue raises questions with respect to how NBC might cover military-related stories.

In addition, the people who sit on the boards of directors of these transnational media conglomerates may also be affiliated with industries that are frequently the subject of coverage by their media companies. For instance, NBC, Fox News, and Time Warner each have a board member who also sits as a director on tobacco producer Philip Morris's board.[32]

Influence of advertising. Because transnational media conglomerates are dependent upon advertising revenue, advertisers exercise enormous influence over the stories that are presented through the media. To illustrate, shortly after the September 11 terrorist attack, Federal Express and Sears pulled their ads from ABC's late-night talk show *Politically Incorrect* with Bill Maher in response to complaints about comments Maher and his guests had made on the program. Immediately, six television affiliate stations "suspended" the show from their viewing schedule. In May 2002, ABC canceled the program.

Cross-promotion. Cross-promotion occurs when media programs are used to promote other programs and products owned by the transnational media conglomerate. To the casual consumer of entertainment, it's almost impossible to detect these linkages. For example, Time Warner employs a series of cross-promotion strategies designed to cultivate audience interest in other Time Warner programming. (For further discussion, see Chapter 9, Applications: Media Literacy Analysis).

Allocation of resources. One would think that one of the benefits of a large transnational media conglomerate buying a media company is that more resources are available for programming. However, this is not the case; budgets are often cut due to the imperative to maximize profit. For instance, shortly after AOL and Time Warner merged in 2000, approximately 1,000 jobs at its subsidiary CNN were eliminated.

Further, many news organizations have eliminated their international news bureaus in order to reduce costs. In 2002, newspapers closing their news bureaus in Tokyo, Japan, included the *Chicago Tribune,* the *Christian Science Monitor,* the *Independent of London, Dagens Nyheter* of Sweden, and *Corriere della Sera* of Italy. Instead, newspapers hire stringers, who are paid by the article.

This new system compromises the quality of news coverage, in several respects. In the past, journalists assigned to a foreign bureau such as London were familiar with the politics and culture of the city. These reporters were able to develop extensive networks of contacts who could furnish valuable information. But now, reporters are based elsewhere and only travel to the site to cover a story. As a result, they have not cultivated a network of sources who can provide insight into a story. In addition, these reporters are no longer in a position to follow a story as it develops. Dave Scott, foreign editor of the *Christian Science Monitor,* said of its coverage of Japan, "We will be bringing in our guy from Beijing (China). I just feel it might be better served by doing more project-oriented pieces. It is not a day-to-day story as it once was."[33]

The concentration of ownership is raising concern within the professional media community. According to Patrick Murphy, American Federation of Television and Radio Artists (AFTRA) national board representative, the concentration of ownership has reduced the number of media professionals working in the field, as well as undermining unions' efforts to stabilize wages, benefits, and pensions:

> We face an increasingly consolidated industry—in every area from film to television, radio and music recording—without the united strength we need to protect our members. Cookie cutter formats—designed to rely less on AFTRA, Writers Guild, and SAG [Screen Actors Guild] talent— offer such thin soup of information and entertainment that public dissatisfaction can be quantitatively measured by steadily decreasing ratings.
>
> But the dangers of consolidation go beyond bland programming and even decreasing employment opportunities within the industry. They touch the very heart of what we have long assumed to be an essential element of our republic—an informed electorate, capable of making informed decisions based on a free flow of ideas.[34]

Recent trends—conglomeration. Beginning in 2001, the dominant transnational media conglomerates began facing a series of crises, which could potentially alter the landscape of global media ownership. The difficulties facing the "big 9" are, in part, a by-product of the global financial downturn. David D. Kirkpatrick and Andrew Ross Sorkin explain:

> "During the Internet boom, when start-ups poured venture capital and public offering proceeds into advertising, many media companies borrowed heavily to make their acquisitions. In fact, even as their earnings

and revenue rose, media companies optimistically borrowed so much that their debt levels rose even faster than their cash flow," said Neil Begley, an analyst for Moody's Investors Service. "Lenders and bond buyers had a relatively high tolerance for risk, so when companies like Disney or the Tribune Company let their credit ratings slide a notch it did not make borrowing much more expensive," Mr. Begley said.

Now lenders and investors are much less tolerant of risk, and the long, deep drop in advertising revenue has left many companies tight for cash. That has pushed the price of media businesses down more drastically than at any time in recent years.

"There is a sea change, where the psychology of the last 30 years—grab more, bigger assets—doesn't work anymore," said Hal Vogel, a veteran media industry analyst. "We are going through a rough patch that in my view is going to last at least a couple of years."[35]

For the first time, major media conglomerates began to report heavy financial losses:

- In 2002, Time Warner reported a 2002 loss of nearly $100 billion —the largest annual loss in U.S. corporate history.[36] Between January 2001 and July 2002, shares of Time Warner declined by 75 percent.[37] In 2003, Time Warner reported an unexpectedly large fourth-quarter of $44.91 billion, or $10.04 a diluted share.[38]
- News Corporation reported losses of $6.27 billion between June 2001 and June 2002.[39]
- Bertelsmann reported a 10 percent decline in sales, and a 91 percent drop in net income in the first half of 2003.[40]
- Disney's share price declined by 65 percent from its high of $43.63 between April 2000 and August 2002.[41] Net income in Disney's first fiscal quarter of 2003 dropped 42 percent to $256 million, or 13 cents a share.[42]
- The Sony Corporation reported a loss in the final quarter of 2002. In 2003, Moody's financial service, a leading provider of independent credit research, ratings, and financial information, downgraded Sony's credit rating for the first time since the agency's records began, citing concern about Sony's profits.[43]
- In 2002, Morgan Stanley financial analyst Richard Bioltti downgraded Viacom stocks from "equal-weight" to "underweight," predicting that advertising revenue won't grow more than 7 percent in 2003.[44]
- In 2002, Vivendi posted a loss of more than $25 billion.[45] In 2001–2002, stock prices declined by 78 percent.[46]

There are also signs of unprecedented instability within the leadership of transnational media corporations. In 2002, two of the media conglomerates dismissed their CEOs: Thomas Middelhoff, chief executive of Bertelsmann AG, and Jean-Marie Messier, ousted by Vivendi Universal. In 2003, Stephen M. Case resigned as chairman of Time Warner. Shortly thereafter, vice chairman Ted Turner also stepped down. Also in 2003, Norio Ahaga, president of Sony, stepped down due to ill health. In 2003, the Walt Disney Company removed Roy Disney, last Disney family member, from its board of directors. Disney then called for the resignation of chairman and chief executive Michael Eisner from the board. Following a vote of no confidence by shareholders in 2004, Eisner resigned as chairman but remained as chief executive.

This pattern of executive turnover disrupts the long-term planning of the conglomerates. According to Steve Case, former chairman of Time Warner, the most pressing task facing the troubled media conglomerates is to "bring stability to the management team."[47]

In addition, several media conglomerates have been the subject of investigation for illegal business practices. In August 2002 the U.S. Securities and Exchange Commission and the Justice Department initiated investigations into Time Warner's accounting practices that may have inappropriately inflated the company's revenue by $49 million between 2000 and 2002. In 2003, securities regulators began investigating potential accounting fraud at Time Warner involving an agreement the company made two years earlier to sell $25 million in advertising to Vivendi Universal as part of a larger deal for its stake in AOL France.

In 2002, French regulators announced an investigation into Vivendi's accounting practices, centering on whether Vivendi communicated its liquidity crisis to investors in a timely fashion. At the same time, Vivendi Universal disclosed that it was also the subject of two criminal investigations in the United States, one by the Securities and Exchange Commission and another by the U.S. attorney's office for the Southern District of New York. In 2003, Vivendi Universal agreed to pay $50 million to settle accusations by the Securities and Exchange Commission that it misled investors in its news releases and financial statements.

Another significant development is that technological developments have enabled smaller competitors to challenge and, in some cases, surpass the dominance of the large conglomerates. To illustrate, Time Warner, which has dominated the global Internet market, relies primarily on dial-up telephone access. However, broadband technology now makes high-speed access over cable lines or satellite faster and more convenient. As a result, America Online's share of the online market in the United States slipped from 41 percent in 2000 to 37 percent in 2002. Indeed, during the third quarter of 2003, the number of subscribers declined by 846,000.[48]

In addition, technological innovations in one subsidiary are undermining operations elsewhere in the corporate empire. For instance, Time Warner's digital cable service enables subscribers to control what and when they watch, including skipping commercials. However, this service harms its Turner Broadcasting and Warner Brothers divisions, which rely on advertising.[49]

Increased international competition also poses a challenge to the dominance of media conglomerates. For instance, Juno and NetZero services from United Online offer Internet services at a significantly lower rate than AOL.

In addition, increased programming competition threatens the international dominance of the media conglomerates. For example, in 2002, Israel's cable television commission granted the country's cable providers permission to remove CNN International from their services. Jim Rutenberg explains:

> [The three Israeli cable companies] say the prices they have traditionally paid CNN . . . are untenable now that they are facing financial difficulty. They recently began to offer their customers CNN's main competitor in the United States, Fox News Channel, a unit of the News Corporation, instead. Ram Belinkov, the acting chief executive of Golden Channels, said, "We gave them a proposal of the maximum we are able to pay. If they meet it, we will not take them off. But so far it looks like they don't want to meet it."[50]

As a result of these corporate setbacks, 2002 marked the beginning of several significant developments on the part of the transnational media oligopoly:

Divestiture of media holdings. Because of their financial problems, the media conglomerates appear to have given up on their strategy to acquire additional media companies. David Kirkpatrick explains:

> A 20-year acquisition spree that turned the major communications companies into behemoths is shifting into reverse as many of them find them-

selves short of cash and looking to sell, leaving few to bid. Vivendi Universal, facing the most severe cash shortage, has put the publisher Houghton Mifflin on the block. It is also considering its options for the Universal film and music studios and theme parks. . . .

Time Warner, under pressure to pay down debts to protect its credit rating, has started preliminary talks to sell its stake in the cable channel Comedy Central to its partner Viacom, said people involved in its plans. Talks to sell its stake in Court TV to its partner in that venture, Liberty Media, are soon to follow, they said. In 2003, Time Warner began to explore the prospect of selling its book publishing division in an effort to pay down some of its debt. The book division includes Little, Brown & Company and Warner Books. Time Warner retained Merrill Lynch to approach publishers and investment funds about a possible deal.[51]

In 2003, Vivendi Universal entered into negotiations to sell its book publication company, Houghton Mifflin into a consortium of financiers led by the Blackstone Group.

One possible scenario is that this movement toward divestiture could lead to further concentration of ownership. For instance, the sale of Time Warner's publishing division has elicited interest from Random House, a unit of Bertelsmann, and HarperCollins, part of the News Corporation.[52]

However, given the current financial straits of the transnational media conglomerates, it is unlikely that any of them would be in position to acquire significant pieces of their rivals' empires: David Kirpatrick explains, "The media industry's collective retreat is an opportunity for the few companies with the wherewithal and inclination to spend, mainly Viacom and Rupert Murdoch's News Corporation. But those two companies can only buy so much."[53]

The divestiture of media holdings by media conglomerates could offer unique opportunities for redistribution of media holdings among smaller companies. Kirkpatrick observes:

> The cable television industry is perhaps most crowded with for-sale signs. Adelphia Communications is in bankruptcy and its cable systems are expected to be sold. . . . The dearth of bidders is already luring some old timers back into the game. Last month, the cable company RCN sold the cable system surrounding Princeton, NJ, in an effort to bolster its balance sheet. With the major companies in the industry all tight themselves, the auction went to Steve Simmons, a former cable system owner who sold his first company in the mid-1990s and spent the last decade writing

children's books. He recently formed a company backed by the Boston investment firm Spectrum Equity Partners to buy up other cable systems. "This is a time when some of the large players in the industry are indeed stepping back and even selling systems that are not in their core strategy," Mr. Simmons said. "We think there will be some wonderful opportunities for us."[54]

Return to national focus. Some transnational media conglomerates are now reevaluating their international outreach and returning to a national focus. Mark Harrington of J.P. Morgan Chase predicts, "Vivendi will eventually dispose of its U.S. assets and move toward a European holding company.[55] Referring to Time Warner, Suzanne Kapner notes:

> [In 2002], AOL Europe, which includes operations in Britain, Germany, and France, lost $629 million (based on earnings before income taxes, depreciation, and amortization) on $905 million in revenue. AOL Latin America, including Brazil, Argentina, and Mexico, had a net loss of $307 million but had revenue of only $66 million. The company does not disclose results for its Canadian and Asian affiliates.
>
> "AOL will have to decide how much assistance to provide money-losing units like AOL Latin America," says Michael Lynton, the president of AOL International.[56]

Collaborative ventures. In order to save expenses, some transnational media conglomerates have began to pool their resources. In 2002, Time Warner began discussions with the Walt Disney Corporation about merging their CNN and ABC News operations.[57]

As they pare back their operations, transnational conglomerates have began to subcontract services. Bertelsmann subcontracted much of the operation of its online music store CDNow to Amazon.com. Through this arrangement, Amazon agreed to operate CDNow's Web site and ship most of the merchandise from Amazon warehouses.

Ultimately, these developments could simply represent a natural correction after the globalization and media boom of the 1990s. How these developments unfold will have an impact on global ownership patterns and on our access and interpretation of media content.

Hybrid Ownership

As a by-product of globalization, the privately owned ownership model has begun to gain entry into countries that had previously operated under the state ownership models. Countries with state-owned media systems, such as Ukraine, China, Romania, and Kyrgyzstan, have begun to allow privately owned media companies in their countries. In 2001, China's Broadcasting Authority announced plans to permit media giant Time Warner to broadcast a cable television channel in China, and Time Warner agreed to carry state-run China Central Television (CCTV) as part of the cable package in major U.S. cities. At the same time, the News Corporation was formally granted cable carriage rights for two channels in southern China.

However, this transition to a hybrid model can be difficult. One major conflict centers around the issue of governmental control over content produced by private domestic media companies. To illustrate, the Chinese government has held up the release of independent films; as a result, the number of films approved for production and distribution fell from approximately 150 per year to 50 in 1999. Stuart Klawans observes:

> For the state film studios, which have lost much of their financing but none of their political responsibility, these contradictory policies have spelled disaster. . . . [Chinese director Zhang Wu Chao] says, "With one hand, the government is still trying to control artistic expression. With the other, it is pushing filmmakers to find independent financing."[58]

In addition, countries that have traditionally operated within the publicly owned media ownership model are now embracing private commercial media companies. For instance, in Germany, where broadcasting had been publicly owned and commerical-free, 36 percent is now commercial.[59]

The influx of the market-driven ownership model has had an impact on programming produced within the established media system. In England, the British Broadcasting Corporation (BBC) provides radio, television, and online services supported by public taxes. However, ITV, a commercial television station, operates within the country as well. In addition, privately owned stations from other countries are accessible by cable or satellite. Newspapers and magazines are privately owned and financed in Britain as well.

This dual system created a competition for the viewing audience that affected the approach and philosophy of the BBC. After slipping behind its rival ITV in the ratings, the BBC was forced to adapt its programming approach. By February 2002, the ratings for BBC television overtook ITV. But critics complained that the BBC was guilty of dumbing down its content in order to pander to the audience. Alan Riding states:

> The charges were that BBC1 and the more elitist BBC2 were filling the screen with soap operas, quiz shows, make-overs, cookery, pets, gardening and loads Easier viewing. Veteran broadcasters had been shoved aside for pretty faces, serious drama had been abandoned and the few surviving current affairs and arts programs were being broadcast at times that ensured small audiences. Greg Dyke, director-general of BBC, declared, "The BBC's role is not only to produce wonderful pieces that are not watched by many people, but also to compete in the marketplace."[60]

Audience

Increasingly, media programming is being directed at a global audience. In 1998, the United States exported $21.8 billion in "cultural goods" (i.e., printed matter, music, visual arts, films, photography, radio, and television) to the rest of the world. And surprisingly, the United States imported $60 billion in cultural goods from other countries during the same period. Sales of imported Latin music in the United States increased by 24 percent between 1997 and 2000, generating sales of $609 million.[61]

One of the major challenges of international communications is identifying the audience. In mass communication, the more familiar you are with your audience, the more you can tailor your comments to their predispositions, interest level, and knowledge of the subject matter.

Many international media communicators employ a *standardization* approach, in which the same media presentation is broadcast to all markets across the globe. However, this approach can result in unintended messages being conveyed to a foreign audience. To illustrate, Va Bene, an expensive Italian restaurant that opened in Shanghai in 2000, was a source of merriment because the Italian name, meaning "It goes well," sounds like Shanghaiese for "not cheap."[62]

An accurate audience profile enables an international media communicator to move to a *localization* approach, in which messages are tailored to a national audience by constructing culturally specific presentations. Barbara Mueller explains the differences as follows: "All humans are confronted with universal needs. For instance, each society must ensure that its young learn the ways of the community, but just how this accumulated knowledge is passed on to the next generation differs from culture to culture."[63]

Demographic characteristics such as nationality, ethnic origin, gender, age, income, and education interact to influence how an individual within a country interprets information. For instance, men are the primary users of the media in developing African nations and traditional countries such as Afghanistan or Turkmenistan; women are not allowed to see a movie or play or listen to foreign music. The income distribution in a country also determines who can afford televisions, computers, or satellite or cable services. (For additional discussion, see Chapter 6, Analysis of National Media Systems.)

Further, a psychographic profile identifies the attitudes and values commonly associated with people who fall within these demographic categories. A person's nationality, gender, race, and class can affect his or her self-concept, primary relationships, significant life experiences, ways of relating to others, ways of dealing with emotion, and personal aspirations.

Localizing media messages enables an international media communicator to devise an effective communications strategy for that particular audience. For instance, in 2000, a cooking program developed by the BBC, which was shown in India, was dubbed in four Indian dialects.

International media communicators localize the style of the presentations for a national audience. For instance, Webster University student Tina Wheeler conducted an analysis comparing the French film *La Femme Nikita* (1990) with an American remake, *Point of No Return* (1993). She arrived at the following conclusion about the stylistic differences in the two films:

> *La Femme Nikita* was very slow paced. The music was drawn out, and Nikita (the main character) did not seem as if she went through much of a transformation.
>
> The remake was very fast-paced, excluded or changed many aspects of scenes, and showed Maggie (the main character in the American remake) going through a complete transformation. A French audience can obviously accept a slower movie that seems darker and ambiguous with little violence. An American audience, however, craves graphic violence, fast pacing, and direct endings that leave nothing to wonder about.[64]

The effective media communicator even tailors the content of the presentation to a specific audience. For instance, the Hollywood film industry now relies heavily on movie testing, a process in which a film studio presents a film to a sample audience before it opens. Based upon the audience's responses, the studio can make changes before releasing the movie to the general public. Michele Willens explains:

> These days, for about $15,000 a screening, the studios hire (almost exclusively) the National Research Group, which recruits people whose demographics match those of the film's hoped-for audience. After seeing the movie, the handpicked audience usually fills out cards answering questions about how they liked the film, and a small number may stay for a focus-group discussion. . . . And movies change as a result.
>
> Characters are softened: with "My Best Friend's Wedding," test audiences found Julia Roberts's character unsympathetic, so the filmmakers eliminated a few scenes of her conniving and inserted a few more guilt-ridden close-ups to turn the numbers around.[65]

The Emerging Global Audience

Global audiences often seek out validation and reinforcement for their experiences through international programming. For instance, "Punjabi youth living in London use domestic and imported audiovisual culture to understand their identities in relation to the family, the nation, the neighborhood, the diaspora and the world."[66]

Programs that attract a large international audience reinforce areas of common interest and concern, promoting the formation of social group identifications beyond national borders. Through a process of "transnational identification," some viewers have discovered that they share similar experiences with people with whom they have, on the surface, little in common. After watching *The Cosby Show*, one Lebanese viewer, a Shiite Muslim and father, observed, "American blacks are a little like us."[67]

International programming can lead to the formation of transnational subcultures, based on race, gender, and class, which transcend national boundaries. For instance, Afro-Caribbean music provides an entrée into Afro-Caribbean culture and countereconomics for working-class, white, British youth. According to S. Jones, "these working-class white youths exhibit a deep affinity with black politics and culture on the basis of shared economic disadvantage."[68]

In the same vein, a white South African commented on his identification with the middle-class African-American characters in *The Cosby Show*:

> The greatest divide between black and white in this country is not the colour of one's skin but the first- and third-world values and attitudes

displayed by the different race groups. . . . Therefore, we do not see the "Cosby Show" as being about black people but we see it as a very entertaining sit-com displaying beliefs and values we can associate with.[69]

Audience Behavior Patterns

Audience behavior patterns vary widely around the globe, affecting how people use and interpret the media. For instance, television is a pervasive presence in the United States:

- Percentage of U.S. households with at least one television: 98.
- Percentage of U.S. households with three or more TVs: 40.
- Time per day that a TV is on in an average U.S. home: 7 hours, 40 minutes.
- Percentage of Americans who always or often watch TV while eating dinner: 40.
- Chance that an American falls asleep with the TV on at least three nights a week: 1 in 4.
- Number of videos rented daily in the U.S.: 6 million.
- Amount of TV the average American watches per day: more than 4 hours.
- Amount of TV the average American 1-year-old watches per week: 6 hours.
- Hours per year the average American youth spends in school: 900. Hours per year the average American youth spends watching TV: 1,023.[70]

In contrast, the Masai, a nomadic community of cattle raisers in Kenya, Africa, spend their lives on the move; consequently, their contact with the media is sporadic. As a result, members of the Masai community did not learn about the September 11 attack in New York until the following June.[71]

The characteristic behavior patterns of a nation's audience affect the development of its media systems. To illustrate, the evolution of laptop computers in America is largely due to the industry's effort to accommodate its highly mobile consumers. New virtual workplaces are being established, as people work from home and collaborate from long distances. Wireless Internet technology was developed, in large measure, to accommodate users who are accustomed to being on the move.

Audience behavior patterns also affect the format of a nation's media productions (Figure 2.2). For instance, in response to the busy American

Figure 2.2   **Percentage of Adults Who Regularly Read the Newspaper**

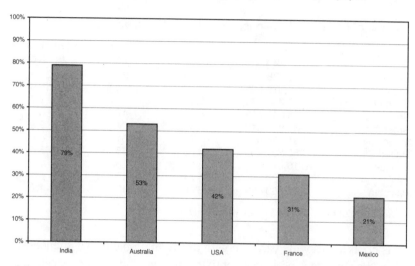

Source: Roper ASW Study, 2003, www.roperasw.com/newsroom/press/
p0211002.html.

way of life, U.S. newspapers have adopted the inverted pyramid style of
reporting, in which the most essential information in an article is included
in the first paragraph. The body of the story then elaborates on the information presented in the lead paragraph. In contrast, in Russia and France,
readers have more leisure time to look through the entire paper to uncover
the news. In France, there is even a cliché, "Newspapers are for slow
reading," meaning that the French enjoy sitting in a café for hours, reading for relaxation. As a result, their newspapers do not depend on the
headline or lead paragraph to entice people to read the entire article.

A population's access to media also varies widely between countries. In the United States, the public is saturated with media messages.
Even for those few who do not own a television set or radio, media
messages are commonly displayed in public spaces. Billboards dot the
roadways. Restaurants and sports stadiums are filled with images and
music. In contrast, the residents of Enoosaen, a village in Kenya, had
no electricity and therefore no access to television until 2002. Up to
that point, villagers relied on battery-operated radio as their primary
mass medium. Estonia, with a population of approximately 1.4 million
people, has only three television broadcast stations and ninety-eight
radio stations.[72]

Table 2.1

Number of Radios, Televisions, and Internet Users per Capita

Country	Population	TVs (millions)	Radios (millions)	Internet users (millions)
United Kingdom	59,778,002	30.50	84.5	34.3
Japan	126,974,628	86.50	120.5	56.0
Czech Republic	10,256,760	3.40	3.2	2.7
South Africa	43,647,658	6.00	17.0	3.1
Argentina	37,812,817	7.45	24.3	3.9
Indonesia	231,328,092	13.75	31.5	4.4
United States	280,562,489	219.00	575.0	165.8
Greece	10,645,343	2.54	5.0	1.4
Iran	66,622,704	4.61	17.0	0.4
Pakistan	147,663,429	3.10	13.5	1.2

Source: Compiled from *The CIA World Factbook, 2003.*

There is also a wide variance with regard to global film audiences. In 1998, the average American went to the movies over five times per year. In contrast, the average inhabitant of Saudi Arabia, Sudan, and Vietnam never went to a movie theater.[73] Although theater attendance is low in some countries, watching films is popular, thanks to media technology such as videocassettes and DVDs. In China, tickets to a movie theater range from $2.44 to $7.34—far more than the eighty-five cents it costs to buy a pirated DVD of the same films. Ciu Jian, China's first Western-style rock star, declares, "In China, the concept of the movie is that it is something that you watch on TV."[74]

Radio is a very popular medium in developing nations. Between 1995 and 1999, ownership of radios increased in Angola, Zimbabwe, Ghana, and Estonia by over 100 percent.[75] This popularity is due to several factors. First, radio receivers are both inexpensive and durable. In addition, the portability of the medium enables people to carry receivers with them. And finally, because the information is conveyed orally, the audience does not need to be literate.

In some countries, television is nearly universal, so that it can serve as a tool for reaching the mass audience (Table 2.1). In the United Kingdom, for instance, children are more likely to have a television set than books in their bedrooms. However, television is not nearly as ubiquitous in other nations. For instance, fewer than 40 percent of the homes in India have television sets.[76] It should be noted that media technology has dramatically increased the availability of television in many countries. For example, in Saudi Arabia, over 60 percent of households now enjoy regular access to satellite TV.[77]

Currently, access to the Internet is uneven across the globe. As of 2002, 42.6 percent of the global online population resided in the United States. China followed with 6.6 percent of total Web-surfing activity, while Japan came in third with 5.2 percent. The United Kingdom trailed Japan with 3.9 percent of global traffic, closely followed by Canada (3.9 percent) and Germany (3.6 percent). Nevertheless, this gap is rapidly closing. For instance, in China, the number of people using the Internet increased by 73 percent from June 2001 to June 2002 (for a total of 45.8 million people).[78]

Case Study, Function: Propaganda

A prime example of persuasion in international communications is *propaganda*. Propaganda is the strategic development and dissemination of information to influence public opinion or to promote the policies of a particular country, organization, or group. The latent function of a propagandistic message is not to inform but rather to influence attitudes among members of the targeted audience.

Although propaganda generally has a negative connotation, it can be used in a positive way as well: to promote national interests, pave the way for diplomatic initiatives, and encourage trade, tourism, and investment. In addition, public service announcements about drug prevention or tobacco use can be regarded as a form of propaganda that promotes the public welfare. Indeed, the term *propaganda* is subjective. What I may regard as propaganda, you may see as simply presenting the truth. To illustrate, organized religions often engage in media campaigns to shape public opinion, working on the assumption that they are presenting the "truth." The critical determinant in defining propaganda, then, must be *intention;* is the function of the media message to inform or persuade?

There are three basic types of propaganda: *internal propaganda, external propaganda,* and *counterpropaganda.*

The purpose of internal propaganda is to enlist and maintain support for public policies, as well as bolster citizens' faith in their government. As an example, the administration of Russian president Vladimir Putin uses popular music as a form of internal propaganda. Steven Lee Meyers explains:

> A new song by a new girl band has burst onto the airwaves with a bouncy beat and adoring lyrics that raise the question of how far Russians, who pretty much invented the cult of personality, will go to pay homage to

President Vladimir V. Putin. "And now I want a man like Putin," sings the band's lead singer, lamenting the brawling, booze-and-drug-addled boyfriend she dumped.

> A man like Putin, full of strength.
> A man like Putin, who doesn't drink.
> A man like Putin, who doesn't hurt me.
> A man like Putin, who won't run away.

It's not exactly a hit—it's not even for sale yet, except in limited editions distributed by the band's promoters—but the song has been playing on two of Russia's pop radio stations and has generated the sort of attention that most bands, not to mention politicians, could only dream of.

Since it appeared, it has been derided by some as a publicity stunt, as the latest manifestation of the cult of personality surrounding Mr. Putin and as the work of a furtive conspiracy to bolster his popularity. It may be all three.

The band sprang from the imagination of a songwriter, Aleksandr M. Yelin, and a spokesman for Russia's Supreme Court, Nikolai V. Gastello. Mr. Gastello said he simply wanted to promote a pop band that would articulate positive feelings about the country. He and Mr. Yelin engaged a public relations company, Kontora, to hold auditions last month and recruit the band's three singers. Mr. Gastello then used his contacts in the radio industry to get the song on the air.[79]

External propaganda is employed to demoralize adversaries and enlist the support of allies. External propaganda emerged as a major geopolitical strategy during the 1930s in Nazi Germany. Minister of Propaganda Joseph Goebbels used all available media (i.e., print, photographs, radio, and films) to promote Germany's message of Aryan supremacy and world domination.

Counterpropaganda is designed to minimize the effectiveness of an opponent's propaganda campaign. For instance, in order to counteract the propaganda messages of Arab extremist groups that U.S. policies are anti-Muslim, the U.S. State Department produced a series of minidocumentaries about the lives of Muslim Americans in 2002, which were broadcast on Indonesian television.

Although propaganda is commonly associated with totalitarian regimes such as Nazi Germany and the former Soviet Union, democratic governments also engage in propaganda campaigns. David Rothkopf, a former official of the U.S. Commerce Department in the Clinton administration, declares, "For the United States, a central objective of an Information Age foreign policy must be to win the battle of the world's information flows, dominating the airwaves as Great Britain once ruled the seas."[80]

As an example, as part of its preparation for the war with Iraq in 2003, the United States embarked on a sophisticated "information warfare" campaign, designed to break down the will of the Iraqi people. Thom Shanker and Eric Schmitt explain:

> American cyber-warfare experts . . . waged an e-mail assault, directed at Iraq's political, military and economic leadership, urging them to break with Saddam Hussein's government. A wave of calls has gone to the private cellphone numbers of specially selected officials inside Iraq, according to leaders at the Pentagon and in the regional Central Command. . . . More than eight million leaflets had been dropped over Iraq—including towns 65 miles south of Baghdad—warning Iraqi antiaircraft missile operators that their bunkers will be destroyed if they track or fire at allied warplanes. In the same way, a blunt offer has gone to Iraqi ground troops: surrender, and live.
>
> Radio transmitters hauled aloft by Air Force Special Operations EC-130E planes are broadcasting directly to the Iraqi public in Arabic with programs that mimic the program styles of local radio stations and are more sophisticated than the clumsy preaching of previous wartime propaganda efforts.
>
> "The goal of information warfare is to win without ever firing a short," said James R. Wilkinson, a spokesman for the Central Command in Tampa, Fla. "If action does begin, information warfare is used to make the conflict as short as possible."[81]

In some instances, the media industry in democratic societies have collaborated with the government to produce propaganda. For instance, during World War II Hollywood director Frank Capra made a series of films for the government entitled *Why We Fight* in an effort to lift public morale. Since the outbreak of the war on terrorism, this partnership between the U.S. government and Hollywood has resumed. Shortly after the attack on New York's World Trade Center, a group called Hollywood 9/11, consisting of studio executives, producers, directors, and writers, met with Karl Rove, senior adviser to President Bush, to discuss ways to support the war effort. This collaboration resulted in several projects, including Chuck Workman's short film, *The Spirit of America,* which was shown on one-fourth of the nation's movie screens during Christmas week, 2001.

But at other times, the media have been unwitting partners in propaganda campaigns devised by the government. During the cold war, America's Central Intelligence Agency (CIA) planted agents in news organizations to propagate its policies. Tim Weiner observes:

> The Central Intelligence Agency had a secret weapon at the Bay of Pigs, the ability to plant propaganda directly on international news wire services, according to a newly declassified CIA document.
>
> The document, a "propaganda plan" issued shortly before the invasion in April 1961, said the agency's headquarters had "the capability of placing items directly on the wire service tickers" as part of its "regular propaganda apparatus."
>
> It has been known since the 1970s that in the cold war the CIA had a handful of "assets," or agents, in place at some news organizations like The Associated Press and United Press International, particularly in foreign bureaus. The newly declassified document says flatly that the intelligence agency could essentially dictate articles and have them sent around the world. It also said the agency would "place specific messages and propaganda lines" on the wire services during and after the invasion.[82]

According to Laurance Zuckerman, the U.S. government has even assumed the secret role of Hollywood producer to deliver propaganda messages.

> Many people remember reading George Orwell's *Animal Farm* in high school or college, with its chilling finale in which the farm animals looked back and forth at the tyrannical pigs and the exploitative human farmers but found it impossible to say which was which.
>
> That ending was altered in the 1955 animated version, which removed the humans, leaving only the nasty pigs.
>
> Another example of Hollywood butchering great literature? Yes, but in this case the film's secret producer was the Central Intelligence Agency.
>
> The CIA, it seems, was worried that the public might be too influenced by Orwell's pox-on-both-their-houses critique of the capitalist humans and Communist pigs. So after his death in 1950, agents were dispatched (by none other than E. Howard Hunt, later of Watergate fame) to buy the film rights to *Animal Farm* from his widow to make its message more overtly anti-Communist.[83]

Today, propaganda is subtly being introduced into the plots, themes, and characters of popular television programs—known as "militainment." In exchange for script supervision, the U.S. Pentagon has provided programs such as *JAG* (CBS), *Military Diaries Project* (VH-1), and *Profiles From the Front Line* (ABC) with free access to military equipment, such as battleships, and locations for episodes of the programs. Katharine Q. Seelye explains:

> An official at the Pentagon elaborated: "We offer our assistance when we think it is in the best interest of the Department of Defense and our people, and it's up to the production company to accept it. If they go on and say, 'Thanks but no thanks, we won't make our character be what you stand for,' we are less inclined to support them."[84]

David James Elliott, *JAG*'s leading man, who in a tribunal episode prosecutes an accused terrorist, described the show's relationship with the Pentagon. "We send our scripts to our liaison and they weigh in on it," he said, referring to Paul Strub, the Pentagon's liaison with the entertainment industry. Elliott said the show hesitated to anger its Pentagon contacts, "because they certainly lend a great deal of production value that we couldn't buy."[85]

As part of its external propaganda campaign, America also sets up its own popular media channels that deliver propaganda messages to a global audience. In 2002, the U.S. government began broadcasting Radio Sawa to the Arab world. This FM station broadcasts a mixture of American popular music and propaganda messages. Felicity Barringer explains:

> Radio Sawa [broadcasts] 85 percent pop music, 15 percent government-generated news, slickly packaged with market research in hand. Anyone who tunes in gets, every half-hour, a dollop of news about President Bush or developments in the Middle East. Three to five minutes later, the station goes back to backbeats.[86]

In 2003, the U.S. government announced the establishment of the Middle Eastern Television Network, a twenty-four-hour satellite television network broadcast to twenty-two countries in the Middle East. The channel presents morning talk shows, sports, news, and children's programs from an American perspective. According to Norman Pattiz, chairman of Westwood One, who heads the Middle East Committee of the broadcasting board of governors, the aim is "to counter the negative images being broadcast right now, the incitement to violence, the hate radio, the journalistic self-censorship."[87] In 2003, the United States also announced plans to launch Al Hurra, a satellite television station, beamed to the Middle East from Virginia.

Photo 2.1a **Media and the Distortion of History**

This original photograph is a portrait of members of the St. Petersburg Union of Struggle for the Liberation of the Working Class, taken in February 1897. Left to right, standing: Alexander Malchenko, Petr Zaporozhers, Anatolii Vanayev. Seated: V.V. Starkov, Gleb Krzhyzhanovsky, Vladimir Ulyanov (Lenin), and Yuli Martov.

Identifying Propaganda Messages

The ability to identify and evaluate propaganda messages undermines the central persuasive function of propaganda by empowering individuals to develop independent judgments about the messages they receive through the media. However, developing an awareness of propaganda is not an easy task, for several reasons. Propaganda is designed to discourage critical analysis by making the messages appear natural. As psychologist Anthony Pratkanis observes, "Most people think propaganda works on everyone else but themselves."[88] To add to the confusion, propaganda messages may consist of a combination of truth and lies. During World War II, the Nazi propaganda machine interspersed facts about achievements such as highway improvements into its anti-Semitic diatribes.

Photo 2.1b **Media and the Distortion of History**

In this retouched photograph, published in 1939, Malchenko has been airbrushed out of the picture. Arrested in 1929 and accused of being a "wrecker," Malchenko was executed in 1930. In 1958, his contributions to the Bolshevik revolution were again recognized, at which time his image was restored in the photograph. (*From* The Commisar Vanishes: The Falsification of Photographs and Art in Stalin's Russia, *by David King. Henry Holt and Company. Reprinted by permission of David King.*)

However, propaganda campaigns, no matter how sophisticated, essentially assign the positives to their side and the negatives to the other side. Propaganda messages establish a simple, absolute worldview in which people, nations, and ideologies are depicted in terms of absolute oppositions: good versus evil, heroes versus villains, friends versus enemies. As a result, propaganda campaigns often employ the same types of images, regardless of the country of origin or its ideology. To illustrate, media historian Leah Bendavid-Val found a striking similarity between propaganda photographs taken in the Soviet Union under Joseph Stalin and pictures taken by photographer Dorothea Lange for the Farm Security Administration during America's Great Depression. Sarah Boxer explains:

In 1933, Dorothea Lange took a shot of Filipino farm workers cutting lettuce in Salinas, Calif., that resembles Arkady Shishkin's 1931 photo of farmers in a commune in the Karelia Region: both show the same bent figures breaking the cracked soil and the horizon line at the same time.

Despite the photographic parallels, the Soviet Union and the United States were worlds apart and their documentarians were making vastly different points.

What accounts for the similarities? In both cases, the photographers were looking for the most persuasive images. In both nations, editors were determining, to some degree, the form and content of the photographs. And they were keenly aware that no matter what the message was, certain subjects and forms were more persuasive.[89]

At the same time, however, some images can have a culture-specific meaning. Richard Leiby describes the U.S. propaganda strategy during the incursion in Afghanistan in 2002: "One official objected to a leaflet showing Afghanistan as a chessboard with bin Laden orchestrating Taliban pawns—until the experts [in Afghanistan] explained that chess is immensely popular in the region and the image would instantly connect."[90]

Frequently, images are manipulated as part of propaganda campaigns. During the Stalin era in Russia in the 1930s, political rivals who had been purged from the party were eliminated from official party photographs. Photos 2.1a and 2.1b (see pages 50 and 51) illustrate how the media can be used to distort historical events. Today, digital photography now makes it even easier to alter people and events by manipulating images.

The use of language must be carefully considered in the analysis of propaganda. Leiby provides the following example from the incursion in Afghanistan in 2001: "In Afghanistan, the psyop-ers deliberately avoided using the word 'surrender' because they knew it would not play well with the Taliban. They substituted appeals along the lines of "Return to your homes and villages."[91] (For more discussion about word choice, see Chapter 5, Production Elements.)

Lines of Inquiry: Process

Function

I. Conduct a media literacy analysis of an international media presentation (e.g., article, newspaper, magazine, television program, film, Web site), focusing on *function*.
- A. What is the purpose (or purposes) behind the media presentation?
  - Description
  - Instruction
  - Information
  - Entertainment
  - Creative expression
  - Exploration
  - Performance
  - Emotional catharsis
  - Exposure to other countries
  - Fostering global communities
  - Maintaining order
  - Persuasion
  - Profit
- B. Can you identify communications functions in addition to the functions discussed in the chapter?
- C. Does the production contain any latent functions?
- D. Does the media communicator want the audience to act in a particular way as a result of receiving the information?
- E. What insight does identifying the function(s) provide with regard to media messages?

II. Analyze a sample of media presentations from different countries, identifying function.
- Name (title) of presentation:
- Medium (e.g., TV, newspaper, Internet):
- Time:
- Briefly describe the media production:
- Functions (Indicate manifest or latent):

Manifest	Latent
_____	_____
_____	_____
_____	_____

A. How many different functions did you identify?

B. Which function(s) appeared most frequently? Indicate which were manifest and which were latent.

C. Did you find any patterns or similarities in function on the basis of:
  • Nationality
  • Medium (e.g., magazines, television, Internet)
  • Genre (e.g., news, advertising, soap opera)

D. What conclusions can you draw from this analysis?

III. Analyze a sample of international news presentations to analyze propaganda:

A. What is the desired result of the propaganda?
  1. Changes in attitudes
  2. Changes in behaviors

B. Who is the media communicator?
  1. Who is providing information?
  2. Why are they providing information?

C. Who or what is the subject of the propaganda (e.g., people, governments, or ways of life)?
  1. Does the propaganda convey a positive or negative message about the subject?
  2. What characteristics are ascribed to the subject?

D. Who is the intended audience?
  1. Internal audience
  2. External audience

E. What is the message of the propaganda?
  1. Does the message associate the object of the propaganda with absolutes (good vs. evil)?
  2. Does the propaganda rely on cultural stereotypes?

F. Do production elements reinforce intended propaganda messages?
  1. Editing
    a. Selected facts
    b. Does the message contain lies, truth, or a combination?
    c. Information that is presented out of context
  2. Connotative words
  3. Connotative images
  4. Music
  5. Camera angle

Media Communicator

I. Conduct a media literacy analysis of an international media presentation, focusing on the media communicator.
  A. Identify the demographic characteristics of the media communicator(s).
    1. Nationality
    2. Gender
    3. Age
    4. Income
    5. Religion
    6. Race/ethnicity
    7. Educational level
  B. What is the affiliation of the media communicator?
    1. Who funds this organization?
    2. What is the mission of the media organization?
    3. Is the media organization national or international?
    4. How does this affiliation affect the point of view of the media presentation?
  C. What is the level of expertise of the media communicator?
    1. Is this person qualified to speak authoritatively on the subject?
    2. Does this person's contribution fall within his or her range of expertise?
    3. What are the criteria for being considered an expert?
  D. Does the media presentation rely on expert sources?
    1. If so, are they identified?
    2. Do these sources share any characteristics (e.g., similar nationality, gender, income, race, ideology, education)?
    3. What are their motives for contributing (e.g., profit, political motives)?
  E. What conclusions can you draw from this analysis?
  F. How does familiarity with the media communicator provide insight into your interpretation of media content? Explain.
II. What is the point of view of the media communicator?
  A. Check a body of the person's work (e.g., a series of news stories or film reviews). Does this shed light on the media communicator's point of view?
  B. Can you detect any embedded values on the part of the media

communicator? Examine word choice, images, and headlines to support your observations.

III. Compare media presentations from different countries. Does the comparison provide insight into the point of view of the media communicators?

IV. Consider the system of media ownership operating in your country.

    A. Under which ownership model does the country's media system operate?

        1. State ownership

        2. Public ownership

        3. Private ownership

        4. Hybrid ownership

    B. How does this ownership model affect the content of media programming?

V. Conduct a media log, identifying the source of the media messages you are exposed to over a twenty-four hour period. As you fill out the media log, consider the following:

- Media formats (e.g., television)
- Media programming (e.g., *The Simpsons*)
- Ownership (e.g., Fox network)

Please note that that this media analysis extends only over one day and therefore is not definitive. However, it does usefully indicate general media consumption patterns.

Media format (e.g., newspaper, TV)	Programming	Ownership
AM		
12–1		
1–2		
2–3		
3–4		
4–5		
5–6		
6–7		
7–8		
8–9		
9–10		
10–11		
11–12		

(e.g., newspaper, TV)	Programming	Ownership
PM		
12–1		
1–2		
2–3		
3–4		
4–5		
5–6		
6–7		
7–8		
8–9		
9–10		
10–11		
11–12		

Data Analysis
   A. Were any media corporations particularly influential with regard
      to the content you received?
   B. Where are you getting your information?
      1. State ownership
      2. Public ownership
      3. Private ownership
      4. Hybrid ownership
   C. What is the origin of ownership?
      1. Local
      2. National
      3. Regional
      4. International
   D. In the case of transnational media conglomerates:
      1. How many different media companies provided you with in-
         formation and/or entertainment?
      2. Did one company provide more than two sources of informa-
         tion and/or entertainment? Explain.
      3. In the case of privately owned media systems, what companies
         owned these media?
VI. Conduct research on a transnational media conglomerate (e.g.,
Disney, Vivendi).
   A. What media companies does the conglomerate own (e.g., TV sta-
      tions, newspapers)?

B. What other businesses does it own (or have an interest in)?

C. Identify members of its board of directors.

    1. What is their demographic profile (i.e., nationality, race, gender, income, age, ethnicity)?

    2. What other companies are they affiliated with?

D. Identify any significant developments that have occurred in the conglomerate over the past year (e.g., mergers, divestitures, profit or loss, personnel changes).

VII. Conduct a media literacy analysis of a specific presentation (e.g., television program, advertisement, or news report) owned by a transnational media conglomerate. In what ways does the ownership of the media presentation have an impact on its content?

A. Support of status quo

B. Homogeneity of content

C. Controlling access to content

D. Programming for profit

E. Programming as product

F. Conflicts of interest

G. Influence of advertising

H. Cross-promotion

I. Allocation of resources

VIII. Examine the influence of one media system (e.g., the private ownership model) on the other ownership models.

A. In a country featuring a hybrid ownership model, what is the impact of one ownership system on the other systems (e.g., the impact of the private ownership model on a state-run system?

B. Compare and contrast media presentations in a country that operates according to a hybrid ownership model, focusing on:

    1. Content

    2. Point of view

    3. Relationship with audience

IX. Conduct research on recent developments with respect to transnational media conglomerates.

- Mergers
- Financial losses
- Management upheaval
- Subject of litigation
- Sale of media assets
- Divestiture of foreign companies

A. What is the status of these developments?

B. What is the impact of these developments on media content?

Audience

I. Select a country and identify the distinguishing characteristics of the national audience.

A. Demographic information

B. Access to media

C. Lifestyle

D. Audience behavior patterns

II. Examine a sample of international media presentations from a single country.

A. How have the messages and themes been developed and presented to reach the intended audience?

B. How does communicating with a global audience affect the communications *style, strategy,* and *content* of the media presentation?

C. Conversely, what do the communication strategy, content, and style of a media presentation reveal about the intended audience?

D. What factors interfere with your ability to interpret the information? Explain.

E. What cues are useful for you in interpreting the content?

3

Context

Historical Context

Media presentations can provide valuable glimpses into the past. Writing about Paris, Michel Reilhac observes, "It's really, truly moving for a Parisian to see, sometimes just in the background of older feature films, how many cars there were, how people dressed, how they walked and behaved. . . . Since we have films dating back 100 years, it really is this idea of trying to keep contact with the past."[1] Nations pass on their historic legacy through their media presentations. To illustrate, in the documentary film *The Unknown War of the East*, filmmaker Dimitri Liakhovitski introduced American audiences to a little-known piece of history, when President Woodrow Wilson sent U.S. soldiers to Russia to fight the Bolsheviks during the Russian Revolution of 1918–1919. As James W. Loewen observes, this obscure historical event had an enormous impact on subsequent relations between the United States and the Soviet Union:

> Few Americans who were not alive at the time know anything about our "unknown war with Russia." . . . Not one of the twelve American history textbooks in my sample even mentions it. [But] this aggression fueled the suspicions . . . that the Western powers meant to destroy the Soviet government if given the chance . . . [This] motivated the Soviets during the Cold War, and until its breakup the Soviet Union continued to claim damages from the invasion.[2]

In addition media programs also provide an *indirect* way for an audience to become acquainted with a historical period. To illustrate, a popular Spanish TV situation comedy, *Cuentame como paso* (Tell Me How It Happened), is set during the dictatorship of General Francisco Franco in the late 1960s and early 1970s. The historical context provides an important backdrop for the plot, which features the misadventures of a middle-class family. Daniel Woolls explains:

> Franco and the worst of his regime are mainly a silent presence. Jailing, repression and execution of political opponents are nowhere to be seen. Spain is now a modern democracy of 40 million people, nearly 40 percent of whom had either not been born when Franco died in 1975 or were too small to remember him.
>
> So for young people—one of the show's several loyal audiences, according to state-run TVE, which broadcasts it—the series is a window on a past they never experienced.
>
> "[The series] reflects where we Spaniards come from, it reflects our immediate history and what that past was like," said series director Tito Fernandez, who at 71 remembers it all vividly. "It is important that people know."[3]

Some historical references found in media programs are universally recognizable. For instance, the term *Waterloo,* derived from French emperor Napoleon Bonaparte's final battle with the British in 1815, has become a familiar metaphor for a watershed moment culminating in defeat. But every country also has its own set of historical references, which are unknown to international audiences. To illustrate, in the United States, the War of 1812 is understood to refer to the conflict between America and Great Britain. However, for Europeans, the War of 1812 is recognized as the French/Russian war, when Napoleon invaded Russia.

A national media program may assume a special significance through its association with a historical event. For instance, the Seventh Symphony by Russian composer Dmitri Shostakovich is known as the Leningrad Symphony because it was written and performed during the blockade of Leningrad by the Nazis in 1942. The subsequent use of this music in films such as *Zoya* (1944), *Simple Folk* (1945), and *Hamlet* (1963) underscored the tragic themes in these movies.

Being able to recognize the historical references embedded in a media presentation can furnish perspective into its themes and messages. For instance, *Star Wars: Episode I—Phantom Menace* (1999) includes a scene of an invading army marching through an archway. Social critic Dr. William Madosky points out that this image is strikingly similar to a famous World War II photograph of the German invasion of Paris, in which the Nazi army marched through the Arc de Triomphe. This historical reference provides perspective into filmmaker George Lucas's commentary about the dangers of capitulation to tyrants.[4]

Many producers now make separate versions of their work for international distribution that include supplementary historical background information, so that foreign audiences will be able to put the presentation into proper perspective. As an example, when the Argentinean film *La Oficial Historia* was released in America, director Luis Puenzo inserted additional historical information into the English subtitles that does not appear in the movie's original Spanish dialogue.

Impact of Historical Sensibility on Media Presentations

The *historical sensibility* of a country—that is, how events have influenced a nation's outlook and attitudes—can affect how a country's media messages are constructed, in several respects.

First, the historical sensibility of a country can influence the selection of topics covered by the media. For instance, the British media focus particular attention on Britain's former colonies, such as the United States, Canada, Ireland, Australia, and India.

In addition, every country has its own *historical taboos*—that is, issues that the media choose not to cover because of past events. As an example, in 2001, a rare concert was held in Israel featuring the work of composer Richard Wagner. However, the concert received no coverage in the Israeli press, largely because of the historical association between Wagner's music and the anti-Semitism of Nazi Germany.

The historical sensibility of a country can also influence the point of view expressed in its media commentaries. To illustrate, when the United States prepared to invade Afghanistan in 2001, the Russian and British media initially expressed skepticism about the mission, in large measure because both countries had unsuccessfully waged war in Afghanistan in the past.

Further, historical sensibility may affect the treatment of subjects that are presented in the media. For instance, in a joint Israeli/Palestinian adaptation of the American children's program *Sesame Street,* the producers took exception to a segment in the American production on littering, showing images of children picking up cans on the street. One of the producers explained, "Our children have been taught not to pick up stray objects. It could be a bomb." Other video footage was substituted, making the container a clear water bottle and showing a child taping the rough edges with the help of an adult.[5]

Media Presentations as Reflection of Historical Sensibility

At the same time, media programming can serve as a text, which furnishes insight into the historical sensibility of a nation. Media-programming can reveal the relative importance that a culture places on particular issues and events. To illustrate, in December 2001, following the events of 9/11, six of the top ten queries on the Internet search engine Google were related to the topics of terrorist attacks and the war on terrorism.[6]

In addition, the retelling of historical events through the media can serve as a barometer of current attitudes. As an example, in 2002, Dream TV, an Egyptian satellite television channel, presented *Horse Without a Horseman,* a forty-one part series that traces the history of the Middle East from 1855 to 1917. The producers of the series incorporated ideas from *The Protocols of the Elders of Zion,* an anti-Semitic document that had been fabricated by Russian czar Nicholas II's secret police. This treatise, which purports to prove that Jewish leaders were plotting world dominion, was used as a pretext for persecution of Jews in twentieth-century Russia and, later, in Nazi Germany. According to Daniel J. Wakin, the reappearance of the *Protocols* in the Egyptian series is evidence of the resurgence of anti-Semitism around the world:

> Anti-Semitic writings and images are on the rise in the Arab world. Some say Israeli actions against the Palestinians are being expressed in anti-Jewish terms. . . . Scholars of the Islamic world, which historically has had a closeness with Judaism, say demonization of both (words and images) is inevitable after such long conflict in the Middle East.[7]

The popularity of media programs may also indicate historical shifts within a culture. For instance, an old American sit-com, *Hogan's Heroes,* set in a Nazi prisoner-of-war camp, resurfaced in Germany during the late 1990s. According to Alan Cowell, the popularity of the series throughout the country demonstrated the degree to which German society has distanced itself from the experience of World War II:

> Those who watch the series are . . . a newer generation for whom the horrors are more distant, for whom being German means living in a peaceful,

comfortable Europe in which nationalism has been subsumed in the striving for a broader, continent-wide identity. That, perhaps, is why the series, produced in the United States between 1965 and 1971 (and still shown in some markets there), took more than 25 years to cross the Atlantic.[8]

Indeed, the content of popular media programming can even *anticipate* historical events. Media communicators look closely at historical trends as material for media presentations. For instance, the Hollywood film *Collateral Damage* (2002), which was shot before the terrorist attack of September 11, 2001, contained some eerie parallels to the tragedy. The film's hero, Gordy Brewer (played by Arnold Schwarzenegger), is a firefighter whose family is wiped out when a Los Angeles skyscraper is bombed by an international terrorist. Director Andrew Davis drew upon previous terrorist incidents, as well as the prevailing sentiments in the Middle East, to develop the plot of the film.

However, entertainment programming frequently distort historical events for dramatic emphasis. Frank Rich identifies the following historical inaccuracies in the 2001 Hollywood film *Pearl Harbor,* a dramatization of the Japanese attack on the U.S. naval base in 1941:

> Among its other idiosyncrasies, this film glosses over Japan's motives for its attack—and, for that matter, never explains why anyone was fighting in Asia or Europe. . . . Though Pearl Harbor is still nominally set in Hawaii, no Hawaiians seem to live there. We also learn that no American servicemen of that time smoked cigarettes, and that at least one of them (Ben Affleck) maintained a coiffure meticulously flecked with blond highlights. And then there's the moment in which F.D.R., trying to rouse his cabinet, miraculously rises from his wheelchair to stand on his own two feet, polio be damned.[9]

Finally, the evolution of a country's media system can serve as a microcosm of historical developments in the nation. To illustrate, Elaine Sciolino draws the following parallels between changes in Iranian cinema and historical events in the country:

> The Iranian cinema has come a long way from the revolution 22 years ago. Ayatollah Ruhollah Khomeini, the father of the revolution, railed against the cinema, putting it in the same category as theater, dancing and sexually integrated swimming. The day after he returned from exile in 1979, he said, "The cinema is a modern invention that ought to be used

for the sake of educating the people, but as you know, it was used instead to corrupt our youth."

. . . In 1982, Iran formally banned films that were judged to encourage wickedness, corruption and prostitution. That policy began to change in the late 1980s, when, as part of a scheme to liberalize the arts, Mohammad Khatami—then the Minister of Islamic Guidance and Culture, now president—declared that "cinema is not the mosque." More conservative clerics resisted, and in 1992 Mr. Khatami resigned, writing that he would rather "fight ignorance and backwardness" on his own.

But his election as president in 1997—and his call for tolerance and the rule of law—signaled an even bolder cultural explosion. In a speech that fall, Mr. Khatami proclaimed, "Our cinema is a vivid and clear reflection of the greatness of our culture, people and Islamic revolution." And although a cultural crackdown a year ago shut down most of Iran's reformist newspapers and put many of its best journalists behind bars, most of Iran's filmmakers have been left alone, in part because they have helped burnish the image of Iran around the world.[10]

Cultural Context

The study of media presentations can provide perspective on the *cultural sensibility* of a country. Cultural sensibility refers to a country's distinctive customs, informal codes of conduct, norms, and mores.

A country's cultural sensibility affects the construction of media messages, as well as how people interpret media programming. To illustrate, China's authoritarian government maintains strict control over the information that appears in the media. However, according to Zhu Ling, deputy editor in chief of the *China Daily,* these controls are as much culturally based as politically motivated: "The Asian way is to respect authority and not be confrontational." Because this respect for authority is so deeply ingrained in Chinese culture, the limits of what journalists can publish are unspoken, but understood. Zhu explains, "We know the rules. No one has to tell me."[11]

Every country maintains its own standards with regard to what types of content it considers appropriate for presentation in the media. For instance, in France, ads depicting nudity, such as Yves Saint Laurent's campaign for Opium perfume, are not uncommon. However, in Great Britain, the Advertising Standards Authority has banned this same Opium perfume ad campaign from its newspapers and television programs.[12]

In addition, a country's media presentations may contain cultural references that are unfamiliar to people in other countries. For instance, the names of American sports legends Babe Ruth, Joe DiMaggio, and Jackie Robinson are largely unknown to people outside of the United States.

Indeed, media programming has emerged as a primary source of new cultural references within a country. For example, in Tanzania, the character of Mkwaju, a truck driver in the radio soap opera *Twende na Wakati* (Let's Go with the Times) became such a symbol of promiscuity within the country that his name has become a metaphor for unbridled sexual behavior (as in the phrase "Don't be a Mkwaju").[13]

Media and Popular Culture

Popular programming reflects a level of acceptance and shared values among large numbers of people. People tend to watch programs that meet their approval. If they are truly offended by violent programs, they would not watch them. In that sense, media programming can be regarded as a text that reflects the attitudes, values, behaviors, preoccupations, and myths that define a culture.

Media Programming as a Reflection of Cultural Attitudes

A popular media presentation can serve as an expression of prevailing attitudes within a culture. To illustrate, South African musician Mbongeni produced a very popular but controversial song, "Amandiya" (Indians) in 2002. The lyrics of the song accuse people of Indian ancestry of having exploited and abused black Africans. Responding to criticism from South African officials, Mbongeni explained that the popularity of the song confirmed the existence of this social problem: "If there wasn't this reality, I wouldn't have written this song. . . . I knew I would be trampling on people's toes. But the emergence of this song has given Africans hope that finally this can be spoken about."[14]

Media Programs as a Reflection of Cultural Values

Psychologist Milton Rokeach defines values as "an enduring belief that a specific mode of conduct or end-state of existence is personally or socially preferable to alternate modes of conduct or end-state of existence."[15] An individual's personal values system is in large measure defined by the prevailing values system in his or her culture.

The study of media presentations can furnish insight into a country's values system. To illustrate, Chinese advertisements reflect the cultural values of family, tradition, and technology. In contrast, American ads emphasize the importance of enjoyment, cost savings, and individualism.[16]

Media Programming as a Reflection of Cultural Preoccupations

A *cultural preoccupation* can be defined by the relative importance that a culture places on a particular issue. To illustrate, a cross-cultural analysis of advertisements reveals that Swedish culture is more comfortable with the process of aging than American society. Thirteen percent of Swedish ads display models over the age of sixty-six as opposed to only 3 percent of U.S. ads.[17] To cite another example, "sex" is the most popular keyword in mainland Europe when buying ad space. In the United Kingdom, however, it ranks fortieth, the most frequent word being "employment."[18]

Media presentations can also provide considerable insight into the nature of a cultural preoccupation. For instance, sex is a pervasive topic in U.S. media programming. However, media historian Barbara Friedman observes that American ads exhibit a more puritanical attitude toward sex that is found in some other cultures:

> In America, the ad campaign for the film *Almost Famous* featured a tight shot of Kate Hudson's face, with the movie title reflected in her sunglasses. But in Paris, the promotion featured a photograph of the actress seated on a bedroom floor, with her knees drawn up to her chest. She was wearing underwear and a camisole. What struck me is that she has the facial and physical features of a young girl. The ad would be considered far more risqué in the U.S. In Moscow, there are billboards everywhere, including government buildings, that display women who are either scantily clad or completely nude. This would clearly be unacceptable in the U.S.[19]

Media Content as a Reflection of Cultural Myths

Cultural myths are sets of beliefs which may or may not be true; nevertheless, cultural myths reveal how inhabitants of a country see themselves, as well as how they are perceived by others. Today, the media have assumed a vital role in the transmission of cultural myths. To illustrate, over 50,000 films have been made about Paris or shot in Paris, reinforcing its reputation as a city of romance. As the French filmmaker Chris Marker once said, "Nothing is more beautiful than Paris, except the memory of Paris."[20]

Regardless of whether or not a cultural myth is true, it often assumes *a mythic reality* over time, as people buy into the transmission of the myth through the media. Indeed, people often make judgments about people and countries based on the messages conveyed through the media. For instance, many South Africans were amused by the ways in which the American reality show *Survivor* played off of cultural myths when taping on location in Africa. Ed Stoddard notes:

> In the opening episode, participants struggled to build a life-giving fire and one of them envisaged an encounter with tigers and bears.
>
> South Africans who know a thing or two about the bush found their antics hilarious. Audiences acknowledged the participants might come across lions and elephants. But tigers and bears? In Kenya? No way.
>
> Then there is the show's concept of where it takes place. The show's tagline, "It's a jungle out there," gets a rise out of viewers because the setting is semi-arid savannah.[21]

At the same time, media programming *reinforces* cultural attitudes, values, behaviors, preoccupations, and myths. Media messages are communicated through the countless hours of media programming that repeat, directly or indirectly, the cultural script. To illustrate, political scientist Farideh Farhi accounts for the popularity of Iranian films as an opportunity for the national audience to "bear witness, and to gain affirmation for their daily experiences."[22]

Finally, the media do not merely reflect or reinforce culture but in fact *shape* attitudes, values, behaviors, preoccupations, and myths. For instance, international media programming can influence a country's customary standards of beauty. In 2002, Miss Nigeria, Agbani Darego, won the Miss World Pageant. According to Norimitsu Onishi, Darego represents a radical departure from the traditional norms of female beauty in her country:

> In a culture where Coca-Cola-bottle voluptuousness is celebrated and ample backsides and bosoms are considered ideals of female beauty, the new Miss World shared none of those attributes. She was 6 feet tall, stately and so, so skinny. She was, some said uncharitably, a white girl in black skin.

The change is an example of the power of Western culture on a continent caught between tradition and modernity. Older Nigerians' views of beauty have not changed. But among young, fashionable Nigerians, voluptuousness is out and thin is in.[23]

The Media and Cultural Imperialism

The media have emerged as a principal means by which ideology is introduced, reinforced, and disseminated throughout the world. Ideology is the system of beliefs or ideas that helps determine the thinking and behavior of a culture. According to media scholar Berle Francis, the global media promote a system of *cultural imperialism*, in which dominant media-owning countries export their culture through the media.[24]

The flow of information has long been dominated by Western culture —particularly the United States. Four of the five major news agencies are Western; these agencies account for 90 percent of the global news flow (for further discussion, see the section on Ownership Patterns in Chapter 2). More than simply providing information, the Western news industry conveys powerful cumulative messages about the legitimacy of the social order, the role of government and laws, a prototype of the class system, and images of success. According to Professor Robert McChesney, American news programming conveys the following cumulative messages:

- The United States is a force for good in the world.
- Opposition to the United States is a sign of evil.
- The United States alone has a right to invade anyone we want for any reason.
- Democracy and capitalism are synonymous.
- The movement toward capitalism is equated with progress.[25]

The international market is saturated with American entertainment programming. Hollywood films account for approximately 85 percent of movie audiences worldwide.[26] Further, American programming makes up approximately 65 percent of global prime-time TV viewing.[27] American music is also a dominant influence worldwide. Over a four-year span, the American pop group Destiny's Child sold more than 15 million albums and singles across the globe. Indeed, during the first week of the release of *Survivor* (2001), the album shot to the number-one-selling slot in ten countries.[28]

The worldview of these entertainment programs sends positive cumulative messages about U.S. culture. Edward Rothstein observes, "American popular culture offers a powerful promise. Luxuriant and prurient passions are partially satisfied; desires for autonomy are offered fulfillment; material pleasures and possibilities become palpable. Choices are freely made. Who can resist such a siren song?"[29] The positive cumulative messages about the United States are so powerful that, although a significant percentage of people throughout the world expressed their disapproval of the U.S. political agenda in 2003, many people remained fans of American culture, as expressed in its music, movies, and TV.[30]

Exposure to Western values through media programming can have a disruptive influence on traditional societies on several levels.

Generational conflicts. In traditional cultures, the older generation serves as curators of its heritage, instructing younger generations about cultural history, art, and values. In contrast, Western media promote a youth culture, in which societal authority has shifted to the younger generation. In these technological cultures, young people have become the source of knowledge; parents depend on their children to program their VCRs, download their music, and fix their computers. Because films, music, and fashion emphasize what is new and contemporary, artistic expression has become the domain of young people. Many films and television programs undermine traditional adult authority by depicting parents as inconsequential, comedic figures, patronized by their all-knowing children. Young audiences have emerged as the primary targets of advertisers, reinforcing the belief that only young people matter.

In the face of these Western media messages, many young people in traditional cultures are rebelling against the societal constraints imposed on them by their elders. Alexis Bloom provides the following example:

> Bhutan, with its policy of placing "Gross National Happiness" ahead of gross national product, is also a country where the police detain or fine adults for not wearing traditional Bhutanese dress—the knee-length gho for men, the apronlike kira for women—in public.
>
> "But we'd like to wear the clothes they wear on MTV," Sherub Dorji said. "At parties we used to wear the kira, but now everybody is wearing pants. Pants and miniskirts."
>
> Fortunately for Sherub's generation, the fashion police don't frequent Club X, the more long-standing of Bhutan's two discos. Young people hunch over the bar, ordering Red Panda beers and potent Bhutanese gin.

The sale of tobacco is prohibited in many Bhutanese provinces, but you'd never guess it from the locomotive puffing of boys with seal-slick hair. Not one person in this basement hideaway is wearing traditional clothing: leather jackets shine, halter tops are clean and pressed. And they're dancing to rock 'n' roll.

This is a change that Kinley Dorji laments. "We have always dressed like this," he said, rubbing the heavy cloth of his gho. "But now the young people want to dress like their new heroes on television, like their favorite movie stars. A generation gap is emerging with great contrast."[31]

Gender conflicts. In traditional cultures, the introduction of new ideas through the media can upset the established social order between men and women. Simon Romero cites this example:

[The] women of the impoverished Wapishana and Macushi tribes of Guyana [in Ecuador] were introduced to the internet in a project sponsored by Bill Humphries, who headed Guyana Telephone and Telegraph at the time and was optimistic about technology's money-making potential. The tribal power structures were shaken.

The women began making money by marketing their intricate handwoven hammocks over the Web at $1,000 each. Feeling threatened, the traditional regional leadership took control of the organization, alienating and finally driving out the young woman who ran the Web site. The weaving group fell into disarray.[32]

Conflicts between urban and rural populations. Although the mass media are well established in the urban areas of many traditional cultures, the global network has not yet reached the outlying villages and farms. Consequently, people living in a large urban center like Bangkok may have more in common with residents of other metropolitan areas like Montreal or London than they do with relatives living in the countryside of Thailand. Bloom provides an example of the growing urban/rural division in Bhutan:

The impish conspirators huddle in a side street of Bhutan's capital, tearing cardboard boxes into strips. Once the strips are trimmed to size, the boys proudly hold them against their waists, like little grooms adjusting cummerbunds. With varying degrees of accuracy, they scrawl "W.W.F. Championship" across the makeshift belts.

"I am the Rock!" screams a child in a yellow T-shirt, grasping a pint-size opponent by the neck. "I am the champion!"

"I am Triple H!" his opponent squawks in reply before he's knocked to the ground.

Less than a mile away, boys the same age chant prayers inside a Buddhist temple. Drawing their wine-colored robes close, the monks, some as young as 5, nod and bow as the wind rattles the prayer wheels outside. This is still a country where rural areas look as they did in ancient times, and where, for every television antenna, a thousand prayer flags flutter.[33]

Class divisions. Poor, uneducated people, who have less access to media, are not in a position to enjoy the benefits of globalization. After traveling to the Angola-Zambia border town of Mwinilunga, Alan Cowell observed, "The question . . . is not so much whether globalization would help the poor in these parts of the developing world, as whether it extended here at all."[34]

However, there have been some recent indications that the global influence of American media programming may be abating. Increasingly, American television programs are being relegated to late night or weekend time periods, with the prime-time slots being taken by nationally produced shows. One reason for this shift is that many countries now produce their own programming. To illustrate, in South Korea, the top-rated show in the third week of September 2002 was *The Era of the Abandoned Hero,* a locally produced soap opera that attracted 22.7 percent of the audience. In contrast, *C.S.I.,* the top-rated television show in the United States, drew just 2.7 percent of Korean viewers tuning in that week.[35] According to Suzanne Kapner, "Foreign viewers often prefer homegrown shows that better reflect local tastes, cultures and historical events."[36]

Recently, the global community has been taking steps to address the inequality of the global information system. UNESCO is providing financial assistance to developing countries as they build their own media communication systems. In addition, a number of independent international organizations are initiating programs to promote the development and use of media technology throughout the globe. The World Economic Forum has created the Global Digital Divide Initiative, which promotes public and private sector initiatives "to transform the digital divide into an opportunity for growth."[37]

Ultimately, of course, the merging of cultures is inevitable, a part of the natural course of events. The mass media have merely accelerated this process. As discussed earlier, the media are simply a channel of communications. Much depends upon how the channel is used, who uses it, for what purpose. Romero declares:

Now, as technology starts to blur the distinction between industrialized countries and developing ones, social transition, if not transformation, has become an issue in some of the world's most remote regions. A recent issue of *Cultural Survival*, a magazine that covers indigenous people and ethnic minorities, described projects to bring the Web to communities as varied as the reindeer-herding Sami of Scandinavia and Northern Russia, the aboriginal peoples of the Northwest Territories in Canada, the ethnic minorities of Burma and native Hawaiians.

These efforts represent a departure from the idea that introducing new technologies to indigenous peoples will bring about negative results. Such thinking, which dates back to Jean-Jacques Rousseau, the 18th-century French philosopher who lured Europe into idealizing the simple lifestyle of the noble savage, appears to be coming undone in the digital age.[38]

Worldview

What kind of world is depicted in a media presentation?

Worldview can be a valuable key to identifying manifest and latent messages contained in media presentations. When producing a program, media communicators construct a complete world based on certain fundamental assumptions about how this world operates. The worldview of a media presentation frequently assumes a disarming naturalness in the narrative; the correctness of this order is never questioned by the heroes and heroines with whom we identify. The worldview of a program also remains unnoticed because it merely provides the background in which the plot and characters operate. To illustrate, the Indonesian film *Ada Apa Dengan Cinta?* (What's Up with Love?, 2002) presents an indirect but compelling worldview of the American system. Jane Perlez observes:

> American icons are everywhere in the film. The school cafeteria serves burgers and fries; a Coca-Cola machine seems to appear in every other scene. Many of the students drive their parents' latest-model pastel colored cars to school. Ms. Lesmana and her crew got some of their film training directing commercials in Jakarta for Western products, and the film has some of the fresh look of American television advertising.[39]

The worldview embedded in media programming sends powerful latent messages about the following:

- What kind(s) of cultures populate this world.
- Who is in control of the world depicted in the media presentation.
- What is important within the world view of the program.
- The way the world operates.
- Measures of success.

To illustrate, the worldview of American media presentations is defined by *consumer culture, modernity, globalization*, and *progress*. These defining characteristics are unified and interchangeable; one cannot exist in isolation from the others.

A Consumer Culture

The world of American media programming is reduced to what we can see, feel, touch—and buy. According to Merle Ratner, American media programming "promotes the love for possessions over the love for people or it promotes the love for people as possessions."[40] In this material world, success is displayed through consumerism. People discover meaning through the acquisition of consumer goods. Indeed, identity has become a disposable commodity. We can become anyone we want on the basis of how we look and what lifestyle we adopt.

At times, the ideology message of a presentation is co-opted, replaced by the worldview of consumer culture. For instance, in 2000, photographer Alberto Korda, whose poster of Cuban guerrilla hero Che Guevara (Photo 3.1) became a symbol of global revolution, sued Lowe Lintas, a British advertising agency, for using the image in a Smirnoff ad for "spicy" vodka. In the ad, the original image of Guevara was overlaid with chili peppers arranged in a hammer and sickle. Korda accused the advertising firm of trivializing the historical significance of the photograph: "So much commercialization of his [Guevara's] image has covered up [his] significance. Capitalism is very intelligent with that. They take any revolutionary symbol and turn it into merchandise to dilute over time the true meaning."[41]

A World That Celebrates Modernity

In American media programming, being stylish and being "cool" are positive attributes. This is in marked contrast with Chinese culture. In 1993, researchers Godwin C. Chu and Yanan Ju found that 91.2 percent of the respondents in a survey were "proud of China's long historical

Photo 3.1   **Che Guevara**

heritage. Pride in China's long historical heritage is often associated with patriotism, which has been endorsed as a core value by Chinese leadership from Mao Zedong to Deng Xiaoping."[42]

A World Based on Achievement

American media programming reflects a competitive world in which success is measured by individual accomplishment. For example, advertising creates a competitive environment in which consumers are continually asked to compare themselves to others. And in entertainment programs, the conclusion usually features the "triumph" of good over evil, getting the girl (or guy), or finding some form of treasure.

A World That Prizes Individualism

American media transmit messages that prize the individual, fostering such values as independence, privacy, mobility, and freedom. Beginning with the Leatherstocking novels of James Fenimore Cooper, American heroes have embodied the ideal of self-sufficiency. A succession of male media heroes (e.g., John Wayne, Clint Eastwood, and the Marlboro Man), play roles in which they are forced to go it alone in the face of adversity and, at the end of the narrative, ride off into the sunset.

This emphasis on individualism in American media programming conflicts with non-Western nations that place importance on collective behavior. To illustrate, when television was first introduced to the country of Bhutan in 1999, Western programs promoting the virtues of individualism clashed with the collective sensibility of traditional Bhutanese culture. Bloom explains:

> Karma Ura, Director of the Center for Bhutan Studies, points to the arrival of a Hallmark shop on Thimphu's main street as evidence of dramatic social change. With indignation, he says that birthdays and the associated cards, cakes and presents were, until now, unheard of in Bhutan. This celebration of individualism, he said, has taken root as a result of Westernization. "They must reflect people's changing patterns of marking social relationships," he said. "The advent of modernization is now reinforced quite powerfully by television. And very soon you will have Christmas celebrations."[43]

International Media Stereotypes

Consider the following joke:

> What is European Paradise?
> A place where Germans are car mechanics, French are chefs, British are police officers, Swedish are hotelkeepers, and Italians are lovers.
>
> What is European Hell?
> A place with Italian car mechanics, British chefs, French hotelkeepers, Swedish lovers, and German police officers.

The humor (or what humor there is) in this joke is rooted in our shared understanding of national stereotypes. Unless we have had personal contact with a country or its inhabitants, our views are colored by national stereotypes depicted in the media. A stereotype is an oversimplified conception of a person, group, or event. Stereotyping is an associative process, based on a common set of assumptions; if there is no general consensus about a group, there can be no stereotype.

Stereotyping is a common coping mechanism. Even people who are victims of stereotyping in turn stereotype others. Thus, stereotyping serves as a kind of shorthand that enables us to make everyday decisions in our lives. A.O. Scott explains:

> Categorizing can be a useful shortcut to an impression, an efficient alternative to the time-consuming business of digging up all the relevant facts. And the category is often at least roughly right. In categorizing people, researchers say, the brain is looking for fast answers to a few key questions: Friend or foe? Competent or not? Can she be trusted?[44]

To be sure, some stereotypes are positive (e.g., the Japanese are good in math, the Russians are proficient in chess, and the Germans are efficient and punctual). However, according to William B. Helmreich, this grouping principle is frequently inaccurate, negative, and dangerous: "Approximately one third of stereotypes can be said to have a good deal of truth to them. . . . The accurate stereotypes are predominately positive, whereas those that seem highly inaccurate tend by and large to be negative."[45]

To illustrate, in American films and television programs, the stereotypical Arab is a depicted as a villain—often a terrorist—who belongs to an extremist Muslim sect. Moustapha Akkad, an Arab-American film producer, declares, "We cannot say there are no Arab and no Muslim terrorists. Of course there are. But at the same time, balance it with the image of the normal human being, the Arab-American, the family man. The lack of anyone showing the other side makes it stand out that in Hollywood, Muslims are only terrorists."[46]

Lines of Inquiry: Context

Historical Context

I. How does the historical sensibility of a country—that is, how events have influenced a nation's outlook and attitudes—affect how a country's media messages are constructed?

Select a country and conduct research on its history. Then conduct a media literacy analysis of a sample of media presentations from that country, focusing on historical context:

A. What topics have been included and omitted?

      1. What does this reveal about the relative importance that a culture places on particular issues?

      2. What does this reveal about a country's historical taboos—that is, topics that the media choose not to cover because of past events?

   B. What topics are emphasized in the country's media presentations?

   C. Identify historical references embedded in media presentations. What insights do they provide into the messages and themes in the media presentation?

II. Popular media programming can furnish perspective on the historical sensibility of a nation. Conduct a media literacy analysis of a sample of media presentations from a country, focusing on the following:

   A. What do the media presentations reveal about the relative importance that a culture places on particular issues and events?

   B. How does the retelling of historical events through the media reflect contemporary attitudes?

   C. Does the media programming anticipate historical events?

III. Conduct research on the coverage of a particular historical event in the media.

   A. What do you learn about the point of view of different countries by examining their media coverage of the event?

   B. Examine an entertainment program based on the historical event. Are there any points of departure from the historical account? What messages are conveyed?

IV. Conduct research on the evolution of a country's media system. What does this reveal about the history of the country?

Cultural Context

I. Examine a sample of media programming originating from one country.

   A. What do the programs reveal about cultural attitudes, values, preoccupations, and myths?

   B. Do the media presentations contain cultural references?

   C. Worldview: What kind of world is depicted in these media presentations?

      1. What culture or cultures populate this world?

         a. What kinds of people populate this world?

         b. What do we know about the people who populate this world?

         c. Does this world present an optimistic or pessimistic view of life?

1. Are the characters in the presentation happy?
2. Do the characters have a chance to be happy?
3. Are people in control of their own destinies?
   a. Is there a supernatural presence in this world?
   b. Are the characters under the influence of other people?
   c. What hierarchy of values is in operation in this worldview?
1. What embedded values can be found in the production?
2. What values are embodied in the characters?
3. What values prevail through the resolution?
4. What does it mean to be a success in this world?
   a. How does a person succeed in this world?
   b. What kinds of behavior are rewarded in this world?

II. Analyze a sample of international media presentations from around the world.
   A. Compare cultural attitudes, values, and myths reflected in international media presentations.
   B. Examine cumulative messages conveyed by media presentations, focusing on:
      1. Gender roles
      2. Measures of success
      3. Attitudes toward other countries

III. Survey a sample of international media programs. Identify stereotypes of different groups.
   A. Identify the characteristics commonly associated with the group being depicted in the media.
      1. Does word choice reinforce stereotypes?
      2. Editing decisions: is information that reinforces stereotypes included in the media presentation?
      3. Connotative images: are images in the media presentation that reinforce stereotypes included in the media presentation?
   B. Are stereotypes more likely to be found in the program of one country?
   C. Compare stereotypical depictions of different nationalities (e.g., English, Germans, Swedes). Identify similarities, differences.
   D. How is your nationality depicted in international media presentations? Construct a stereotypical profile from foreign films, television programs, advertisements, or magazines.

4

Framework

Framework refers to areas of inquiry related to the form and structure of media programming.

The introduction of a media presentation can provide cues to media messages. The opening credits of films and television shows acquaints the audience with essential information about the worldview of the presentation and foreshadows events that occur later in the narrative. In like fashion, the covers of magazines and tabloid newspapers announce what the media communicators consider the most important story in the publication.

Comparing the headlines in newspapers can disclose striking differences in how information is being presented. A useful example can be found in the headlines of stories about the Middle East "roadmap for peace" in two American newspapers on May 24, 2003: "Israeli Leader Accepts U.S. Peace Plan"[1] and "Sharon Gives Plan for Mideast Peace Qualified Support."[2] These headlines provide very different interpretations of the event. While the first headline declares that Prime Minister Sharon has accepted the U.S. proposal, the second headline frames Sharon's statement as more provisionary.

The introduction of a TV news broadcast can also furnish perspective on its point of view. Discussing international television coverage of the 2003 conflict in Iraq, Daoud Kuttab observed the following:

> A question of terminology has been a subject of heated debate around the AmmanNet office in recent days—whether to refer to the situation in Iraq as an invasion or a war. Arab television stations tend to use the term "invasion" as part of their regular war logo. Al Jazeera uses the logo "War on Iraq" (and not war in Iraq). The Lebanese Hezbollah station Al Manar uses the phrase "Invasion of Iraq"; the Lebanese Broadcasting Corporation uses "Iraq in the Middle of the Storm." And the Saudi station Al Arabiya uses a more neutral phrase: "The Third Gulf War." (The Iraqi

war against Iran was the first; the war following Iraq's invasion of Kuwait was the second.)[3]

The *premise* of a media program can also provide insight into its point of view and ideology. A premise can be defined as the initial circumstances, situation, or set of assumptions that serve as the point of origin in the narrative. A description of a premise usually answers the question, "What is this program about?" According to poet Samuel Taylor Coleridge, our response to fictional narratives is accompanied by "willing suspension of disbelief"—the audience accepts the premise of the program, no matter how outlandish. This suspension of disbelief enables us to participate in the fantasy world of Harry Potter or *The Lord of the Rings*: once the initial premise of the program has been accepted, the remainder of the narrative progresses in a logical fashion.

The premise of a news program affects the construction of the messages that constitute the program. To illustrate, in an article profiling the Arab television station al-Jazeera, Sharon Waxman observes the following set of assumptions:

> From watching the network for any length of time, it's clear that al-Jazeera takes a consistently hostile stance toward the United States. In al-Jazeera's world, the Taliban is invariably an underdog force, the United States looms as an occupying power, and Egypt and other moderate Arab states have knuckled under to the superpower's pressure. The channel's other central topic is Israel's persecution of Palestinians, a constant litany of suffering and aggression. Otherwise there is little on al-Jazeera except sports.
>
> All American-based news networks . . . make the unspoken assumption that the state of Israel has a right to exist and that Osama bin Laden is evil. In the Arab world, that looks like bias.[4]

As you begin to watch a film, see an ad, or read the newspaper, identify the underlying assumptions behind the premise of the presentation. At that point, you can decide whether or not you are willing to suspend your disbelief.

Affective Response

Affective response refers to people's emotional reactions to what they hear and see through the media. Visual and aural media initially touch you on an emotional level. When you hear a song on the radio, your immediate response is to move to the rhythms of the music or, perhaps, sing along. Indeed, one of the fundamental reasons that people enjoy media presentations is for the emotional experience, which explains the promotional category "Feel-Good Movie of the Year."

Media communicators frequently use affective appeals to influence the attitudes and behaviors of the audience. Dr. Donna L. Mumme found that even very young children are able to respond to the emotional cues delivered through a television screen: "They are able to pick up where a person is looking, and of course, they pick up the emotion. It was quite striking that one-year-olds were able to gather that much information from a 20-second television clip."[5]

Advertisements that display animals or babies are intended to evoke a warm response, which the media communicator hopes will be transferred to the product. And political figures routinely arrange for "photo opportunities" with children, elderly people, and their own family members in hopes that the audience will feel positively toward them and, as a result, support them and their policies.

Visual and aural elements can create a mood that reinforces manifest messages or themes in the production. For example, manipulation of lighting, music, and screen space in horror films arouses, intense feelings of terror in the audience. Production elements can also be manipulated in news presentations to influence the attitudes and behaviors of the audience. To illustrate, Thomas Friedman reports the following:

> On my way to Jakarta I stopped in Dubai, where I watched the Arab News Network at 2 A.M. ANN broadcasts from Europe, outside the control of any Arab government, but is seen all over the Middle East. It was running what I'd call the "greatest hits" from the Israeli-Palestinian conflict: nonstop film of Israelis hitting, beating, dragging, clubbing and shooting Palestinians. I would like to say the footage was out of context, but there was no context. There were no words. It was just pictures and martial music designed to inflame passions.[6]

Production elements such as color, lighting, camera angle, movement, editing, music, and costume send clear signals of approval or disapproval to the audience. For instance, the appearance of villains in a narrative may be accompanied by a discordant musical theme throughout the narrative, so that the audience learns to associate their appearance with something negative. Neal Gabler explains:

Viewers get a set of signals, a kind of code, that advises them how to respond.... You watch most television sitcoms and, just by the rhythm of the banter and the laugh track, you know how you are supposed to respond, whether the jokes are funny or not. Sitcom writers call this "likeajoke" because it has the form of a joke without the content. Or you go to a big commercial movie, and just by experiencing the rapid cutting and thumping music you know how you are supposed to respond, whether the action engages you or not.

[Audiences] are sophisticated enough to know that a certain cadence of speech means funny and a certain editing pattern means action and certain saccharine music means melodrama.[7]

Although emotional reactions such as fear, happiness, and anger are universal, the stimulus that provokes these reactions may vary from country to country. For instance, people from different countries have divergent opinions of what is considered humorous or offensive. Sandra Basso, a student from Croatia who attends Webster University in St. Louis, Missouri, remarked, "If somebody tells a bad joke at home, then someone else might say, 'What is that, an American joke?'"[8]

Narrative Elements

Narrative elements such as plot, theme, and characterization can serve as useful keys to interpreting media content.

A *plot* is a series of interrelated actions that progress through an introduction, body, and conclusion. The foundation of plot is conflict: opposing forces clash before coming to a resolution.

Examining the plot of a program can furnish insight into the cultural sensibility of a country. To illustrate, a popular Thai soap opera featured a plot in which a young girl was faced with the task of informing her parents that she had earned a low grade in school. This plot indicates the degree to which education is taken seriously in Thailand.

Narratives often contain a series of secondary stories, called *subplots*. Subplots may initially appear to be unrelated; however, because the characters operate within the same worldview, the subplots often comment on different aspects of the same thematic concerns. Consequently, identifying the connections between the subplots can reveal messages in the presentation. To illustrate, a news broadcast generally consists of a number of separate stories, selected on the basis of their importance and appeal to the audience. However, identifying linkages between these seemingly unrelated stories can disclose cumulative messages and themes. In his documentary film *Bowling for Columbine* (2002), Michael Moore observes that the numerous stories in news broadcasts about crime contribute to a climate of fear that adds to (rather than diminishes) violence in America.[9]

A *theme* is the central idea expressed in a narrative, whether implied or explicitly stated. Thematic expression enables artists to make observations about the human experience. This abstract idea is given expression or representation through a character or plot. It is the expressed intention of the artist that the audience should emerge from the production with a clear understanding of this central idea.

Universal themes raise issues pertaining to the human condition, the nature of good and evil, and the limits of human mortality. Universal themes are mythic in nature, in that they have been told and retold countless times in different forms throughout the world. These mythic themes correspond to the stages of human development, such as birth (or creation), adolescence, adulthood, and death. Many themes deal with issues presented by the rite of passage from one stage of human development to the next.

Films and television programs with universal themes resonate with international audiences. According to Nadene Nohr, managing editor of Granada Group, a British independent television consortium, the British television series *London's Burning* and *The Knock* have done well abroad because "they tap into universal themes of teamwork and adventure."[10] Other popular media presentations focus on themes related to sibling rivalries, parenting problems, and romantic relationships.

However, media programming may also reflect culture-specific themes that reflect the attitudes, concerns, and myths of a country. For instance, Elaine Sciolino discusses several national themes found in Iranian films:

> The tyranny of tradition in a patriarchal society is a theme that resonates deeply with Iranian audiences, particularly women. *Two Women*, directed by Tahmineh Milani, became the biggest box office hit in Iranian history when it was released in the summer of 1999. . . .
>
> Still another kind is the emotionally direct film that explores the tensions, restrictions and grimness of everyday life. This type deals with the gritty: suicide, murder, war, mental illness, divorce, infertility, polygamy, tribal oppression, unemployment, adultery, cross-dressing, social inequality, mixed-sex parties, drug addiction, wife-beating, child abuse and, recently, prostitution. Abbas Kiarostami's *Taste of Cherry* (1997) deals with

suicide; Dariush Mehrjui's *Leila* (1997) with infertility and polygamy (although I have yet to find an Iranian woman who found this tale of a modern, educated, infertile woman insisting that her husband take a second wife plausible).

A third type is the film about innocent children, often in a rural or village setting, with a combination of sentimentality, exotica and unreality that is easy to get past government censors. Jafar Panahi's *White Balloon* (1995), about a little girl trying to buy a goldfish for a New Year's celebration, was a breakthrough film.[11]

Examining *characterization* in a narrative is also a useful line of inquiry into media messages. According to Rollo May, the hero or heroine has a universal quality as the embodiment of our aspirations, our ideals, and our beliefs. May observes, "In the deepest sense we create the hero; he or she is born collectively as our own myth. This is what makes heroism so important; it reflects our own sense of identity and from this our own heroism is molded."[12] Conversely, the villain is a projection of those dark qualities that reside in all of us. Villainous characters enable the audience to come to terms with evil in the world, in others, in us.

Characters can be considered embodiments of ideological positions, based upon whose interests they represent. Daniel Chandler points out examples of these ideological oppositions:

East/West	Rich/Poor	Male/Female
Us/Them	Old/New	Black/White
Freedom/Constraint	Individual/Society	Gay/Straight
Inner/Outer	Private/Public	Old/Young
Insider/Outsider	Producer/Consumer	Good/Bad
Successful/Unsuccessful	Honest/Dishonest	Faith/Godless[13]
Caucasian/Asian	Religion #1/Religion #2	

In addition, characterization can be culture-specific. Heroes and heroines epitomize the dominant values operating within a culture. Conversely, villains represent threats to the system.

Consequently, examining characterizations can provide insight into a country's cultural identity and values. For example, the lead character in the American film *A Streetcar Named Desire* is Stanley Kowalski, an uncouth member of the lower class. His marriage to the aristocratic Blanche generates much of the tension in the narrative. In creating this character, playwright Tennessee Williams depicted Stanley as being of Polish extraction, drawing upon many Americans' disparaging stereotypical attitudes about this ethnic group. In 1993, an adaptation of *A Streetcar Named Desire* was made in Thailand. In *Ri luo ka men*, director Alfred Cheung designated Stanley's character as Chinese, reflecting the underclass status of Chinese people in Thailand.

Changes in characterization can also indicate shifts in a country's historical and cultural landscape. For instance, cold war films like *The Russians Are Coming, The Russians Are Coming* (1966), *The Hunt for Red October* (1990), and *Rocky IV* (1985) cast Americans as heroes and the Soviets as villains. However, in post–cold war films such as *Enemy at the Gates* (2001) and *K-19: The Widowmaker* (2002), Soviet soldiers were depicted as heroes. In their stead, a new cast of villains appeared that reflected changes in U.S. and British foreign policy. Arabs were cast as villains in a number of films, like *Air Force One* (1997), and North Koreans were tabbed as villains in the James Bond film *Die Another Day* (2002). In response, the North Korean Central News Agency denounced the Bond film as a "premeditated act of mocking at and insulting the Korean nation."[14]

Stock characters appear so frequently in the media that they transcend programs and genre. We instantly recognize stock characters—we have met them a thousand times before. Examples include the sidekick in a western, the blonde hostess on a game show, the honest friend, the talkative old woman, the suave gambler, the simple country boy, the blundering drunkard, the supersleuth, the eccentric scientist, and the folksy TV weatherman.

Decisions about how to cast the parts of stock characters also furnish insight into cultural attitudes. For instance, the 1960s American sit-com *Hogan's Heroes* enjoyed surprising success in Germany as a syndicated series during the 1990s. In the German version, the dialogue of the stock buffoon character, Sergeant Schultz, was dubbed with a Bavarian dialect. According to Alan Cowell, this decision "played on regional stereotypes to underline the notion that [Bavarians] are comic figures."[15] (For further discussion, see the section on Cultural Context in Chapter 3.)

A new category of international film stars and musicians have emerged, who embody the interests, experiences, and mind-set of a group of fans who transcend national boundaries. As an example, action film star Vin Diesel resonates with young male fans in countries throughout the world. Rick Lyman observes:

> Young people—especially young males—who make up the bulk of the summer movie audience are finding it increasingly difficult to relate to

the kind of black-tie, martini-sipping super-spy who has dominated the genre since Sean Connery first cocked an eyebrow. [Diesel] not only reflects the young audience's romantic image of itself—general indifference to authority mixed with contempt for conformity—but even personifies the multi-ethnic, multicultural face of current youth culture.[16]

Diesel's multicultural persona appeals to the growing global audience of young males. Todd Gardner states, "He is a guy who every culture has adopted as its own. You look at him on the screen and you listen to him and you cannot pin down what cultural group he fits in best with. . . . He is the Everyman."[17]

Genre

A *genre* is a standardized format that is distinctive and easily identifiable. Examples include horror films, romances, science fiction, situation comedies, reality shows, and the evening news. A genre is not confined to one medium. For instance, at one time or another, soap operas have appeared in print and on radio, television, and film.

Some genres enjoy worldwide popularity and acceptance. For instance, over 400 million people in 110 countries tune in daily to soap operas like *The Bold and the Beautiful.* David Andrews, professor of politics and international relations, declares, "Soap operas are the closest thing we have to a world religion."[18]

Genres with a strong visual appeal transcend language barriers. For instance, the graphic violence found in the action adventure genre is a powerful and entertaining form of nonverbal communication. Live musical performances and costume dramas also resonate with a global audience. Children's programs and factual programs also enjoy international popularity. Claire Murphy explains, "Kids' shows are often animated, making them simple to dub, while factual programs are generally narrated by an easily dubbed voiceover."[19]

However, the popularity of particular genres in certain countries reflects cultural tastes and preoccupations. Elaine Sciolino provides this example:

Today, Iranian films fall into a number of categories. One is the commercially popular junk film—the slapstick comedy or adventure film about murders or mummies. Another is the propaganda film, the kind that is shown on government-owned Iran Air's foreign flights and that invariably depicts a character gone wrong who is redeemed through prayer and the power of the Islamic Republic.[20]

The *formula* of a media genre furnishes cues which are helpful in interpreting international programming. Formula is defined as patterns in structure and plot. John Cawelti explains, "Individual works are ephemeral, but the formula lingers on, evolving and changing with time, yet still basically recognizable."[21]

Genres often adhere to a *formulaic structure*—that is, an identifiable, unvarying organizational pattern that is characteristic of a particular genre. The standard narrative structure for many genres, including comedies and dramas, is order/chaos/order. Programs begin in an initial state of harmony, with unquestioned assumptions about the correctness of this order. However, this initial order is soon disrupted. This chaotic stage consumes most of the program and is the source of much of its drama or humor. Finally, in the last stage, order is restored. The reestablishment of the status quo reaffirms the prevailing belief system of the narrative.

The formulaic structure of the soap opera typically features multiple subplots interweaving throughout the episode. These subplots are typically in different stages of development in a given program; one subplot may be at the initial stage, another is at midpoint, and a third could be moving toward resolution. In this way, some subplots remain unresolved from week to week. Even works that challenge the parameters of the genre are highly conscious of the formula. For instance, American television dramas such as *Charmed* and *7th Heaven* have borrowed from their poor relative, the soap opera, so that some subplots remained unresolved from week to week. This variation in the formulaic structure enables the producer to comment about contemporary American culture.

A *formulaic setting* is a standard background against which the action takes place (e.g., the set in a television news broadcast). In addition, *formulaic trappings* such as props and costumes are also common to a genre.

Examining nuances within the formula of a genre can furnish insight into a culture. For instance, although Nigerian movies routinely feature basic genres such as action stories and romances like those in Hollywood movies, many have Africa-specific nuances. To illustrate, *Ekulu* (1994) is a love story about an African slave and a white woman who frees him. They become outcasts and must flee into the jungle.

Tracing the evolution of a genre can provide insight into corresponding changes within a culture. For instance, beginning with *The Matrix* (1999), the action genre has moved away from simple plot-driven stories toward greater thematic and character complexity. Jeanine Basinger, chairperson of the film studio's program at Wesleyan University, declares, "*The Matrix* gave this type of movie a brain. It really did change everything. Filmmakers now realize that action doesn't have to be dumb."[22]

In part, this evolution is a result of sophisticated computer-generated special effects, which enable dramatic actors to assume leading roles previously reserved for stars who were better known for their athletic prowess. Todd Gardner notes, "*The Matrix* has opened up this world where anything is possible. So you don't need action stars who can really do those things. You can hire people for their acting skills instead."[23] In addition, special effects enable producers to add action elements to dramatic films that would previously have been more static. As a result, the supernatural physical exploits of action heroes can serve as thematic metaphors. For instance, in *The Matrix,* Neo (Keanu Reeves) learns to defy the laws of gravity and the time/space continuum in order to join the resistance against an advanced race of predators who have subjugated humankind. But, more importantly, Neo's physical exploits are a manifestation of his discovery of the limitlessness of the human mind and spirit.

Finally, identifying the emergence of new genres can reveal contemporary developments and ways of seeing the world. To illustrate, the "urban generation" genre emerged in China in the 1990s, largely in response to two defining events: the Tiananmen Square massacre and the onset of the government's drive toward privatization. Stuart Klawans explains:

> In *On the Beat* (1995), [Ying] Ning invites us to tag along with the bicycle-riding cops in an old neighborhood of Beijing, one of those warrens of courtyards, lanes and two-story flats that are fast being replaced by high-rises. Since the worst malefactor the cops meet is a three-card-monte player, the film on its surface is all shaggy-dog charm. Beneath, it's a catalog of frustrations, at everything from senseless policies at work to crumbling relationships at home.
>
> Lu Yue's *Mr. Zhao* (1998) follows the same pattern: amiable and even humorous on the outside, unsettled within. Set in Shanghai, it's the cleverly constructed story of a philandering middle-aged professional who betrays, with exquisite clumsiness, his wife, his mistress and his own best possibilities.

Mr. Zhao and *On the Beat* are exceptional in maintaining an aura of rueful humor and focusing on characters with respectable jobs.

If any figure defines the Urban Generation film, it's the ne'er-do-well, whose estrangement from society is portrayed with notable sympathy.

In the epic-length *Platform* (2001), Mr. [Hongwei] Wang Wang plays a member of an acting troupe whose experiences mirror those of the Urban Generation. Having started in the 1970s by performing musical tributes to Chairman Mao, the character winds up after privatization playing rock music to an audience of dozens. In both roles, Mr. Wang is never without his cigarette, his slouch and an ill-concealed vulnerability.

The story [these filmmakers] tell about themselves may be dismal, but it suggests that Beijing's dingiest housing compound may contain energy and willpower, kept under high pressure and straining for release.[24]

Lines of Inquiry: Framework

I. Introduction
   A. What does the title or first scene in a film or television program foreshadow about the themes, characters, and plot of an international media presentation?
   B. Analyze an international media presentation, focusing on premise:
      1. What is the premise of the presentation?
      2. Is the premise logical?
      3. Does the presentation flow naturally from the premise?
II. Analyze a media presentation produced in a foreign country, focusing on affective response.
   A. How does the media communicator want you to be feeling at particular points in the plot?
      1. Do the intended affective responses provide insight into media messages? Explain.
      2. What production elements are used to evoke an emotional response?
         a. Music
         b. Camera angle
         c. Lighting
         d. Color
         e. Editing
      3. Why is the media communicator attempting to elicit that intended emotional response from the audience?
      4. How did you react during the media presentation?

a. At what points did you react emotionally?

b. What does your reaction reveal about your personal belief system?

B. Do the circumstances depicted in the presentation generate a universal response, or is the expected affective response culture-specific?

III. Narrative Elements

A. Conduct a media literacy analysis of an international media presentation, focusing on the following narrative elements.

1. Plot/Subplot

2. Theme

3. Characterization

B. Compare two similar programs from different countries. Are there differences in plot, theme, and characterization? What does this comparison reveal about differences between the cultures?

C. Analyze a feature film, focusing on character development:

1. Have the major characters changed as a result of the events in the story? How? Why?

2. What have the characters learned as a result of their experience?

IV. Genre

A. Identify the formulaic elements belonging to a genre (e.g., reality shows).What would you expect to see in the genres listed below?

B. Select one of the following genres:

1. Detective show

2. Quiz show

3. Afternoon talk show

4. The network news

Focus on the following formulas in the analysis: function, premise, structure, plot motifs, and conventions.

C. Analyze a sample of programs from a particular genre (e.g., reality shows, TV news broadcasts). What media messages can you identify through an analysis of genre? Focus on the following:

1. Formulaic structure

2. Formulaic set

3. Formulaic conventions and trappings

D. What accounts for the popularity of certain genres in particular countries?

E. Trace changes in the formulas of a genre. What do these changes indicate with respect to corresponding cultural and historical changes?

F. Compare programs belonging to the same genre but originating in different countries. Can you identify any differences between the programs? What do the differences reveal about differences in the countries?

G. Select a genre. What messages are conveyed by the conventional trappings and plot motifs in the genre?

H. Identify the emergence of new genres that appear internationally. What do these genres reveal about new cultural and historical developments?

I. Identify the emergence of new genres that appear within a particular country. What do these genres reveal about new cultural and historical developments within that country?

J. Identify any new genres that emerge as an expression of contemporary developments and ways of seeing the world.

5

Production Elements

Production elements refer to the style and quality of a media presentation. Production values such as shape, color, lighting, editing, relative space, and sound are roughly analogous to grammar in print, influencing:

- The way in which the audience receives the information.
- The emphasis, or interpretation placed on the information by the media communicator.
- The reaction of the audience to the information.

In the early twentieth century, many countries developed their own distinctive media aesthetic styles, in large measure because these countries existed in relative isolation. For instance, until World War I, Germany was relatively self-contained and insulated from other countries' media presentations. In this environment the Germans could develop their own forms of expression. As a result, they were able to extend their own artistic traditions into photography, music, and film. German films such as *The Cabinet of Dr. Caligari* (1919) and *Nosferatu* (1922) were influenced by German Expressionism, an art movement that also influenced German painting, literature, and theater. The dramatic use of light and shadow and of exaggerated sets resulted in a distortion of two-dimensional space as an expression of internal states of consciousness. As documentary filmmaker Kathy Corley observes, "In many instances, you can make a good case for associating a style of cinema with a country. For instance, you would never confuse a German film like Fritz Lang's *Metropolis* with a Japanese film such as Akira Kurosawa's *Shichinin no Samuari* (Seven Samurai)."[1] After World War II, German filmmakers were exposed to international cinema—most notably Hollywood films. At the same time, German refugees like Fritz Lang, Billy Wilder, and Karl Freund emigrated to the United States, further contributing to the synthesis of the German and Hollywood styles.

Today, many artists are influenced by cultural traditions from around the world. As an example, the musical heritage of the Yoruba religion, which originated in West Africa, was carried to the New World in the holds of slave ships. The rhythms and forms of the Yoruba religion have influenced the development of many forms of American music, including jazz, rhythm and blues, and rock 'n' roll. In an article about American rock 'n' roll legend Bo Diddley, Bernard Weinraub notes, "The syncopated Bo Diddley beat—bomp ba-bomp bomp, bomp bomp has been traced to . . . the drumbeats of the Yoruba and Kongo cultures."[2] In turn, American rhythm and blues artists like James Brown and Booker T were the inspiration for the "funk and soul" sound that emerged in Ghana, Africa, in the 1970s.

Economic considerations have also played a role in the movement toward a global aesthetic synthesis. Transnational media conglomerates now produce many of the films on the market and distribute them throughout the globe. In addition, independent film companies increasingly depend on international sources of financing, which can then have an impact on story content and casting decisions. As Corley observes, "It's hard to separate aesthetics and economics."[3]

However, this convergence of aesthetic styles is far from complete. Countries that have remained relatively isolated from the global community have managed to preserve their artistic traditions. As an example, Iranian films have maintained a distinctive cinematic style, including landscape, editing and pacing, and visual elements, free from the influence of Hollywood. Elaine Sciolino observes:

> Iran's cinema is a world unto itself, the most creative expression of the country's imagination, so much so that it has earned a reputation as one of the most vibrant and prolific cinemas in the world. As filmmakers scoop up more and more prizes at international festivals, filmmaking has become one of the most popular professions for young people in Iran. They are buying cameras, writing scripts and competing for both the few places at film schools and the privilege of working on the sets of famous directors.[4]

Some artisits have made a concerted effort to preserve artistic traditions. Dogma 95, a collective of contemporary filmmakers are committed to "pure cinema." These filmmakers, many of whom are from Denmark, have limited resources, relying instead on the story, acting, and creativity, in response to the highly stylized filmmaking that has become predominant today. This movement has produced a number of films that have received high critical acclaim, most notably *Idioterne*, or *Dogma 95* (1998), a Danish film directed by Lars von Trier; *Festen*, or *The Celebration* (1998), directed by Thomas Vinterberg; and *Mifunes Sidste Sang*, or *Mifune* (1999), directed by Soren Kragh-Jacobsen.

Production elements have assumed an increased importance as a way to transcend language barriers in the global arena. Media scholar George Gerbner observes that one of the reasons that violence is so prevalent in American film and television programs is that this form of nonverbal communication is highly exportable to other cultures.[5] Programming with spectacular visual effects is also especially popular with global audiences. For instance, *Harry Potter and the Chamber of Secrets* and *The Lord of the Rings: The Fellowship of the Ring,* were enormously popular in China.

Production elements have universal properties, which are rooted in human experience. In his discussion of the universal properties of color, Wallace S. Baldinger observes:

> Owing to association with certain experiences and objects, we feel that certain hues are "warm" and others "cool." By association with late-afternoon sunshine, fire, or heated iron, on the one hand, and with nightfall, water, ice, snow, on the other, we group yellow, orange, and red together as warm hues and green, blue, and violet together as cool. The artist draws on the ideas which we thus connect with color when he selects and organizes hues, sometimes even making us feel hot or cold by reaction to them.[6]

However, production elements may also have culturally specific meanings. In most Western cultures, black is associated with mourning. However, in many Asian cultures, white is the color associated with bereavement. Thus, while you would wear black to a funeral in the United States, white would be the appropriate color in Japan. In Bosnia, green is associated with the Muslim religion—not because of any connection with the Koran but because of the color of the Bosnian flag. The cultural meaning of color is sometimes tied to historical context. In Croatia, blue has a negative connotation because, according to Webster University student Sandra Basso, after the war in Croatia, blue became associated with military police and militia during the conflict in Croatia. Media communicators can make grave errors by ignoring the cultural significance of colors. Craig S. Smith observes, "One multinational company giving gifts from Tiffany [had to] replace the white ribbons on the famous jeweler's robin's-egg-blue boxes with red ribbons after the company's Shanghai employees pointed out that white in China signifies death, while red is lucky and is used for celebrations."[7]

By recognizing that production elements may convey unintended messages in another culture, the media communicator is in a position to substitute other production elements that achieve the intended purpose of the original production.

Editing

Editing is defined as the selection and arrangement of information. Editing decisions influence the audience's understanding of the world as presented through the media. As author Thomas Wolfe observed, "Fiction is fact selected and understood, fiction is fact arranged and charged with purpose."[8]

Before you read a newspaper, an editor has decided what topics will be covered, what information about the subject will be included, and how much importance should be attached to the story. In like fashion, because the finished version of a film typically contains only one-tenth of the original footage, the filmmaker exercises enormous control over what the audience sees.

Recognizing the following editing principles can be valuable in the interpretation of media messages.

Inclusion and Omission

Time and space constraints limit the number of stories that can be included in a media presentation. Media communicators generally focus only on those stories that they perceive to be of immediate concern to them and their audience. Consequently, comparing international sources of news can disclose stories that do not appear in your country's newspapers, magazines, and television coverage. To illustrate, Caryn James found different stories being presented about the war on terrorism by the British Broadcasting Corporation and American media in 2002:

> From the time the antiterror coalition was formed, the BBC has offered a stark view of its fragility, something the American media have just begun to focus on. . . . And in the midst of covering anthrax, foreign-based

programs have continued to report regularly from Jerusalem and the West Bank, offering a sense of how volatile the Israeli-Palestinian conflict has become. For American television, with its relentless focus on a single issue, covering anthrax and the Middle East at the same time is the news equivalent of walking and chewing gum.[9]

Because of the time and space constraints of newspapers and television, those stories that do appear assume an exaggerated importance. For instance, in the 1980s, the American press carried stories about a bomb scare at the airport in Rome, Italy, that affected the Italian tourist industry. Even though this was only one isolated incident, the bomb threat was the only story about Italy that appeared in the American press that week, leaving the impression that Italy was a dangerous place to visit.

At the same time, the international media underreports many important stories. Obviously, it is difficult for an audience to take note of stories that do not appear in the media. However, several organizations, including Project Censored, track underreported stories. In addition, Doctors Without Borders identifies the most underreported humanitarian stories each year. In 2002, this list included the following:

- End of war reveals nutritional emergency in Angola
- Civilians caught in increasing violence in Colombia
- War and lack of health care in the Democratic Republic of Congo
- Food aid and refugee protection in North Korea
- Hundreds of thousands displaced by civil war in Liberia
- War, disease, hunger, and lack of health care contribute to mortality in Somalia
- Violence, health, and access to aid in Sudan
- Pressure rises on civilians escaping war in Chechnya
- World's poor still die for lack of access to medicines
- Disregard for humanitarian law erodes protection for war-affected people[10]

In addition decisions about which *aspects* of a story to include have an enormous impact on the audience's understanding of a story. Examining international news programming can furnish additional layers of information to what we might ordinarily know by relying solely on our national news accounts. An example can be found in the international media coverage of an attempt to depose Venezuelan president Hugo Chavez in April 2002. Military personnel, backed by the oil and media industries, captured Chavez and installed a new government. However, after two days of massive protests by the citizens of Venezuela, Chavez was released and returned to power. The U.S. government denied any role in the coup attempt. Deputy Secretary of State Richard L. Armitage declared that the Bush administration "didn't have any involvement" in the effort to oust Chavez. However, international newspapers furnished information about the American role in the coup that did not appear in American news accounts:

- The British *Guardian* broke the story that a few weeks before the coup attempt, U.S. administration officials had met Pedro Carmona, the business leader who took over the interim government after President Hugo Chavez was arrested.[11]
- Both the *Guardian* and the London *Times* reported that the Venezuelan army's chief of staff, General Lucas Romero Rincon, had traveled to Washington, D.C., the previous December and had met the assistant secretary of defense for western hemispheric affairs, Otto Reich.[12]
- Agence France Presse first broke the story that a U.S. military attaché had been with the planners of the coup at the armed forces inspector general's office at Fort Tiuna, Venezuela, in the hours before Chavez was overthrown. A retired general confirmed the report on condition of anonymity, saying that "a number of reliable eyewitnesses on the scene" had assured him of its veracity.[13]
- The London *Times* reported that after Chavez was restored to power, alleged coup leaders Isaac Perez Recao and Vicente Perez Recao flew by private helicopter to their $500,000 beachfront flat in Key Biscayne, Florida. Under U.S. law, the secretary of state has the power to deny entry visas or revoke their issuance to persons deemed to have "potentially serious adverse foreign policy consequences for the United States." Although this statute was applied to President Chavez in 1992, after he had led an unsuccessful coup attempt in Venezuela, it was not invoked in this case.[14]

Media presentations may also contain *extraneous inclusions*—that is, information added to a story that, on the surface, appears to be irrelevant. However, the inclusion can serve as a subtle commentary by making connections between apparently unrelated ideas, events, or people.

To illustrate, in 2001, Arab television station al-Jazeera aired a documentary about Osama bin Laden, "Biography and Secrets." The documentary included footage of Che Guevara, the Cuban revolutionary who died in 1967. Although the two men had never met, the inclusion of Guevara was designed to add to the mystique of bin Laden as a revolutionary. Fouad Ajami explains:

> The episode's subject matter was, of course, allegorical. Before bin Laden, there was Guevara. Before Afghanistan, there was Bolivia. As for the show's focus on CIA operatives chasing Guevara into the mountains, this, too, was clearly meant to evoke the contemporary hunt for Osama, the Islamic rebel.[15]

Whether a media presentation provides *context* also has an impact on the audience's understanding of a story. Greg Philo found that audiences of television news are often misinformed because of a lack of background information. However, providing additional context—for example, presenting the international economic and political links that underpin the continuance of a war—can radically alter both the attitudes and the level of audience interest.[16] To illustrate, in 2002, the American press reported that the North Korean government had reinstituted its nuclear program, in violation of its 1994 treaty with the United States. However, as Laura Stuhlman, a graduate student at Webster University, points out, the American news accounts consistently omitted a key piece of information that would have added important information about the crisis:

> While most of the American mainstream newspapers demonized North Korea for a flagrant breach of the 1994 Agreed Framework, other news sources around the world reported that the U.S. was also in violation of the agreement. In November 2002, *Maclean's*, a Canadian business and culture magazine, reported, "In 1994, in return for North Korea suspending nuclear weapons development, the U.S., South Korea, Japan and the European Union promised to build two big reactors for electrical power. With the program five years behind schedule, North Korea has become convinced the Americans are stalling, anticipating a total collapse of the regime. Washington also promised to normalize relations and stop making threats. It hasn't happened." Other media outlets that reported the story of North Korea included *European Report*, based in Belgium, *The South China Morning Post*, *The Korea Herald*, *The Moscow Times*, and Agence France Presse, based in Paris.[17]

Selective Emphasis

The amount of attention devoted to a story sends a message about its significance. Lengthy segments indicate that a story is important, whereas a brief account signals that it is of little consequence. To illustrate, Fouad Ajami observes that the Arab television station al-Jazeera's emphasis in its newscasts on anti-American demonstrations in the Middle East exaggerates the magnitude of these events:

> In its telling, the Pakistani street is forever on the boil, with "huge throngs" in Rawalpindi and Peshawar and Islamabad. Anti-American demonstrations are, of course, eagerly covered by the Western news media as well. But by television standards, the Al-Jazeera video was notably extended—close to a minute long.[18]

Sustained Coverage

Sustained coverage keeps an issue or event in the public consciousness, reinforcing its importance. On the other hand, stories that are covered infrequently are discounted as being of little consequence.

Sustained coverage can also generate an affective, or emotional response from the audience that influences their attitude toward the subject. For instance, in 2001, al-Jazeera repeatedly showed the heartrending footage of Muhammed al-Durra, a twelve-year-old boy who was shot in Gaza and died in his father's arms. This sustained coverage fueled resentment among Palestinian sympathizers.[19]

Sequence of Information

The order in which information appears in a media presentation also affects the audience's interpretation of its content. The first position cited in a newspaper article is generally regarded as the legitimate perspective; the second position challenges the initial viewpoint. Sequencing is very important in the construction of visual and audial presentations as well. Sequencing one shot after another gives a producer an opportunity to comment on the consequences of events. For instance, in November 2001, CNN aired a report on the American bombing of Afghanistan that included a visual montage: the video of the bombing was immediately followed by footage of the September 11 destruction of the World Trade

Center. The juxtaposition of these images reminded viewers that the U.S. bombing was in retaliation for the attack of September 11.

Relative Position

Where a character or object appears on the screen (or page) sends distinct messages to the audience. Objects stationed toward the front attract immediate attention, whereas items appearing in the background are generally considered of secondary importance. The arrangement of stories *within* a single page also affects the audience's perception of content. Stories on the top half of the page are accorded greater importance by the reader than stories appearing near the bottom.

Human beings tend to look for balance—that is, an equal distribution around the center. Because of this natural predisposition to order, or *gestalt*, the audience tends to feel unsettled if all the activity is placed on one corner of the screen. The media communicator can take advantage of the audience's natural desire for order to convey a particular message.

The media communicator can employ relative position to comment on the relationship between objects and events. For instance, by juxtaposing two apparently unrelated shots, a filmmaker can establish relationships between people and events or create an entirely new meaning.

Readers often regard the composition of a newspaper page as a collection of separate stories. However, by seeing the page as a whole, they can draw connections between events and identify cultural preoccupations and concerns. For instance, consider the page of the *New York Times* shown in Figure 5.1. The article on the left-hand side of the page, "U.S. Focuses on Iraqi Links to Group Allied to Al Qaeda," discloses that there was evidence that members of the terrorist organization al Qaeda were found in northern Iraq. This article, which raised the possibility of links between Saddam Hussein and the extremist terrorist network, lent credence to U.S. president Bush's rationale for invading Iraq. The article on the right side of the page, "Some U.S. Forces in Northern Iraq, Military Chief Says," reports that members of America's military forces were operating in northern Iraq, organizing opposition forces against Saddam Hussein.

Although these two stories are ostensibly unconnected, by putting these two stories together, a third story emerges. Clearly, at that time, northern Iraq was an unrestricted zone that was not under Saddam Hussein's control. The presence of al Qaeda (or Americans, for that matter) in that region was no proof of a link to Saddam.

Figure 5.1   **Relative Position:** *The New York Times*, **Thursday, January 30, 2003**

THREATS AND RESPONSES: G.I.'s Already in Iraq, and Growing Suspicions

TERRORISM

U.S. Focuses on Iraqi Links To Group Allied to Al Qaeda

By DAVID JOHNSTON and DON VAN NATTA Jr.

WASHINGTON, Jan. 29 — After months of scouring for hard evidence of a connection between Iraq and Al Qaeda, the Bush administration is focusing on possible links between Saddam Hussein and Islamic extremists who may have produced poisons in northern Iraq and a Qaeda terrorist leader who spent time in Baghdad last year.

A group in north Iraq is suspected of developing poisons.

Secretary of Defense Donald H. Rumsfeld and Gen. Richard B. Myers, chairman of the Joint Chiefs of Staff, at the Pentagon yesterday.

Some U.S. Forces in Northern Iraq, Military Chief Says

By ERIC SCHMITT

WASHINGTON, Jan. 29 — Small numbers of American military forces are now operating in northern Iraq, the chairman of the Joint Chiefs of Staff acknowledged today.

An employee of the local Kurdish government at work last week at Bakravo airfield in northern Iraq, where American forces are now operating.

PREPARATIONS

Source: Copyright © 2003 by The New York Times Co. Reprinted with permission.

Word Choice

Word choice plays a monumental role in the way that international media messages are shaped, received, and interpreted. Because there are over 2,200 different languages and dialects in the world, understanding the use of language is a vital aspect of media literacy analysis.

The choice of words in a media production can provide insight into the *historical sensibility* of a country. To illustrate, Paul Theroux observes that Great Britain's language reveals "a weariness about the world" as a result of the enormous sacrifices that the British endured during both world wars:

> The English have a lot of phrases for delay—"I'm doing it." "We're seeing to it." "It's in the pipeline." "I'm dealing with that." "It's in my in-tray." "Yes, that's vexing us at the moment." "I'm very exercised by it." These are phrases and words for inaction, which are either to delay action or not to do something. It's an elegant or obscure way to avoid taking a decision or doing something. Talking can be a way of avoiding action, of being elegantly in repose.[20]

At the same time, however, the English language also includes numerous synonyms describing the nuances of "sharing," reflecting a generosity of spirit that typifies the British people.

Word choice can also furnish perspective on the *cultural sensibility* of a country. To illustrate, the following words originating in the American cultural experience became so pervasive that they were added to *Merriam-Webster's Collegiate Dictionary* in 2000:

- fashionista: a devout follower of fashion trends
- digerati: computer geeks
- eye candy: attractive person[21]

Words may assume a special significance in a country that transcends their denotative meaning. To illustrate in the 2003 song, "Who Can Bwogo Me," Kenyan rap artists GidiGidi MajiMaji coined an expression that captured the optimistic mood and spirit generated by the first real free elections in Kenya's history. Based on *bwogo,* the Luo word for "scare," *unbwogable* (pronounced un-BWOH-gable) is translated as "unshakable":

> I am unbwogable
> I am unbeatable
> I am unsueable
> So if you like my song
> Take it from me
> Who can bwogo me
> I am unbwogable.
> Oh, you should remember great people.
> You should remember those who have helped you
> You should remember those who have uplifted you.
> I am unbwogable.

This term assumed such significance in Kenya that incoming president Mwai Kibaki referred to Kenya's song in his 2003 inaugural address, to the approval of the audience: "We are unbwogable. Nothing will defeat us."[22]

International media communicators must be particularly sensitive to the nuances of language. To illustrate, in 2001, an American reconnaissance plane collided with a Chinese fighter plane over Chinese airspace, causing an international incident. In the collision, the Chinese plane was destroyed and its pilot killed. The American fighter plane was forced to land, and its crew was captured. The Chinese government demanded a formal apology from the United States as a condition for returning the American servicemen. The United States refused to apologize, and tensions grew. Finally, after a period of intense negotiations, U.S. secretary of state Colin Powell issued a formal statement expressing "regret" over the incident. This wording enabled both sides to save face. For Americans, the connotation of "regret" is an expression of sorrow, without admitting guilt. However, for the Chinese, the translation of the term suggests a degree of culpability. William Safire explains:

> Using the syllable "qian" in [the] translation of [Powell's] letter . . . allowed the Chinese to infer an admission of wrongdoing. It's the informal alternative to sorrowful, based on sorg, which first appeared in "Beowulf" around 725, meaning "grief, sorrow, care."
>
> Sorry, with its "y" suffix—meaning "full of" but also used to form pet names—seems more colloquial than regret. It was seized upon by the Chinese as "a form of apology," enabling them to claim satisfaction.[23]

Given the intricacies of word choice, it was particularly ironic that the American newspaper *USA Today carelessly* published the following headline the next week: "Bush Scolds China as Crew Returns to Hero's Welcome." The verb "to scold" is commonly used in reference to someone younger or in an inferior social or political position.

Word choice often furnishes clues about the point of view of the media communicator. To illustrate, in the ongoing Middle East conflict, a number of Palestinians strapped explosives on their bodies, killing Israelis (and themselves in the process). While the Israeli and American press describe these individuals as "suicide bombers," Egyptian journalists refer to them as *shahid,* or "martyrs" and "self-sacrificers" who were carrying out acts of "resistance" against their Israeli oppressors.[24]

Certain forms of language can be used to alter the essential meaning of a concept:

Labels are connotative words or phrases that describe a person or group. Labels often appear with such frequency in the media that they no longer simply describe but, in fact, define the group. To illustrate, during his 2002 State of the Union address, U.S. president George W. Bush used the term "axis of evil" to describe Iraq, Iran, and North Korea, to the dismay of the international community. Much of this alarm was due to the derivation of that term, from the Axis powers (i.e., Germany, Italy, and Japan) of World War II. Bush's use of this term therefore implied that the three countries had formed an alliance, when, in fact, they have different histories and ethnic compositions and have no political connections to one another.

Euphemisms are neutral terms that are intended to minimize the reaction of the audience. An example can be found in the United States' use of the term "regime change" to describe its policy toward Iraq under the rule of Saddam Hussien, William Safire observes:

> Secretary of State Colin Powell laid it on the rhetorical line: the Bush administration "is committed to regime change" in Iraq. He repeated to the Senate that "a regime change would be in the best interests of the region." That's a euphemism for "overthrow of government" or "toppling Saddam."
>
> Why, then, did he not say "we intend to throw him and his motley crew of mass murderers out of Baghdad, replacing them with a government that will allow the Iraqi people free elections"? Because that sort of talk is undiplomatic or even impolitic. "Overthrow" and "topple" are hot, vigorous verbs; "regime change" is a cool, polite noun phrase suggesting transition without collateral damage.[25]

Euphemisms are often used in international diplomacy, requiring a vigilant eye (and ear) to interpret messages. To illustrate, in his address to the United Nations articulating the American justification for invading Iraq, Secretary of State Powell displayed satellite photographs of a site that he described as a poisons and explosives factory that was supported by both Baghdad and al-Qaeda. Two days later, Iraqi officials allowed international journalists into the camp. It contained no evidence to support Powell's claims. The buildings had no plumbing and only limited electricity supplied by a generator. Roughly half the buildings in the compound appeared to have recently been civilian homes, and the remaining structures served as fighters' barracks and a television and radio station for the Islamic party.

In response to questions by journalists about this discrepancy, a State Department official maintained that, despite the lack of evidence, Powell's characterization of the compound was accurate: "A poison factory is a *term of art* [italics added], and it doesn't necessarily mean that people are pumping out thousands of gallons a year."[26] In this case, "term of art" was a euphemism for a deliberate deception.

Language collectives are a form of personification that ascribes human qualities to a large, all-encompassing organization or entity (e.g., "the European Union said today," or "Poland claimed"). However, it is impossible for an organization to talk. This misuse of language sends several messages to readers. First, language collectives make absolute claims, overlooking individual dissent or disagreement among people within the organization. Second, a language collective invests the organization with an aura of authority.

To illustrate, in May 2003, a group of American marines guarding the United States Embassy in Afghanistan opened fire on a group of allied Afghan soldiers, killing at least three and wounding two others. An article in the *New York Times* included this passage: "The American Embassy said it regretted the loss of life. Heightened tensions led to a live-fire incident today between U.S. marines defending the embassy and Afghan military forces. This incident, unfortunately, caused a loss of life."[27]

This use of language deflects responsibility for the act by having the American Embassy apologize. The last sentence is even more intriguing, as the incident *itself* becomes the agent of responsibility.

Obfuscation words are intended to conceal, rather than clarify, meaning. As an example, in an article appearing in the *Herald Sun* (Melbourne, Australia) in 2003, Royal Australian Air Force chief Angus Houston discussed the success of the Australian military during the U.S.-led invasion of Iraq as follows: "A major reason . . . is the fact that the two [Iraqi] divisions were heavily engaged by air forces over the last week and they obviously *attrited* [italics mine] to an extent where they've lost a lot of their fighting capability and perhaps the will to fight."[28] In this case, *attrited* is a verb that confuses the meaning of the statement, which is that the Iraqis suffered heavy casualties. The term is derived from an obscure military term "attrition."

Antitheticals go a step further by not just covering up but actually controverting the actual meaning of the term. To illustrate, in 2002, the Bush administration backed out of the Kyoto Environmental Treaty. In its place, it offered programs called "Healthy Forests" and "Clear Skies" which, in fact, rolled back regulations on environmental limits.

Translation

The translation of written materials from one language to another adds yet another layer of complexity to the communication process. The precise meaning of words can easily be lost in translation. To illustrate, in 2003, French president Jacques Chirac was criticized for rebuking thirteen Eastern European countries that had expressed support for the U.S. actions in Iraq. Chirac said that these countries "ont manqué une bonne occasion de se taire," which was translated in the American and British press as "missed a good opportunity to shut up." However, according to Eleanor and Michel Levieux, it was the translation of the phrase that made it appear insulting:

> Mr. Chirac's words were a significant notch above [a level of insult]. To be sure, he could have been quite formal and said "ont manqué une bonne occasion de s'absentir de tout commentaire" ("refrain from making any comment"), or "garder le silence" or "se garder de s'exprimer" ("keep silent" or "say nothing"). And of course, he also could have taken a much lower road and said "ont manqué une bonne occasion de fermer leur gueule" or "de la fermer"), which would indeed mean, "to shut up." The verb Mr. Chirac chose, "se taire," was neither elegant nor rude, simply neutral.[29]

In some cases, the literal translation from one language to another simply does not make sense. As an example, *The Gods Must Be Crazy* (1979), a film made in Botswana, was shown in a movie theater in Tokyo, Japan, that catered to an English-speaking audience. Rather than simply showing the original English version of the film, the Japanese distributors inexplicably decided to retranslate the film from Japanese back into English. Consequently, the title of the film that appeared on the marquee was *Nice to Meet you Mr. Bushman.*

Some words are so unique to the cultural sensibility of a country that they defy translation. To illustrate, there is no term for *impeachment* in Russia, since the concept is foreign to its past and present systems of government. On the other hand, the lexicon of the United States has no equivalent word for *Propiska,* a Russian term that refers to a national identification card.

Similarly, idiomatic expressions are often tied to the cultural life of a nation and, consequently, do not translate easily into another language. For example, the American phrase *It's no picnic* (which means "it's not easy") is unknown in countries that do not engage in this type of social function. American idioms such as *can't get to first base* and *hit a home run* are based on its national pastime, baseball, and make little sense to people in countries that are unfamiliar with the sport.

Slang expressions are an informal form of expression that operates outside of its formal syntax and vocabulary. A person learning a language in school would not be exposed to these terms. Consequently, international audiences can easily be confused by slang expressions. To illustrate, Marc Lacey observes:

> When a Kenyan asks for a little tea, he may or may not have a hot beverage in mind. Tea is a popular drink here, usually served with healthy helpings of milk and sugar. But "a little tea" is also the slang used by bureaucrats, police officers or anyone else with an outstretched palm to ask for a bribe. In "Ncluya Kitu Kidogo," a new Kiswahili song that has taken Kenya by storm, Eric Wainaina tells those desiring a little tea to visit a popular tea-growing area in central Kenya. He recommends that those in need of a soda—another word for bribe—refresh themselves with a Fanta.[30]

Translation problems can lead to serious misunderstandings within the international community. In 2002, relations between North Korea and the United States were strained after North Korea's admission that it had restarted its nuclear weapons program. On April 18, 2003, tension reached a fever pitch when North Korea's state-run KCNA news agency issued a statement in English that it had already begun reprocessing its spent nuclear fuel into bomb-grade plutonium: "As we have already declared, we are successfully reprocessing more than 8,000 spent fuel rods at the final phase, as we sent interim information to the U.S. and other countries concerned early in March after resuming our nuclear activities from December last year." However, on April 21, the North Korean government asserted that the statement was inaccurate and offered another translation: "We are successfully completing the final phase to the point of the reprocessing operation for some 8,000 spent fuel rods." This translation suggested that North Korea was preparing to reprocess spent nuclear fuel rods, rather than having already done so—a subtle but very important distinction.

Connotative Image

In a world characterized by different languages and dialects, the use of images can be a powerful communications vehicle. Although many images possess universal associative properties, other images derive their meaning through cultural context. As an example, long before the swastika became the emblem of the Nazi Party in the 1920s, it was regarded as a positive symbol throughout the world. The word *swastika* is derived from the Sanskrit word *svastika*, which means "well-being" and "good fortune." The earliest known swastikas date from 2500 or 3000 B.C. in India and in Central Asia. Synagogues in North Africa, Palestine, and Hartford, Connecticut were built with swastika mosaics. Indeed, Buddha's footprints were said to be swastikas. In the early twentieth century, the swastika was a common icon in the United States as well. Coca-Cola issued a swastika pendant as part of an advertising promotion. And during World War I, the American Forty-fifth Infantry Division wore a shoulder patch adorned with an orange swastika. Only after the Nazis adopted this symbol was the swastika associated with evil.

Within that context, the analysis of connotative images can furnish insight into the attitudes and preoccupations of a country. For instance, anti-Semitic images have become more prevalent in Islamic popular culture since 2000, reflecting an increasing frustration with the political situation in the Middle East. Susan Sachs observes:

> Pick up a newspaper in any part of the Arab world and you regularly see a swastika superimposed on the Israeli flag. The use of Nazi imagery and newspaper caricatures of Jews . . . is now embedded in the mainstream discourse concerning Jews in much of the Islamic world, in the popular press and in academic journals. The depictions are not limited to countries that are at war with Israel but can be found in general-interest publications in Egypt and Jordan, the two countries that have signed peace agreements with Israel, as well as in independent religious schools in Pakistan and Southeast Asia.
>
> In the view of many scholars of Islam, such texts are a sign that the Arab-Israeli conflict has been transformed in Muslim culture from a political, nationalist and territorial battle into a cosmic war between religions and, indeed, between good and evil.[31]

The choice of which images appear in media presentations has an enormous impact on the audience's response to a story. To illustrate, in 2003, the pictures of the conflict in Iraq that appeared in American media were vastly different from the images displayed elsewhere in the world. The reluctance of American news outlets to show pictures of civilian casualties fed into criticism that the U.S. media were biased in support of the war. In contrast, the Arab media emphasized images depicting the harsh realities of the war, which helped marshal public opinion against the United States. Nihad Awad, executive director of the Council on American-Islamic Relations, declared, "There are two wars. One that's shown around the world through the eyes of Arab and European networks and the other that Americans see through American networks."[32]

An example of the messages conveyed by connotative images can be found on the cover of the November 18, 2002, issue of *Newsweek* magazine (Figure 5.2). American president George W. Bush is dressed in an air force flying jacket, raising his thumb in the air. The headline, "Top Gun," ostensibly refers to his party's victory in the 2002 congressional election. However, the image conveys a latent message about America's military superiority in anticipation of the war in Iraq: Bush (and the United States) are "top guns" in the world. The cover is also a cultural reference to the motion picture *Top Gun* (1986), an action/romance film starring Tom Cruise as a dashing fighter pilot. Thus, the photo reinforces the image of Bush as a daring military hero.

Media communicators use the following imaging techniques to influence the audience's interpretation of content:

Imagistic layering occurs when two images combine to form a third meaning. To illustrate, in August 2002, President Bush gave a speech at the site of Mount Rushmore (Figure 5.3). In the photograph of the speech, the president is captured off-center (which is highly unusual), capturing the likeness of the other presidents in the photo. The image of Bush's profile aligned next to America's most beloved presidents adds to the legitimacy of the Bush presidency by conveying the message that he is a part of the tradition of great American presidents.

Symbolic representations are images that serve as symbols of other objects (e.g., subway signs), people, or concepts (e.g., churches). For instance, after the events of September 11, 2001, Fox Television News anchors wore American flag lapel pins on the air. According to Barbara Friedman, this image undermined the objectivity of the news broadcasts: "When you see patriotic symbols [American flag] on the screen during a news broadcast, it suggests that the press is working for or with the government and is not being the independent observer it should be."[33]

Figure 5.2   **Connotative Image**

Metonymy is a process in which an image stands for a group of attributes. For example, Marlboro ads associate smoking that brand with individuality, freedom, independence, heroism, and, ironically, health. In liquor and beer advertisements, the consumption of the product stands for such attributes as fun, friends, youth, happiness, and fitness.

Infographics

Infographics are various pictorial (as opposed to photographic) representations that appear in the media, including illustrations, logos, graphs, maps,

Figure 5.3   **Imagistic Layering**

Source: AP/World Wide Photos, Ken Lambert.

typefaces, and political cartoons. Infographics offer a way to communicate information despite problems posed by language barriers or illiteracy.

Evidence of infographics predates written languages. Five thousand years ago, the Egyptians developed the first calendar that divided time into 365 days a year. They also drew maps of the earth to chart events such as the flooding of the Nile River. Infographics are particularly well suited for the presentation of certain kinds of information. They can display a sequence of events, so that the audience can see how the parts of an event fit together. Graphic representations such as pie charts can clearly show numerical data. Maps are the most effective means of orienting people with regard to location. In general, infographics are used for emphasis, drawing the viewer's attention to information.

Two forms of infographics worth particular consideration in the study of international communications are logos and political cartoons.

Logos

Logos are visual symbols that represent organizations, products, and ideologies. The logo must be instantly recognizable, regardless of culture and language barriers.

Logos can serve several different functions:

To Convey Information

Logos are commonly used to provide directions or as warnings to the public (e.g., street signs). Logos also serve as visual notification of quality assurance. For instance, in 2002, the Marine Products Export Development Authority of India introduced a new logo that certifies that the products have met quality standards that make them eligible for export.

To Generate a Positive Emotional Attitude Toward the Company

As an example, in 2002, International Confex, a company that organizes and presents industry trade shows, introduced a new logo to promote its new Event Therapy concept. Paula Lorimer explained, "Event Therapy will provide participants with everything they need to fulfill business objectives within the framework of a relaxing day. The new logo and colour ways have been devised to enhance the relaxed and luxury feel of the [trade] show."[34]

To Establish Identity

Corporate logos are designed to embody the image of the company. In 2002, the Taiwan Bicycle Exporters Association introduced a new logo as part of its promotional campaign to ship more Taiwan-made bikes to the world market. Officials of the association said the new logo would help consumers and buyers to "think of Taiwan whenever they think about bicycles."[35]

Logos may also be used to express personal identity. To illustrate, graphic designer Margo Chase describes a logo she designed in 2002 for American pop star Cher's final concert tour:

> The logo we created for Cher's tour is in the form of a cross with wings, constructed with the letters in her name. The wings symbolize the enduring spirit of Cher's music, while the cross refers to the religious symbols used in the stage production. . . . The cross also nods to the gothic, Cher's most recognizable style.[36]

The tourist divisions of various countries have begun to use logos as a means of establishing their global identity. In 2002, Poland adopted a logo to attract tourists (Figure 5.4). According to Szymon Gutkowski,

Figure 5.4   **Polish Logo**

strategic director of Corporate Profiles, DDB, the national logo, in the form of a kite, connotes "youth, freedom, playfulness and hope in any language, any country." Reporter Sarah Boxer adds that this logo also conveys another latent message: "The hope is that the kite will lift Poland up and let it float gently away from its past and toward the prosperity of Europe."[37]

To Announce Significant Changes

Logos are an effective way to draw attention to significant changes such as company mergers. For instance, the banking and insurance company of Holland, the ING, which has increased its stake in Vysya Bank, came out with a new logo that incorporated visual elements of the Vysya and ING logos into a new design, visually communicating the message that the old companies were joining forces to form a new company.

To Conceal Meaning

A logo may be used to disguise the central focus of the organization. As an example, the process of irradiating food has come under considerable criticism by members of the scientific community, who are concerned that the irradiation process interacts with pesticides found in foods to create toxins like benzene and formaldehyde.[38] In response to this negative publicity, the industry designed a logo resembling the logo of the U.S. Environmental Protection Agency (EPA) (Figure 5.5). Accord-

Figure 5.5   **EPA Logo, Irradiation Industry Logo**

The "radura" is a symbol that indicates a food product has been "treated with irradiation instead of chemicals to control insect infestation." The term "radula" stems from the Latin verb *radio, radiare*, "to gleam, emit rays, radiate" and from the Latin noun radius, "a staff, rod, stake, spoke of a wheel." This word has been used on occasion with the noun *sol, solis* to indicate a "beam of light." This logo is strikingly similar to the EPA logo, which stands for safeguards for good health.

ing to the Organic Consumers Association, this logo sends the message that irradiation is a natural, healthy process:

> People have a good feeling about the EPA, because it is supposed to be a watchdog for the people.
> People don't have a good feeling about irradiation, because it often uses radioactive materials, and it benefits meat and poultry packers and producers, not the consumer.
> The EPA symbol appropriately shows water, the sun and a flower.
> The radura shows a flower in a broken circle, symbolizing the radiation.
> The radura distracts your attention from the fact that irradiation is mostly about "sterilizing" feces-contaminated food, not about preserving flowers.[39]

The visual design of a logo is carefully crafted to convey messages to the audience. To illustrate, in 2002, Malayawata Steel Company announced that it was adopting a new corporate logo "to better reflect the company's current image and corporate culture" (Figure 5.6):

> Executive chairman Lim Kiam Lam said the symbol, which consists of a perfect circle and a geometrical square in its centre, signifies precision at the core management and operational levels. "Precision is the key es-

Figure 5.6   **Malayawata Steel Berhad Logo**

sence which enables Malayawata to chart significant progress time after time," he said. Lim said the logotype, which consisted of two bars, reflected strength and resilience.

"The corporate blue denotes the will power to succeed—a personification of our commitment to excel in every aspect of our operations. It is also a symbol of integrity and farsightedness. Orange represents a vibrant, competent workforce that embraces the spirit of teamwork; the embodiment of a strong corporate culture."[40]

Political Cartoons

Political cartoons surmount the obstacles of illiteracy by relying predominantly on drawings, which require a minimum of explanation to comment on world events, leaders, and ideologies. Christina Michelmore observes, "Cartoons do not just illustrate the news. They are graphic editorials, and like all editorials they analyze and interpret a situation; they pass judgment. They tell readers what to think and how to feel about what is happening—amused, sympathetic, chagrined, angry, afraid."[41]

The humor in political cartoons is based on hyperbole—that is, exaggeration of a situation or issue. Cartoons may also depict a caricature of a person's appearance or behavior to make a point. But in the process, political cartoons provide serious commentary on the people and issues being lampooned. In the eighteenth century, political cartoonist James Gillray helped prepare England for war against France and its emperor, Napoleon Bonaparte. This famous cartoon, "The King of Brobdingnag and Gulliver," shows George III holding a tiny Napoleon in his hand and frightening himself half to death by looking at the emperor through a pair of binoculars (Figure 5.7). This political cartoon influenced public opinion and England's decision to go to war. Another historical political cartoon appeared in British papers soon after the Nazi invasion of France

Figure 5.7 **Political Cartoon Using Caricature**

The KING of BROBDINGNAG and GULLIVER

in 1940. It depicts Winston Churchill standing on the white cliffs of Dover (Figure 5.8). The caption captures the sense of isolation felt by the British population at that time, along with the strong sense of resolve to continue the fight: "Very well, alone."

Examining contemporary political cartoons can be an effective way to gauge current global opinion on world events. David L. Paletz declares:

Figure 5.8 **Political Cartoon as Text**

" VERY WELL , ALONE "

If Americans want to understand the hostile feelings many people in the Arab/Muslim world have about the U.S., its leaders and their policies, they should take a hard look at the striking cartoons from the region. Post–Sept. 11 political cartoons in Arab/Muslim newspapers draw a moral equivalent between the war in Afghanistan and terror attacks, ridicule the United States for its incompetence in locating Osama bin Laden and portray the U.S. as a powerful yet often blind or misled soldier.[42]

Today, the Internet has broadened the scope and audience for political cartoons. Political cartoons appear on numerous Web sites, including *The Village Voice*, *Mother Jones*, Salon.com, and Netzeitung.de, which provide new arenas for political cartoonists. Some of these political cartoons are animated, with audio and video capabilities, which attracts younger audiences.

Music

Music can have a subtle, yet powerful influence on individuals. Music evokes an affective response in the audience, enhancing their moods or distracting them from their immediate concerns.

Music can also foster a sense of national cohesion and identity. For instance, national anthems inspire patriotic feelings. The musical tradition of a country is also an expression of its history, religion, and ethnicity. To illustrate, the distinctive rhythms, uses of instruments, and vocalization found in the music of the Yoruba people of West Africa are derived from their religious traditions. In the Yoruba religion, music is a major element in the worship of the Orishas (Divine Beings). Each Orisha has devotional songs, dances, and rhythms associated with Him or Her, and singing and drumming are a part of most important ceremonies. Depending on the nature of the celebration, percussionists and drummers (often playing the sacred three-piece *bata* drums) play precise rhythms directed to specific Orishas, while those present sing call-and-response songs in archaic Yoruba. This ceremony induces the Orishas to descend and possess initiated priests and priestesses of the religion.

Music serves as a major form of communication between cultures. A large percentage of the popular music that young people around the world listen to is in English, spreading Western ideas, lifestyle, and values. But at the same time, the widespread distribution of international music has contributed to the continued evolution of musical forms. To illustrate, in 2000, a Web site, jhblive.co.za, carried South African home-grown dance music to an international audience when the first live streaming of local disk jockeys was staged in Johannesburg as part of a "cyber summer party." The event was designed to highlight local talent and encourage international communication in the dance music industry. The Webcast proved so popular that the organizers found themselves confronting serious bandwidth limitations.[43]

Music can be used as a narrative device in film and television presentations, furnishing subtle cues that reinforce themes and messages. The choice of major or minor keys and harmonic or discordant notes in a musical score can signal approval or disapproval of characters, situations, or the ideology of the presentation. The genre of a musical selection can also convey messages. For instance, the use of classical music can underscore the sophistication of a program—and the audience as well.

Music is used not just in entertainment programming and advertising but is also employed in news programs as well. Michael Colton observes:

> Among [musical themes] for Fox News is the sultry lite-jazz used on Judith Regan Tonight ("It has a sex vibe to it, and it's intelligent," says Scott Schreer of NJJ Music). The company has also finished Fox's theme for the 2000 presidential campaign, a slow, regal piece featuring trumpet, tympani, and gong. [Richard O'Brien, vice-president/creative director of

Fox News Channel] says he asked Schreer for something "grand and heroic, majestic and inspiring, with a hint of patriotism."[44]

News events, such as the conflict in Iraq, are given their own distinctive theme music on CNN. Gary Anderson, creator of the *Headline News* theme on CNN, says, "Any network and any TV program needs an audio identification, or 'idents.' It's the 'kitchen factor': The viewer is in the kitchen, the music comes on and they go running to the next room to see what's going on."[45]

Performance

Nonverbal behavior is an effective and sophisticated form of communication. According to communications scholar J.S. Philpott, over two-thirds of the total impact of a message is the result of nonverbal factors.[46] In visual media (e.g., photographs, film, and television), nonverbal behaviors such as body posture, accents, subtle facial expressions, and eye movements convey messages and reinforce themes. Even in radio, which relies only on sound, vocal modulation, rhythm, and pitch have an enormous impact on the attitudes of the audience.

For instance, the nonverbal behavior as anchors or reporters deliver the news can provide very subtle but powerful editorial commentary. For instance, according to media critic Paul Farhi, Shepard Smith, the host of the *Fox Report* on the Fox News Network, interjects his conservative ideology into the news through his nonverbal behavior: "Smith isn't shy about letting viewers know where he stands; a quick eye roll is usually enough to convey his thoughts on a particular story."[47]

Nonverbal behaviors can furnish clues about media messages, on several levels:

- Nonverbal communication provides insight into the character and disposition of the media communicator. Independent of the content, nonverbal behavior such as posture, body type, and dress sends messages about the speaker's self-image, competence, confidence, and trustworthiness.
- Nonverbal communications analysis identifies ways in which media communicators use "scripted" nonverbal strategies to create a particular image or impression. Media figures carefully orchestrate their nonverbal behaviors to make their verbal messages more convincing. The study of nonverbal communication can furnish

perspective on the communications strategy, style, and content of a media presentation.

• Nonverbal communications analysis furnishes individuals with tools to detect "unscripted" behaviors, which are at variance with the verbal message. People who are interviewed on-camera often are unable to express their true feelings verbally. However, their non-verbal behaviors may divulge their actual thoughts and feelings.

Nonverbal responses are an intrinsic aspect of human behavior; all humans smile, frown, and gesture. However, the circumstances that trigger these reactions vary between cultures. As a result, the meanings people attach to nonverbal cues differ between countries. For instance, a non-verbal behavior that you might intend to be reassuring may be regarded as offensive by someone from another country. Larry A. Samovar and Richard E. Porter explain:

> Cultural norms often dictate how, when, and to whom [nonverbal behaviors] are displayed. Even what calls forth a specific expression is related to our cultural experiences. For example, not all cultures have the same definition of what is humorous. What produces a smile in one culture may elicit a frown in another. Cultures that value the elderly would not find jokes about old people the least bit amusing.[48]

To complicate matters further, subcultures within a country may exhibit distinctive nonverbal behaviors. To illustrate, Craig S. Smith observes, "In the South [of China], people tap two fingers on the table to say thanks, but people in the North might think the gesture is just a nervous tic."[49]

Nonverbal communication can present a fascinating subtext, in which the latent, nonverbal "conversation" is a commentary about relationships, power, and control. For instance, Samovar and Porter observe that males and females often display different nonverbal behavior:

> Women in many settings often hold their arms closer to their bodies than do men. They usually keep their legs closer together and seldom cross them in mixed company. Their posture is also more restricted and less relaxed than the posture of males.[50]

Other issues of status are also addressed in the ways that people interact nonverbally. For instance, certain forms of eye contact, proximity, and touching behavior are acceptable for people in positions of authority but are not permissible for subordinates.

Facial Expressions

People express a range of facial responses, including evaluative judgments (e.g., pain, pleasure, superiority, determination, surprise, attention, and bewilderment), degree of interest or disinterest in the subject, and level of understanding. Some facial cues to be alert for include the following:

- Raised eyebrows indicate surprise.
- A set jaw reveals anger, determination, tension, resolve, or decision.
- A chin retraction is a protective action or a signal that something is scary or frightening.
- Flared nostrils express anger.
- A nose wrinkle signifies dislike, disapproval, or disgust.

Facial responses may also have culture-specific meanings. In China, people are conditioned by their culture to remain stoical as a way, literally, to "save face." But in many Mediterranean cultures, inhabitants exaggerate their facial expressions to convey emotions.

Gaze

A person's gaze offers a range of communication options: establishing eye contact, avoiding eye contact, looking down, shifting the eyes, squinting, staring straight ahead, and closing the eyes. According to Dale Leathers, the eyes fulfill the following communication functions: (1) they indicate degree of attentiveness, interest, and arousal; (2) they influence changes in attitude and behavior; (3) they regulate interaction; (4) they communicate emotions; (5) they define power and status; and (6) they assume a central role in creating and maintaining an impression.[51]

Cultures vary with respect to the amount of eye contact that is acceptable among their people. In the United States, people are regarded as honest if they "look you straight in the eye," whereas in Japan, extended eye contact is a sign of disrespect. Indeed, Japanese children are instructed to direct their gaze to the region of their superior's Adam's apple.

Posture

Posture is the stance or positioning of the body or body part. Postures can communicate a range of personal information about a person. Hav-

Figure 5.9 **A Body Cant**

In this posture, the person moves the head and shoulders from an upright position. In China, this gesture is a sign of respect. *(Photo by Lee Kuehner.)*

ing good posture—standing tall—is an indication of confidence, integrity, empowerment, authority, and rank in society. A slumping posture signals meekness, sadness, carelessness, depression, or cowardice. Posture also can indicate the speaker's attitude. Leaning toward a person expresses a positive disposition, while slumping is a sign of disrespect.

However, posture may possess culture-specific meanings as well. In Japan, females often stand in a "cant" position, in which the head or body is bowed (Figure 5.9). The latent message of this body language is deference, submission, and subordination. In Germany and Sweden, slouching is a sign of rudeness, sloppiness, and incompetence.

Gestures

Gestures are the act of moving the limbs or body as an expression of thought or emphasis. Some specific gestures and their meanings include: the chin stroke suggests pensiveness and concentration; the chin rub suggests dubiousness and questioning; the chest beat indicates strength and power. Another common gesture is the palm punch, in which the fist

Figure 5.10 **Japanese Palm-Up Gesture**

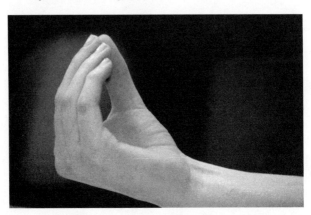

(Photo by Lee Kuehner.)

hits the palm of the other hand. According to Desmond Morris, this is an angry gesture that has a primal, symbolic significance: "This has a common meaning of a mimed blow against an enemy, redirected onto the palm of the gesturer. In such cases the gesture indicates a state of barely controlled rage."[52]

Openness gestures (e.g., unbuttoning coats, uncrossing legs, moving toward the edge of the chair) convey a sense of confidence, encouraging interaction. On the other hand, defensive and nervousness gestures are considered unattractive and undesirable. Crossed arms and crossed legs suggest that the communicator is inaccessible and defensive. Fidgeting, tugging at clothing, and playing with objects signal that the communicator is nervous.

Gestures may also assume a specific cultural significance. For instance, Li He points out that in China, tapping a person on the shoulder "is a wish to convey bad fortune. It's not done in a casino or during a mah jongh game."[53] Indeed, the meaning associated with a particular gesture may vary widely in different countries. In Japan, the thumb and forefinger making a circle with the three other fingers up in the air is used as a symbol for money (Figure 5.10). In the United States, this gesture means A-OK. In Brazil, Spain, and Denmark, this gesture is regarded as obscene and insulting. In France, it means "zero" or "worthless."

Proxemic Communication

Proxemic communication refers to the ways in which space configurations convey meaning. The use of space falls into two distinct categories:

Personal space consists of the space immediately encircling our bodies which each of us considers our own territory. The boundaries of personal space may be culturally determined. Members of Arab nations typically stand closer when conversing than do Europeans. The boundaries of personal space may also vary within particular subcultures. For instance, in the United States, women tend to stand closer together than men do.

Group formation refers to the arrangement of people in relation to one another. Where people are positioned in relation to one another may indicate status. Group formation also indicates whether the assemblage of people forms an open or closed society.[54] People standing in a closed formation are excluding others, while groups in an open formation are more inclusive. A football huddle is an example of a closed formation. A classroom seating arrangement in a circle is an example of an open formation.

The meaning attached to group configurations may vary in different cultures. In America, people at the head of the table are in control. The individual seated to the left of the head of the table often has the least status in the group. In Japan, the most important person sits at one end of a rectangular table, with those nearest in rank at the right and left of this senior position. The person with the least status typically sits at the opposite end of the table, nearest the door.

Tactile Communication

Tactile communication, or touch, can signal support, reassurance, intimacy, sexual interest, anger, or exhilaration. Touching violations can be an assertion of power and control by high-status individuals.

Touching behaviors can reinforce verbal content or convey independent latent messages. For instance, politicians have mastered the art of holding a handshake for an instant longer than is normally expected, sending a message of personal regard, intimacy, and trust.

Other factors also influence the meanings associated with touch:

- *The nature of the relationship:* Family members touch each other in different ways than mere acquaintances do.
- *Region of the body:* A tap on the shoulder has a different meaning than a pat on the bottom.
- *Age:* Young and old people touch most frequently when communicating.
- *Context:* The place and occasion in which the touching behavior occurs help determine its meaning. What might be acceptable at a drive-in movie might not be suitable at the office.
- *The type of touching behavior exhibited:* There are subtle yet discernible differences between pats, squeezes, brushes, and strokes.

Some cultures are more inclined than others toward touching as a form of communication. Examples of these high-contact cultures include Arab, Latin American, and southern European countries. Low-contact cultures include northern European, Asian, and North American countries. For instance, Greeks and Italians often express themselves through pats on the shoulder, prodding with a forefinger, hugging, and kissing on the cheek. But in Thailand, people would regard these tactile behaviors as rude and intrusive.

Costumes

Wardrobe can communicate a range of information within a culture, including ethnic affiliation and social class. However, apparel that conveys these messages often varies widely between countries. In Germany and Spain, businessmen adhere to a very strict dress code, consisting of a dark suit, tie, plain shirt, and dark shoes and socks. But for Arab males, proper business attire consists of a long loose robe called a dishdasha or *thobe* and a headpiece, a white cloth kaffiyeh, secured by a black cord, or *egal.*[55]

Clothing can therefore serve as a code, which conveys cultural messages. Craig S. Smith provides the following example:

> A Washington State agriculture official who was touring China a few years ago handed out bright green baseball caps at every stop without noticing that none of the men would put them on or that all the women were giggling.
>
> Finally, a Chinese-American in the delegation took the man aside and informed him that "to wear a green hat" is the Chinese symbol of a cuckold.[56]

Vocalic Communication

Vocalic communication refers to the quality of the voice that conveys meaning, independent of the meaning of the words that are spoken. Dialect, tonal quality, inflection, speed of delivery, and accent transmit a wide range of information about the speaker's educational level, class, cultural orientation, and nationality. Psychologist Richard Wiseman declares that vocality can be a more accurate barometer of the communicator's intention than eye contact or gestures: "If you want to find out if a politician's lying . . . you're better turning away or shutting your eyes and just concentrating on the sound track."[57]

Countries vary in their vocalic communication behaviors. Samovar and Porter observe:

> The Thai people, as well as people from the Philippines and Japan, speak so softly that it almost sounds as if they are whispering. For them a gentle and soft voice reflects good manners and education. When interacting with Americans, people from cultures that speak softly often believe that Americans are angry or upset because of their relatively loud speech.[58]

Vocalic communication consists of the following elements:

Volume refers to relative loudness or softness in the voice. Loudness can signify dominance and conviction, or it can be interpreted as anger or insistence. Low volume may suggest insecurity, submissiveness, or evasiveness; on the other hand, it can reflect sensitivity, good manners, and education.

Tone is the characteristic quality or timbre of the voice. A deep tone suggests authority, power, and confidence. Nasal voices are judged unattractive, lethargic, and foolish. Breathy voices are judged to be youthful and artistic in males, but artificial and high-strung in females.

Pitch refers to the relative position of a tone in the musical scale—that is, whether the voice is high or low. Flat voices are seen as sluggish, cold, and withdrawn. On the other hand, variety in pitch is often regarded as dynamic and extroverted. A high-pitched voice may signal lying. An elevated pitch at the end of a sentence signals that the speaker is asking a question. However, this rise in pitch also indicates that the speaker is uncertain about what he or she is saying. Conversely, lowering the pitch at the end of a sentence conveys certainty and authority.

Rate refers to the pace or rhythm of delivery—how rapidly or slowly a person speaks. A person is generally regarded as speaking with greater intensity and earnestness as the speaking rate increases.

Duration is the length of time a communicator takes to emit a given sound or sounds. Taking too much time during a conversation is a dominance device used by a speaker seeking to control the conversation, including the topics of conversation.

Diction refers to the clarity of pronunciation and articulation. Garbled diction can convey confusion, ignorance, or deceit.

Silence is the absence of sound. Silence can be a dominance device, used for control and intimidation. However, as Seva Gunitsky, research associate at Center for Defense Information points out, in Japan and Scandinavia, silences that occur during a conversation are not considered uncomfortable, but natural and productive.[59]

Laughter is an involuntary, physical release of emotion. Laughter expresses a variety of emotions, including joy, approval, surprise, discomfort, anxiety, sympathy, and ridicule. Various types of laughter convey different meanings. In television, laugh tracks punctuate programs with chuckles, giggles, snickers, and guffaws, instructing the audience not only what is funny, but how funny the situation is. The context of the laughter also determines meaning. People who are nervous or feel that they are in a subservient position often laugh at inappropriate times.

Accent, meaning the way in which a person pronounces words, can disclose a person's geographic origin. A British acquaintance claimed that he could identify a person's exact neighborhood of origin in London by his or her accent. An accent can also disclose a person's level of education.

It should be mentioned that nonverbal behaviors sometimes have quite innocent explanations. For instance, a person may stand in a particular posture just because his or her back hurts. As Groucho Marx commented, "Sometimes a cigar is only a cigar."

Lines of Inquiry: Production Elements

I. Examine a body of work produced in a particular country, focusing on aesthetic style.
   A. Can you identify a national aesthetic style?
   B. Can you identify aesthetic influences from other countries, cultures, or traditions (e.g., the influence of African music on American jazz)?
II. Examine international media presentations, focusing on universal and culturally specific meanings.

A. Identify universal meanings associated with production values in the presentation.
1. Where do they appear in the presentation?
2. When do they appear in the narrative?
3. What does the appearance of these universal production values reveal about the themes and messages in the presentation?
B. Identify culturally specific meanings associated with production values in the presentation. Are there choices of production values that run counter to the meaning normally assigned to it in your culture (e.g., a Japanese film in which white is the dominant color at a funeral)?

III. Color
A. Colors can evoke a wide range of emotional responses. Examine a sample of international media presentations, focusing on the affective properties of color.
1. How does the color set the mood and tone of a production?
2. What feelings are evoked by the use of colors?
3. Do the colors convey meanings that correlate with or contrast with the content of the production?
B. Conduct research on a particular country, focusing on the culture-specific meanings assigned to colors. Compare the uses of color in media presentations in your own country.
C. Examine a sample of international media presentations, focusing on connotative properties of color.
1. How does the use of color reinforce messages and themes in the presentations?
2. Do the colors in the presentations convey particular messages and themes?

IV. Examine the impact of *editing* decisions on the construction of meaning. How do the following editing decisions affect the construction of meaning?
A. Inclusion and omission. Compare the media coverage of an issue in several countries.
1. Identify stories that appear in the media of some countries but not others. What accounts for this inclusion and omission?
2. What information can you find in the media of one country that does not appear in the media of another?
3. Do the stories provide context about the subject?
4. Does the arrangement of information vary between the stories?

  5. Selective emphasis: What aspects of a story are given promi-
     nence? Does this comparative analysis furnish perspective
     on the biases of a country's news? Does your analysis pro-
     vide insight into the prevailing attitudes in other cultures?
     Explain.
B. Sustained coverage
  1. Trace the coverage of an issue in a sample of international news
     sources.
     a. Which stories receive sustained coverage?
     b. Do some stories receive sustained coverage in some national
        sources but not others?
  2. Collect articles (e.g., environmental changes) on topics that have
     been covered sporadically in a newspaper. When seen collec-
     tively, what messages are being conveyed?
C. Relative position. Conduct a gestalt analysis. Construct your own
   front page using international sources of news (newspapers, TV).
  1. What news is included?
  2. What countries are included?
  3. What stories about these countries are included?
  4. What stories about these countries could have been included?
D. Films are often edited before being distributed in other countries,
   leaving out content that would be considered objectionable in that
   culture. For instance, *Idioterne* (*Dogma 95*), directed by Lars von
   Trier, eliminated sexually explicit content for distribution in
   America. Compare film versions to see what is included and excluded. What does this tell you about the cultures?

V. Word Choice
A. Analyze a sample of international presentations (print, broadcast,
   or Internet). What does word choice in the presentation reveal
   about a nation's
  1. Historical sensibility
  2. Political life
  3. Cultural sensibility
B. Identify examples of the following forms of language. How do
   they alter the meaning of the presentation?
  1. Labels
  2. Euphemisms
  3. Language collectives
  4. Obfuscation terms
  5. Antitheticals

C. Translation. If you have skills in a foreign language, translate a newspaper article into your native tongue.
   1. Is the translation accurate?
   2. Does the translation affect the meaning of the presentation?

VI. Connotative Image
A. Analyze a sample of international presentations (print, broadcast, or Internet). What do the images in the presentation reveal about the following:
   1. Historical sensibility of a country
   2. A nation's political life
   3. Cultural sensibility of a country
B. Analyze a sample of international media presentations dealing with the same topic, focusing on *image*.
   1. Identify universal images.
   2. Identify national images.
      a. Are images used in one country interpreted differently in your culture? Explain.
      b. Does the appearance of an image in the media furnish perspective on cultural attitudes, preoccupations, and myths?
C. Examine several images, focusing on *point of view*.
   1. How do the images reflect the points of view of the productions?
   2. How do the images affect the interpretation of the audience?
D. Identify examples of the following manipulations of images. How do they alter the meaning of the presentation?
   1. Imagistic layering
   2. Symbolic representation
   3. Metonymy
E. Identify connotative images in the media presentation.
   1. What is the connotation of the image?
   2. Why was the image included in the media presentation?

VII. Infographics
A. Analyze a logo, focusing on the following:
   1. What entity does the logo represent (company, individual, government)?
   2. What is the function of the logo?
      a. To convey information
      b. To generate a positive emotional attitude toward the company
      c. To establish identity
      d. To announce significant changes
      e. To conceal mission

3. What design elements are employed to convey the message?

B. Political Cartoons

1. Examine a political cartoon.
   a. What is the intended message of the political cartoon?
   b. What are the latent functions?
   c. What attitudes and stereotypes does the cartoon reveal?
   d. What does the style of the political cartoon reveal about the cartoonist's attitude toward the (1) issue, (2) people?

2. Analyze a range of international political cartoons focusing on the same topic.
   a. What do you learn about the issue by examining the cartoons?
   b. What are the different perspectives on the issue?

3. Analyze a sample of political cartoons on a variety of subjects from different media sources within a particular country.
   a. What issues appear to be of interest or concern?
   b. What is the range of opinions about these issues?

4. Examine a sample of international political cartoons focusing on a contemporary issue.
   a. What can you learn about global attitudes about the issue?
   b. Identify different perspectives and attitudes toward the issue.
   c. Do these political cartoons provide any perspective on the prevalent attitudes in your country?
   d. What messages are conveyed by the drawing?
   e. What is the central message of the cartoon?
   f. What is the function of the political cartoon?

5. Examine a sample of national political cartoons to identify national attitudes toward other groups, issues, and ideologies.

6. Examine political cartoons, focusing on caricatures.
   a. What is the nature of the exaggeration?
   b. Is this caricature an expression of the cartoonists' attitudes toward the subject? Explain.
   c. Is the caricature tied to cultural or political stereotypes?
   d. What political or ideological statement is made by the caricature (e.g., the person looks greedy)?

VIII. Music

A. What does a country's indigenous music reveal about its culture?
   1. History

2. Religion
3. Ethnic makeup
B. What do the lyrics of contemporary songs reveal about the following?
1. Current conditions in a country
2. Attitudes toward issues
3. Attitudes toward other countries
C. Does the music in a media presentation fulfill one of the following functions?
1. Influencing behaviors and attitudes
2. Eliciting an affective response
3. Punctuating the visuals
4. Providing editorial comment
5. Conveying narrative cues to the audience
D. Examine how the use of music reinforces messages and themes in the media presentation.
IX. Analyze a media presentation, focusing on performance elements.
A. Universal meaning
B. Culture-specific meaning
C. Scripted behavior
D. Unscripted behavior
E. Facial expressions
F. Eye contact
G. Posture
H. Gestures
I. Space configuraions
J. Touch
K. Wardrobe
L. Vocalic communication

II

Comparative Analysis
National Media Systems

6

Analysis of National Media Systems

People who have never traveled outside of their native country may not realize the degree to which media systems vary throughout the globe. National media systems actually are as distinctive as their countries of origin. Interpreting a country's media presentations requires an awareness of the following aspects of a nation.

Political Systems

In many countries, the mass media have assumed a central role in attaining, maintaining, and influencing power:

- The media inform the public about the political life of the nation.
- The media provide public exposure for politicians.
- The media influence public attitudes toward politicians and issues.
- Politicians use the media to establish the political agenda.
- Politicians use the media to influence the public response to policies and events.
- The media have emerged as a key to geopolitical relations between nations.

A nation's system of government affects its concept of *freedom of the press*. Freedom of the press refers to standards that determine: (1) the openness of a country with respect to the flow of information; (2) access to national and global information by the public; (3) access to information by the media (including information from its own government); (4) the kinds of information being conveyed through the media; and (5) the relative importance of freedom of the press within the country.

According to the Freedom House ratings of press freedom, as of 2000, 33 percent of the countries in the world are rated not free, 27 percent are categorized as partly free, and 40 percent are identified as free.[1] A report from Reporters Without Borders, which included a worldwide index of countries according to their standards of press freedom, declares (see Table 6.1, pp. 140–141), "[Press] freedom is under threat everywhere, with the 20 bottom-ranked countries drawn from Asia . . . which contains the five worst offenders: North Korea, China, Burma, Turkmenistan, and Bhutan." The criteria for the index were based on a range of press freedom violations, including the number of murders or arrests of journalists, censorship, pressure, punishment of press law offences, and regulation of the media.[2]

Significantly, this survey suggests that a country's political system is a bigger influence on its media than the state of its economy: "The top end of the list shows that rich countries have no monopoly of press freedom. Costa Rica and Benin are examples of how growth of a free press does not just depend on a country's material prosperity." And conversely, relatively rich countries such as Kuwait maintain strict limits on the freedom of the media.[3]

Political systems fall into three general categories: totalitarian, democratic, and countries in transition.

Totalitarian Political Systems

In totalitarian systems, the primary function of the media is to support the political agenda of the government. Totalitarian governments control the production and dissemination of information as a means of maintaining order and shaping public opinion.

The government limits all forms of expression, including information conveyed through the channels of mass communication. Dissension and criticism are permitted only with the approval of state authorities. State agencies routinely monitor programming to insure that it promotes the national interest. In the former Soviet Union, members of the secret services (KGB) monitored every newspaper article, radio show, and television program before it could be presented in the media. These government agents were actually part of the staff, usually holding the nominal title of "deputy editor." But their presence served to intimidate reporters, insuring that the topics and stories were in keeping with the state guidelines.

Under this system, media communicators are part of the political establishment as well. For instance, in the former Soviet Union, all employees of the state media were required to be members of the Union of Journalists of USSR, a Communist organization. This arrangement created conflicts of interest with respect to their coverage of governmental activities.

As of 2000, forty-five totalitarian countries had placed restrictions on Internet access for their citizens.[4] The Chinese government exercises the most extensive Internet censorship in the world, denying a vast majority of its 46 million Internet users access to 19,000 political, educational, and religious Web sites that it regards as dangerous, including *Playboy,* the Dalai Lama, and the *New York Times.*[5] The Chinese government controls access to information on the Internet in other ways as well. Erik Eckholm explains:

> Newly trained "Internet police" patrol Web sites and chat rooms, weed out seditious thought and pornography, and read the e-mail of those suspected of crimes. The government is also trying to impose stricter registration of cafe users and recording of their online travels.
>
> Beyond blocking access via standard Chinese servers to hundreds, perhaps thousands of "anti-social" Web sites, the cyberpolice have also learned how to jam e-mail they deem threatening. In a continuing race of offensive and defensive technologies, dissident groups abroad were flooding the country with e-mailed newsletters, but these have been largely suppressed. The government has also started trying to block e-mailed news reports from the Voice of America, and popular chat rooms, some of which are forums for lively debate on current affairs, must maintain a full-time monitor who can filter out postings that enter vaguely defined forbidden zones.[6]

Totalitarian governments also screen entertainment programs for ideological messages. For instance, the Chinese government delayed the release of the film *Go for Broke* for over a year. Government censors cited concerns about the image of workers in the film, objecting that the characters looked poor and were shown swearing and gambling. The film was finally released in 2002.[7]

Media content may also be suppressed for what is considered objectionable moral content. In 2001, the government of Tanzania closed down Swahili-language publications on the grounds that these tabloids were encouraging the spread of the AIDS virus among their readers.[8]

In totalitarian countries, journalists frequently risk personal harm for violating government restrictions on information. Over the past decade,

Table 6.1

2003 Press Freedom Index, Reporters Without Borders

Rank	Country	Rank	Country	Rank	Country	Rank	Country
1	Finland	—	Peru	—	Mongolia	109	Liberia
—	Iceland	38	Bulgaria	—	Sierra Leone	110	Malaysia
—	Norway	39	South Korea	75	Kenya	111	Brunei
—	Netherlands	40	Italy	—	Mexico	112	Ukraine
5	Canada	41	Czech Republic	77	Venezuela	113	Democratic Republic of the Congo
6	Ireland	42	Argentina	78	Kuwait	114	Colombia
7	Germany	43	Bosnia and Herzegovina	79	Guinea	115	Mauritania
—	Portugal	—	Mali	80	India	116	Kazakhstan
—	Sweden	45	Romania	81	Zambia	117	Equatorial Guinea
10	Denmark	46	Cape Verde	82	Palestinian National Authority	118	Bangladesh
11	France	47	Senegal	83	Guatemala	119	Pakistan
12	Australia	48	Bolivia	84	Malawi	120	Uzbekistan
—	Belgium	49	Nigeria	85	Burkina Faso	121	Russia
14	Slovenia	—	Panama	86	Tajikistan	122	Iran
15	Costa Rica	51	Sri Lanka	87	Chad	—	Zimbabwe
—	Switzerland	52	Uganda	88	Cameroon	124	Belarus
17	United States	53	Niger	89	Morocco	125	Saudi Arabia
18	Hong Kong	54	Brazil	—	Philippines	126	Syria
19	Greece	55	Ivory Coast	—	Swaziland	127	Nepal
20	Ecuador	56	Lebanon	92	Israel	128	Tunisia
21	Benin	57	Indonesia	93	Angola	129	Libya
—	United Kingdom	58	Comoros	94	Guinea-Bissau	130	Iraq

Rank	Country	Rank	Country	Rank	Country	Rank	Country
—	Uruguay	—	Gabon	95	Algeria	131	Vietnam
24	Chile	60	Yugoslavia	96	Djibouti	132	Eritrea
—	Hungary	—	Seychelles	97	Togo	133	Laos
26	South Africa	62	Tanzania	98	Kyrgyzstan	134	Cuba
—	Austria	63	Central African Republic	99	Jordan	135	Bhutan
—	Japan	64	Gambia	—	Turkey	136	Turkmenistan
29	Spain	65	Madagascar	101	Azerbaijan	137	Burma
—	Poland	—	Thailand	—	Egypt	138	China
31	Namibia	67	Bahrain	103	Yemen	139	North Korea
32	Paraguay	—	Ghana	104	Afghanistan		
33	Croatia	69	Congo	105	Sudan		
—	El Salvador	70	Mozambique	106	Haiti		
35	Taiwan	71	Cambodia	107	Ethiopia		
36	Mauritius	72	Burundi	—	Rwanda		

Source: Reporters Without Borders, www.rsf.fr/article.php3?d-article=4118

366 journalists have been killed in the line of duty. Sixty reporters were killed in crossfire and 277 were murdered in direct reprisal for their work. Of the remaining twenty-nine casualties, the motives for murder are undetermined. In 2002, the two most dangerous countries in which to practice journalism were Colombia (ten dead) and Russia (seven dead).[9]

In countries with totalitarian political systems, journalists may also be jailed for violating their government's restrictions on freedom of speech. In retaliation for their reporting, 136 reporters were imprisoned by their governments in 2002.[10] For instance, Iranian law authorizes the courts to prosecute journalists (and their editors) for publishing any information deemed offensive to the government.[11]

Traditionally, foreign reporters have been granted immunity while working in totalitarian nations; however, in recent years, this protection has been rescinded. To illustrate, in 2001, Zimbabwe declared that foreign correspondents would be treated as terrorists.[12] In 2002, Daniel Pearl, an American reporter for the *Wall Street Journal,* was kidnapped and murdered by Pakistani militants. Also in 2002, Israeli soldiers lobbed grenades at foreign journalists covering an Israeli incursion into Palestinian territories.

Totalitarian governments may also employ a number of indirect strategies to curb freedom of the press in their countries. For instance, the governments of Botswana and Namibia prohibit the placement of ads in publications they find objectionable, thus driving them out of business. In Burma, all stories must first pass a government review board before they can be published. If an article is deemed unacceptable, it must be not only removed but also replaced by a story of an equivalent length so that readers do not see the traces of censorship. Because these additional expenses can be financially ruinous, magazine and newspaper editors are understandably reluctant to publish controversial stories.

Nevertheless, in recent years, it has become increasingly difficult for totalitarian governments to maintain strict control over media content. The rapid expansion of private media operations within a country makes it nearly impossible for the government to monitor the flow of information. Throughout China, for instance, over 2,000 small newspapers had sprung up by 2001—far too numerous for tight government oversight. As a result, the Chinese government can only prosecute violators on a selective basis. Consequently, the Chinese press was able to inform the public about numerous sensitive issues and events. For example, in 2002, *China Economic Times* reported on a bridge collapse, concluding that the government casualty numbers were faked; *China News Weekly* examined sexual abuse of students by teachers, focusing on recent cases in Beijing; and *Worker's Daily* reported that nearly half of important government-owned coal mines had dangerously high levels of gas and that almost the same number had no safety monitoring.[13]

In addition, developments in media technology enable individuals to circumvent government censorship. Despite the restrictions placed on the Internet discussed earlier, individuals still manage to access the Web. Eckholm provides the following example from China:

> Among the many paradoxes of 21st-century China, consider this one: It is actually easier and cheaper for the average Zhou in Beijing to hook up with the internet than it is for most Americans.
>
> In many cities of this totalitarian Communist state, you don't even need to sign up with an internet service provider or pay any monthly minimum. From any modem you can just dial 95963, 95700 or a number reserved by an internet company and dive directly into the World Wide Web—for charges of 36 cents an hour that are paid with the phone bill.
>
> Although Beijing shut down many unlicensed Internet cafes after a deadly blaze in June, one can still hang out in more than 200,000 cybercafes around the country and cruise the Web with a high-speed connection—and usually at even lower cost [than rates for people in the U.S.].
>
> "Now, young people rush to the internet cafes rather than rushing to newsstands to buy *People's Daily*," said Liu Junning, a liberal political scientist who cheers the long-term effects. "The internet has fundamentally undermined people's dependence on the government-controlled media."
>
> On the grand concourse of the World Wide Web, though, [censorship] measures hardly even serve as speed bumps. New site names are limitless, and those who really want to read the Dalai Lama's opinions could use proxy servers or other methods to evade the official firewall. And the subtler, inherently subversive effects are too numerous to imagine.[14]

Further, media communicators have devised a number of tactics to circumvent censorship in totalitarian countries. Seth Mydans provides the following example:

> In Burma, as in other repressive states, writing under censorship is an art form in itself, for both the writer and the clever reader. Many of its rules are universal. . . .
>
> "The trick is in the presentation," said U Tin Maung Than, a Burmese writer and editor who played the game hard, bobbing and weaving, wink-

ing and nudging, honing his metaphors, comparisons and historical references until it all became too much and he fled . . . from Myanmar for safety.

Writing under censorship is an intricate and multilayered exercise that consumed Mr. U Tin Maung Than. . . . Sometimes you aim too low and the readers miss your point entirely, he said. Sometimes too high and the censors catch you.

It is a game played by all independent-minded writers in the military dictatorship of Myanmar, the former Burma: the writer versus the censor. The stakes are high; at the worst, the penalty box is prison. . . . "Two or three years in prison is O.K.," he said in an interview here. "But more than 10 years, the cost is too high."

"You cannot criticize," Mr. Tin Maung Than said. "You have to give hints that you are being critical, that you are talking about the current system. The hints are in your choice of words and your tones and your composition. You use words with double meanings."

"If we want to talk about fear, we cannot talk about fear in the political context," he said. "So we talk about children's fear and its impact on society. The key is that you have to give little hints that you are not really talking about children."[15]

Democratic Political Systems

In countries with democratic political systems, the government maintains a relative distance from the production and distribution of information. Indeed, one of the responsibilities of government is to protect its citizens (and the media) from infringements of freedom of the press. To illustrate, the First Amendment to the U.S. Constitution declares that "Congress shall make no law . . . abridging the freedom of speech, or of the press." Over the years, the term *Congress* has been expanded to include any local or federal governmental body. The First Amendment was established on the premise that the United States is a marketplace of ideas. All forms of ideas should be expressed, and all people must be able to make their own decisions about what is right and appropriate.

In addition, the U.S. Freedom of Information Act, enacted in 1966, guarantees that not only journalists, but all citizens have equal access to the records of federal agencies. Jane Kirtley, a professor of media ethics and law at the University of Minnesota, explains: "The Freedom of Information Act is a crucial piece of legislation for journalists, researchers and investigators trying to get to the truth of how our government operates. The act is crucial for the protection and general education of the public."[16]

At the same time, however, all democratic governments are charged with imposing some limitations on freedom of the press. For instance, the U.S. Supreme Court has ruled that certain categories of speech—obscenity, false advertising, "fighting words" inciting to riot, and defamation—are not protected by the First Amendment. The government is charged with determining the scope and the limits of these categories.

Surprisingly, in the survey ranking freedom of information in different countries conducted by Reporters Without Borders, democratic countries such as Colombia (114th) and Bangladesh (118th) are ranked very low. In these countries, armed rebel movements, militias, or political parties constantly endanger the lives of journalists. These governments fail to do all they can to protect journalists and fight the immunity very often enjoyed by those responsible for such violence. The United States ranks at seventeenth place in the index, primarily because of the number of journalists arrested or imprisoned. Most of these reporters have been arrested because they refuse to reveal their sources in court; others, in the wake of 9/11, have been arrested for crossing security lines at some official buildings.[17]

Democratic governments are faced with the challenge of striking a balance between freedom of information and national security. This tension between freedom of expression and national security is most evident in wartime. During World War II, the United States and Great Britain imposed strict controls about what information could be reported (e.g., troop movements, weapons specifications, attack targets). Before reporters could send their stories for publication, the copy first was reviewed by military censors.

News organizations also adhered to a system of self-censorship by withholding sensitive information that might aid the enemy. Journalists, filmmakers, and radio personalities also produced programs designed to boost public morale. However, at times, this "voluntary" censorship code was enforced through government pressure. Barbara Friedman explains:

> U.S. President Franklin D. Roosevelt's Office of Censorship was charged with managing voluntary censorship among American journalists and news organizations. In 1942, the Office published a "Code of Wartime Practices for the American Press" which detailed to publishers, broadcasters,

and reporters what would constitute improper handling of information regarding the war effort. While censorship was "voluntary," it was imposed by the threat of prosecution via the Espionage Act of 1917. In addition, reporters could be left out of briefings, denied battlefield access or access to sources if the military or administration didn't like what was being written.[18]

As part of the war on terrorism, the Bush administration has removed public records, such as specifications about bridges and highway construction, from Web sites that could be used by terrorists. In addition, the Bush administration restricted the availability of federal records by reinterpreting the guidelines for the Freedom of Information Act. Attorney General John Ashcroft announced that the new administrative policy would support the withholding of documents as long as there was a "sound legal basis for doing so." (The previous standard had been to withhold documents only if "disclosure would be harmful.") Jane Kirtley declared, "What's so troubling about this is the message it sends to records custodians: When in doubt, don't give it out."[19]

Alarmingly, the U.S. wartime censorship policies may become permanent. Shortly after the September 11 attack, President George W. Bush declared that the war on terrorism was an ongoing conflict, so that these wartime measures would continue indefinitely. Consequently, the revamped U.S. media policy resembles that of another democracy, Israel, which maintains an ongoing censorship code because the country is in a constant state of war.

Countries in Transition

As countries move from one political system to another, their media are also frequently caught in transition. Russia offers a good example of how the shift from a totalitarian to a democratic political system can be problematic, as reflected in the relationship between the government and the media. Even though Russia ostensibly supports an independent media system, the state continues to control the production and distribution of media programming. Thus, privately owned television stations are dependent on state-owned transmitters to broadcast their programs. The state still has the principal rights to all radio frequencies, left over from the Soviet era. The allocation of these rights is granted to individuals who are friendly to the government. Similarly, Internet providers are primarily dependent on telephone companies, which are still controlled by the Russian government. In addition, the state assists favored media outlets by giving tax relief and free rent on warehouses and other government-owned buildings.

At the same time, the Russian government penalizes private media companies that are considered unfriendly to the administration. Russian journalist Aleksander Grigoryev recounts:

> My newspaper was publishing articles that were critical of the local system of state medical insurance. The day after it was published, the tax police with masks and guns broke into the office, frisked the employees, and closed the office for two days, on the pretext that they needed tax information. Afterward, we published the next article in the series and they returned to harass us.[20]

In some cases, efforts by the Russian government to control the private media are even more overt. In 2002, the Russian government shut down TV-6, Russia's last independent television network. With this move, the government expanded its control of national television from one state-controlled network in 1999 to three in 2002, leaving NTV as the only national independent TV station. The deputy chief of the Russian Democratic Party Yabloko, Sergei Ivanenko, declared that the network's closure "is the most striking manifestation of the development of controlled democracy in this country."[21]

Regulatory Systems

Media regulations place controls on the content and dissemination of information conveyed through the channels of mass communications. Regulations fall into the following categories:

Acquisition of Media Outlets

Some countries have established regulations that govern how media operations are procured. For instance, in 2003, the U.S. Federal Communications Commission (FCC) proposed relaxing the regulations governing acquisition of media companies:

- Companies could own television stations that reach 45 percent of the U.S. population, up from 35 percent.

- In local markets with five or more TV stations, a company could own two; in markets with eighteen or more, a company could own three.
- In markets with nine or more TV stations, media companies could own newspapers and TV stations or TV stations and radio stations in the same market.
- In markets with at least forty-five radio stations, one company could own eight. In markets with thirty to forty-four stations, a company could own seven; in markets with fifteen to twenty-nine, ownership would be limited to six; and in markets with fourteen or fewer, ownership would be limited to three.

In contrast, countries such as Russia have no restrictions on cross-ownership of broadcast and print media, so that a company can hold television, radio, newspaper, and magazine outlets in a single marketplace. According to Bill Kovach and Tom Rosenstiel, changes in these regulations would have enormous implications:

> What will happen to communities if the ownership rules are eliminated? Among the possibilities is that one or two companies in each town would have an effective monopoly on reaching consumers by being allowed to control the newspaper, radio, TV, billboards and more—with costly consequences for businesses that need those outlets for advertising. Such a monopoly on information would also reduce the diversity of cultural and political discourse in a community.[22]

As of January 2004, these proposed FCC guidelines are being contested in the U.S. Congress.

Limits on Foreign Ownership of the National Media System

One major area of concern in international communications is the growing dominance of transnational media conglomerates. To illustrate, prior to 2001, Russia had no restriction on foreign ownership of its media. Consequently, Independent Media, which controls Russian publications such as *Vedomosti*, and the *Moscow Times*, was completely owned by foreign interests—90 percent by Dutch interests and 10 percent by a Lausanne affiliate of the bankrupt Menatep Bank. An editorial in the *Russia Journal* warned about the potential danger of no restrictions on foreign ownership: "It could lead to genuine threats to strategic interests, as there is no guarantee that a foreign owner of a media outlet would not use it first and foremost as a means of increasing his or her own nation's interests over that of Russia."[23] In response, Russia passed an amendment to its mass media law in 2001, stipulating that only 49 percent of its media operations could be owned by foreign interests.

Several other countries have established quotas that limit the proportion of media outlets that can be owned by foreign interests:

- In 1993, the European Community (EC) adopted its Television Without Frontiers directive, limiting the number of imported foreign television programs and films.
- In 1955, India imposed a ban on foreign ownership of newspapers and TV stations.
- In 1998, the Israeli Parliament passed a bill requiring that half the songs on national radio stations be sung in Hebrew, Israel's official language.

However, some transnational media conglomerates have circumvented this quota system by creating "strategic alliances" with domestic media companies, such as joint ventures, formal and informal agreements, and cooperative partnerships.[24]

In the face of global economic pressure, some countries are beginning to relax their quotas on foreign ownership. In 2002, India announced plans to ease its restrictions on foreign ownership of its print media. Hungry for foreign investment to offset a swelling current-account deficit, the government said that with certain conditions, foreign owners could acquire stakes of up to 74 percent in technical journals and other nonnews publications and up to 26 percent in newspapers and current-affairs periodicals. Editorial and management control would have to remain in Indian hands, the government said, and in the case of news publications, foreigners could not be the largest shareholders. Each deal and each foreign owner would have to obtain clearance from the government. In 2002, the Chinese government doubled its quota of Hollywood films permitted in the country—from ten to twenty per year.[25] (For further discussion, see the section on Ownership Patterns in Chapter 2).

Ownership of Content

Regulations pertaining to intellectual property—the ownership and distribution rights to media productions—are complicated by the global marketplace. New technologies make it difficult for producers to maintain control over sales and distribution. For example, within days after the premiere of *Harry Potter and the Sorcerer's Stone* (2001) in London and New York, pirated videotape copies of the film were being sold in Beijing, China.

In Russia, over 80 percent of mass-produced films on video and DVD are produced illegally.[26] In response, the Russian government established regulations in 2002 that required each producer of DVDs and CDs to obtain a license from the Press Ministry, the agency responsible for intellectual property issues. Desperate to protect their illegal operations, these "video pirates" have resorted to mob-style violence. In 2002, Konstantin V. Zemchenkov, the chief of a task force fighting illegal video and DVD production, was murdered by a gunman who fired seven shots at Zemchenkov's car.[27] Other countries have launched a crackdown on media piracy as well. In China, law enforcers confiscated 114 million illegal CDs, VCDs, and DVDs in 2001.[28]

Ownership of content is also an issue in the recording industry. Individuals are now able to download music on the Internet, bypassing recording companies and musicians. Sites like Napster, an online music service, have been taken to court for intellectual property and copyright infringements.

Standards of Morality

In some countries, regulations forbid media content that undermines the religious and moral beliefs of the culture. In Iran, for instance, censors can require that filmmakers make changes in dialogue and action to meet the moral standards of the country. In the Iranian film *Unforgiven*, film star Mahaya Petrossian played a young woman who had to come to terms with her dying father. Petrossian recalls, "There is a scene in which I'm crying and begging him to forgive me and I couldn't touch him, I had to use my expressions and my voice instead. It dupes the audience because in real life a father and daughter would touch."[29] In addition, countries such as Australia, Canada, and the United States have developed their own broadcast policies governing children's television.

Accessibility to Media Programming

Some countries have established regulations to insure that their citizens have access to media programming. Singapore, a multilingual society, requires that broadcast television be available in English, Chinese, Malay, and Tamil. In the Netherlands, programming time is distributed among many social and political groups based on the proportion of their sub-culture among the general population. Production facilities (complete with crews) are made available upon request. In the United States, regu-lations mandate that television sets come equipped with closed caption capabilities to assist people who are hearing-impaired.

Protection of the National Media Industry

In some countries, local communities have instituted regulations de-signed to protect and promote local media outlets. For example, in order to protect the viability of local cinema theaters in Paris, laws have been established limiting the number of video and DVD rental shops in a given area.

In addition, numerous countries, including France, Norway, Denmark, Russia, Spain, Mexico, Canada, and South Africa, have established regu-lations that enable them to compete with transnational media conglom-erates. In France, a percentage of the income generated from ticket sales at movie theaters is channeled into the French film industry. In that way, the French government commits $400 million annually to support film production in the country.

However, media technology has made the enforcement of these regu-lations considerably more complicated. The Internet, which transcends national borders, strains the ability of an individual country to enforce its own set of laws and regulations. To illustrate, although the United States has its own laws restricting pornography, an Internet user need only tap into a Web site originating in another, more permissive country in order to circumvent U.S. laws.

Alarmed by this situation, some nations have asserted their regula-tory authority over information coming into the country via the Internet. In 2001, a French judge, Jean-Jacques Gomez, ordered Yahoo! to block French Web users from accessing pro-Nazi sites or from purchasing Nazi memorabilia through Yahoo's on-line auction site. The French court was enforcing French law, even though Yahoo is an American company. In addition, judges in Germany, Italy, and Canada have ruled that national regulations apply to the virtual world. In 2002, Australia's highest court ruled that an Australian businessman had the right to sue a U.S. news organization (in this case, Dow Jones & Company, pub-lisher of the *Wall Street Journal*) in his home country over a story carried on the Internet. However, the debate regarding the jurisdiction of national regulations is far from settled. Internet providers such as Yahoo are contesting these court rulings. In addition, civil liberties groups such as the American Civil Liberties Union, are concerned about preserving freedom of speech on the Web.

Computer software offers the possibility that national regulations can now be enforced. Geotracking programs can establish jurisdiction by pinpointing the physical location of a Web user.

Currently, there is some movement in the direction of nations agreeing on a common set of regulations. For instance, in anticipation of its acceptance into the World Trade Organization in 2001, China has amended both its copyright and patent laws to meet international standards. In 2003, the World Health Organization adopted a treaty, called the Framework Convention on Tobacco Control, that would prohibit advertising and sponsorship of television programs and entertainment by tobacco companies as a step to discourage cigarette smoking and reduce the estimated 5 million deaths it causes each year.[30]

Geographical Elements

The following geographical features of a region can affect how a national media system presents information:

Size

Residents of large countries such as the United States or China are often isolated from other nations. As a result, residents of these countries tend to regard events occurring outside of their borders as having no relevance to their own lives. In contrast, Europeans routinely interact with people from other countries. This exposure to other countries is reflected in increased media coverage of other countries.

Proximity

A nation's media coverage may be particularly attuned to the activities of adjoining countries. For instance, Lesotho is completely surrounded by one country—South Africa (see Figures 6.1a and 6.1b.) Consequently, the media coverage in Lesotho focuses a great deal of attention on the activities of its much larger neighbor.

Figure 6.1a **Map of Lesotho**

Figure 6.1b **South Africa, Surrounding Lesotho**

Source: The CIA World Factbook, 2003.

Neighboring countries often share a common history, language, culture, religion, and terrain. In addition, they are often exposed to the same natural disasters, such as earthquakes and drought. Neighboring countries may also serve as important strategic and economic partners. For example, the Mexican media routinely include information about the United States because of the close ties between the two countries.

The construction and interpretation of media messages may also be affected by territorial disputes between countries with shared borders. To illustrate, in 2002, an advertisement by Cadbury India for Temptations Chocolates created a political controversy between India and Pakistan, two countries that have been embroiled in a long-standing conflict over the territory of Kashmir. The ad displayed a map of India that included the disputed territory. The text of the ad read, "I'm good. I'm tempting. I'm too good to share. What am I? Cadbury's Temptations or Kashmir?" A political firestorm ensued; protest rallies were held outside Cadbury India's office in Mumbai and newspaper editorials criticized the company for its insensitivity. Eventually, Cadbury India retracted the ad and issued a public apology.

Climate

The climate of a country can also affect the story selection and emphasis in a country's media coverage. For instance, agricultural countries depend on weather information; indeed, weather information is often front-page news in drought-plagued regions of Africa. And in countries that rely on tourism, reports on sea conditions or the amount of snowfall are major news.

In addition, the climate can have a bearing on audience behavior patterns within a country. In the United States, for instance, the television audience is generally larger in winter, when outdoor activities are curtailed in much of the country. Climate can even affect which media are commonly utilized within a country. For instance, because film stock deteriorates in tropical climates, residents of these countries often rely on radio or television as primary media.

Resources

The availability of natural resources plays a role in the development of an individual country's media system. For instance, the availability of paper and ink determines whether print media are widespread in a country.

The transportation infrastructure of a country also has an impact on its media system. Roads, railways, and rivers play a major role in the distribution of newspapers and magazines throughout a country. For instance, in central Russia, national daily newspapers can be delivered to small towns and villages only once a week. Readers are then required to catch up on the week's news by reading back issues. However, in technologically developed countries, the Internet has facilitated the distribution process. Newspaper content is being e-mailed to different towns and printed and disseminated locally.

Ethnic Composition

Ethnic groups share a number of characteristics, including race, religion, cultural background, and language. At one time, ethnicity was tied to a person's place of national origin; however, many ethnic groups are now widely dispersed throughout the globe.

In countries like Norway, which have a relatively homogeneous ethnic population, it is easy to identify a clear target audience and construct media messages accordingly. However, many other countries are composed of numerous ethnic groups, adding to the challenge of international communications. For instance, China comprises a number of distinct ethnic groups, including Han Chinese, Zhuang, Uygur, Hui, Yi, Tibetan, Miao, Manchu, Mongol, Buyi, and Korean. These ethnic groups speak a variety of languages and dialects, such as Standard Chinese or Mandarin (Putonghua, based on the Beijing dialect), Yue (Cantonese), Wu (Shanghaiese), Minbei (Fuzhou), Minnan (Hokkien-Taiwanese), Xiang, Gan, and Hakka.[31]

The ethnic composition of a country can affect the selection and emphasis of news stories by its mainstream press. For example, the Russian media are very sensitive to the concerns and interests of the country's 20 million Muslim residents.

In addition, tensions between ethnic groups in a country can affect how information is presented in the media. For instance, Myanmar's ethnic minorities, which make up one-third of the population, continue to suffer from a wide variety of human rights violations. The media are the province of the dominant culture; ethnic subcultures are discouraged from having their own media. In this case, it can be a mistake to regard the mainstream media as representative of the entire country. Indeed, media presentations may present vastly different points of view, depending on the ethnic subculture of the media communicator. To illustrate, journalists covering the civil war in the former Yugoslavia during the late 1990s included Serbs, Bosnians, and Montenegrins, who looked at the war through their own particular ethnic lens.

At the same time, ethnic traditions, humor, and culture often find their way into mainstream films, advertisements, and news programs. For instance, the U.S. film *My Big Fat Greek Wedding* (2002) was particularly popular among the Greek-American population.

Religious Orientation

It might surprise some Americans that the religious life of a country can influence how the media messages in a country are constructed. The United States operates under a system of religious pluralism, in which many faiths, churches, and religious movements coexist. The U.S. Constitution guarantees separation of church and state, so that there is no official state religion. Consequently, even though the predominant religion is Protestantism, other religions are tolerated as well. As a result, numerous newspapers, publishing houses, radio stations, and television programs throughout the country serve the Catholic, Jewish, and Muslim communities.

In contrast, many countries have a tradition of only one officially sanctioned state religion. For example, in Saudi Arabia, the media were established by clerics as a way to impart the tenets of Islam. Consequently, Islamic principles influence the selection and presentation of stories that appear in the media. In 2003, the government of Saudi Arabia ordered the removal of the editor in chief of *Al Watan,* the daily newspaper that had been critical of Islam for propagating extremist views that contributed to terrorism. The paper had raised a number of issues related to the political role of the Islamic religion in Saudi Arabia, including questioning the central role of the religious police in Saudi society. The Islamic community protested against the newspaper, with a senior Muslim cleric issuing a religious fiat declaring it a sin to buy the paper.[32]

Even when media stories escape government censorship, the interpretation of the audience may be colored by its religious sensibility. In 2002, Nigeria hosted the Miss World beauty pageant. A riot broke out when the daily newspaper, *This Day,* declared that the Prophet Muhammad might have favored marrying one of the contestants. In the ensuing conflict between Muslims and Christians, over a hundred people were killed, and the newspaper office was burned to the ground.

In countries such as Italy, Britain, and Russia, the official restrictions on religious groups have been removed. However, media messages continue to be influenced by the dominant religion in the country. For instance, even though there is no law regulating media coverage of the Catholic Church in Italy, criticizing the church or church leaders would violate a clear, if unstated, cultural understanding.

Media communicators must be sensitive to religious references in the construction of media messages. To illustrate, after the events of September 11, 2001, President Bush addressed an international audience, proclaiming that "this crusade, this war on terrorism, is going to take a while." However, by using the term *crusade,* Bush inadvertently transformed the conflict into a religious war between Christians and Muslims. William Safire explains that the word *crusade*

> has a religious root, meaning "taking the cross," and was coined in the 11th century to describe the first military expedition of the Crusaders, European Christians sent to recover the Holy Land from the followers of Muhammad. . . . In this case, a word that has traditionally been used to rally Americans was mistakenly used in the context of opposing a radical Muslim faction, and the White House spokesman promptly apologized.[33]

The ability to recognize religious references in international media presentations can be useful in the interpretation of media messages. To illustrate, in 2002, a message allegedly from Osama bin Laden, broadcast on al-Jazeera, referred to U.S. president George W. Bush as "Pharaoh." On the surface, this allusion to ancient Egyptian rulers appears incongruous. However, as Verlyn Klinkenborg explains, "Invoking Pharaoh's name is a moral allusion, unbound by any regional associations. . . . Pharaoh lives still, not as a tyrant of flesh and blood but as an apotheosis of secular evil."[34]

Educational Systems

The educational system of a country plays a significant role in an individual's selection and use of the media. A country's educational curriculum—what subjects students are exposed to—affects their ability to interpret the information being conveyed through the channels of mass media. In societies in which the literacy rate is low, people are unlikely to depend on print media. According to Berle Francis, a media literacy scholar from Jamaica, "When I was a youngster, there was a very high rate of illiteracy in most English-speaking Caribbean countries, so radio held sway."[35] Indeed, 125 million children around the globe have never been inside a classroom. And in sub-Saharan Africa, 40 percent of primary-age children have no opportunity for schooling.[36]

The American educational system does not emphasize the study of foreign languages, which limits students' exposure to foreign newspapers, magazines, and films. As a result, most Americans must rely on the accuracy of the translation of international media presentations. In contrast, countries throughout Africa and Europe emphasize foreign language instruction in school, so their citizens, have a wider access to print and film presentations in their original form.

In addition, American students are unfamiliar with world history. In 2002, only 10 percent of American high school seniors were considered proficient in history, based on their scores on the National Assessment of Educational Progress Exam. Asked which of the following nations was an ally of the United States in World War II, 18 percent of high school seniors identified Germany, 9 percent said Japan, and 24 percent selected Italy.[37] This lack of historical consciousness means that American students frequently lack the context to interpret international news. It also has an impact on American journalists' ability to put the events of the day into meaningful perspective, as well as their judgment about what is considered newsworthy.

The subject of geography is also generally overlooked in U.S. schools. As a result, American high school students are largely unaware of where countries are situated on the globe. In one survey, conducted by the National Geographic Society, only 13 percent could find Iraq on a map, only 71 percent could find the Pacific Ocean, and 10 percent could not locate their own country on a blank map of the world.[38] Knowing where countries are located—or, indeed, if they exist—is an essential step in developing a global consciousness.

An emphasis on science and technical subjects such as engineering instruction can determine whether a country develops trained personnel who can install, operate, and maintain media equipment.

Countries that include a media and journalism programs in their schools produce media communicators who have learned to present information in a professional, insightful fashion. Significantly, a number of countries, including Canada, England, and Australia, emphasize media literacy throughout their school curricula. This critical thinking skill empowers students to decipher the information being conveyed through the channels of mass communication. Other countries have also made significant inroads into the field of media literacy, including New Zealand, Chile, India, Scotland, South Africa, Japan, France, Italy, Spain, and Jordan.

Finally, there is a wide disparity in the media technology available in schools throughout the globe. In 2000, 78 percent of students in Sweden were able to access the Internet from their schools, as opposed to only 25 percent of students in France and Germany.[39] As a result, students in some countries do not have technological support for their research. Further, these students are not formally instructed about the various applications of the Internet.

Systems of Media Ethics

Ethics can be defined as professional standards of conduct, based on a set of moral principles—in this case, applied to the media. Behavior that would be considered a violation of ethical standards in one country might be considered perfectly acceptable in others.

One of the ethical issues facing media communicators throughout the globe is the objectivity of the press. The American Society of Professional Journalists' Code of Ethics declares:

> Good faith with the public is the foundation of all worthy journalism.
> Truth is our ultimate goal.
> Objectivity in reporting the news is another goal, which serves as the mark of an experienced professional. It is a standard of performance toward which we strive. We honor those who achieve it.[40]

Unlike the United States, however, some other countries do not regard objectivity as an ethical standard. As mentioned earlier, in totalitarian countries like Vietnam, the function of the media is not to inform the people but, instead, to maintain control over the populace. Consequently, state agencies slant information to achieve this goal. For a country like Iran, a religious theocracy, the objective is to sustain Islamic traditions. As a result, the goals of the media may conflict with objective reporting. (See earlier discussion on Religious Orientation.)

It must be noted that even in the United States, the ideal of objectivity is impossible to attain. The ideal of objectivity assumes that an absolute truth exists and that journalists are in a position to determine what that truth is. However, editors and reporters have to make numerous decisions, including the selection of quotes, placement of stories, and selection of pictures, that shape how the information is presented and interpreted. Many members of the American audience, deceived by this illusion of objectivity, suspend their critical judgment of the information they receive through the media.

Another ethical issue involves conflicts of interest. In the United States, it is considered unethical for journalists to accept gifts or favors from sources. For example, in 2003, columnist George Will wrote positive articles about Conrad Black, chairperson of media conglomerate Hollinger International, without mentioning that Will was a paid advisor to Hollinger. Columnist Paul Krugman declares:

> Now, I thought there were rules here. First, if you're a full-time journalist, you shouldn't be in that kind of relationship. Second, whoever you are, if you write a favorable article about someone with whom you have a personal or financial connection—like . . . Mr. Will's March column praising Lord Black's wisdom—you disclose that connection.[41]

However, in Eastern Europe, it is not uncommon for interested parties to pay journalists to publish favorable articles or comments in their paper. In Russia, journalists routinely supplement their low annual income by writing favorable articles about people, in return for a fee. During Boris Yeltsin's election campaign in 1996, his staff gave TV journalists suitcases of money, cars, and free apartments in order to ensure favorable stories and comments.

A third ethical issue involves standards of privacy. Different countries have varying conceptions of privacy. For instance, in the United States, people can be subjected to media scrutiny as "public figures" if they meet the following criteria:

- They voluntarily stepped into the spotlight.
- They assumed an important role in the resolution of important public issues.
- They had an impact on a public issue.
- They became a public figure through means other than simply media attention.[42]

Within this framework, criminals are considered celebrities in the United States, and the media routinely cover their exploits. In contrast, in some other countries, like France, Russia, and Ukraine, government officials are regarded as public figures, whereas celebrities (at least in theory) are entitled to a degree of privacy. To illustrate, in 2001, a French political adviser caused quite a disturbance by writing a book that overstepped his culture's unwritten rules of decorum. Suzanne Daley explains:

> In the corridors of power [in Paris], everyone was in a twitter this week: an unwritten rule of French politics had been broken. Olivier Schrameck, the up-to-now discreet, bespectacled chief of staff of the Socialist prime minister, Lionel Jospin, has written a book about the relations between his boss and the Gaullist president, Jacques Chirac.
> Mr. Chirac's supporters could hardly contain their outrage at what they saw as underhanded pre-election politics dressed up in a 200-page book, called "Matignon, Rive Gauche 1997–2001." Government officials, they argued, had an obligation to wait until they were out of office before spilling the beans.[43]

In this era of globalization, these different systems of media ethics are creating conflicts within individual nations. For instance, British tabloid newspapers are frustrated by their country's interpretation of privacy, which might explain why they incessantly publish stories about American celebrities.

Lines of Inquiry: Analysis of National Media Systems

The following defining characteristics of a country can be useful in the analysis of its media system: political system, geographical elements, ethnic composition, religious composition, educational system, and system of media ethics.

I. Select a country and, using the defining characteristics cited above, describe its media system.
    A. What is the political system of the country—totalitarian, democratic, or transitional?
        1. How does the country's political system affect its media system?
        2. What is the relationship between the country's political system and its media system?

3. How does the government influence the flow of information?
4. How does this country define freedom of the press?
   a. What kinds of information are permitted?
   b. What kinds of information are prohibited?
   c. What kinds of tools can the government use to defend the freedom of the press?
   d. In what ways do the following factors affect the country's freedom of the press?
      1) The government
      2) The business community
      3) The audience
      4) Cultural considerations
5. Conversely, in what ways does the country's media system reflect the country's political system? What does analysis of the relationship between the government and the media industry reveal about the country's political system?

B. Does the media content in the country submit to any set of regulations?
   1. What is the balance between individual, local, national, and global regulations?
   2. If so, what are the parameters of these regulations?
      a. What kinds of information are permitted?
      b. What kinds of information are prohibited?

C. Do geographical considerations affect the construction and interpretation of media content?
   1. How does the size of the country affect its media coverage?
   2. How does the country's proximity to neighboring countries affect its media coverage? Focus on:
      a. Geopolitical context
      b. Economic and cultural impacts of neighboring countries
      c. Territorial issues
   3. How does the climate of the country affect its media coverage?
   4. How does the availability of resources affect the country's media system?
      a. How do the technical resources of the country affect its media system?
      b. How do the natural resources of the country affect its media system?
      c. How do the trained personnel of the country affect its media system?

      d. How does the distribution system of the country affect its media system?

D. How does the ethnic composition of the country affect the production and interpretation of media content?

    1. What is the ethnic composition of the country?

    2. Is the ethnic composition of the country homogeneous or mixed?

    3. In the case of a country with multiethnic composition, consider the following:

      a. Do the media represent the dominant ethnic culture?

      b. Are there media that express the perspective of other ethnic groups?

      c. Are there tensions between the ethnic cultures that might affect the presentation and interpretation of content?

    4. Can you identify ethnic references (e.g., words, humor, and culture) in media presentations that provide insight into media messages?

E. Religious composition

    1. What religion(s) exist within the country?

    2. Is one religion dominant within the culture (either officially or unofficially)? If so, does this have an impact on the selection of stories, point of view, inclusion and omission of information, etc.?

    3. Can you identify religious references (words, humor, and culture) in media presentations that provide insight into media messages?

F. Educational system

    1. What subjects are emphasized in the country's schools?

    2. What subjects are de-emphasized in the country's schools?

    3. How does this affect the presentation and interpretation of media messages?

G. How does the system of media ethics in the country affect media content?

    1. Objectivity of the press

    2. Conflicts of interest

    3. Privacy.

II. Using the defining characteristics cited above, compare the media system in your country to the media system of another country.

7

Case Studies

National Media Systems

This chapter consists of a collection of monographs written by distinguished media scholars throughout the globe, describing the media system in their own country. These case studies identify the distinctive characteristics of the national media system, and how they affect the construction of content and the interpretation of information by the national audience.

Each author responded to the following questions:

1. What are the distinguishing characteristics of the media system in your country?
2. Who owns the media in your country?
3. How much of the media is owned by foreign companies?
4. How much of the programming is produced in other counties? Which countries?
5. Which media are predominant in your country (e.g., Internet, film)?
6. How is your media system organized?
7. How is freedom of the press defined in your country? Are there any limits with regard to the content delivered by the media system (e.g., religious, political, criminal, medical, ethnic stories)?
8. Is the media system changing in your country? If so, how and why?
9. Do your country's media furnish insight into its cultural, political, and economic systems? Explain.

As you read the case studies describing national media systems, identify patterns that emerge: What are the points of similarity and contrast?

Mass Media in China: Controlled Transformation
Juyan Zhang

Propaganda Tools and Guided Commercialization

The mass media in China have been strictly controlled by the Communist Party of China (CPC) as its ideological vehicle and propaganda tool since 1949, when the party took the state power through revolution, and the rigid mouthpiece function of the mass media has since seldom been challenged. Meanwhile, commercialization guided by the CPC has been fundamentally transforming the landscape of the mass media in the past two decades since China launched its reform in 1978.

The strict control of media by the CPC has its theoretical foundation in the Marxist and Leninist theories about ideology and the press, which held that the press should work to promote state policies and to educate, organize, and mobilize the masses. Although the Chinese Constitution cherishes speech freedom, it at the same time monopolistically stipulates that "the state promotes the development of literature and art, the press, broadcasting, and television undertakings."[1]

Almost all of the mass media in China are owned and operated by the state and were financed by the state before their commercialization during the 1980s. The radio, film, and television stations are under the supervision of the State Administration of Radio, Film and Television (SARFT), and the press, books, and magazines under the State Press and Publications Agency. The Central Propaganda Department of the CPC operates behind both of these governmental bodies. The Internet as a new medium is under supervision of a special leadership group of the State Council, which coordinates the operation of the Ministry of Information Industry, the State Bureau of Industry and Commerce Administration, the Culture Ministry, the Public Security Bureau, and other bodies involving the management of the Internet and its content.

Since the 1990s, the Chinese government has actively promoted corporatization of the media industry, forming forty-seven state-owned media groups, including twenty-six press groups; eight radio, film, and television groups; six publishing groups; four distribution groups; and three film groups. Commercialization has driven the media, although still under tight control of the CPC, to seek more daring and lively content to attract audiences, and advertisers and the media increasingly have become critical of the negative aspects of the society.

Figure 7.1   **China**

Population	1,284,303,705 (July 2002 est.)
Ethnic groups	Han Chinese 91.9%, Zhuang, Uygur, Hui, Yi, Tibetan, Miao, Manchu, Mongol, Buyi, Korean, and other nationalities 8.1%
Religions	Daoist (Taoist), Buddhist, Muslim 1%–2%, Christian 3%–4% note: officially atheist (2002 est.)
Languages	Standard Chinese or Mandarin (Putonghua, based on the Beijing dialect), Yue (Cantonese), Wu (Shanghaiese), Minbei (Fuzhou), Minnan (Hokkien-Taiwanese), Xiang, Gan, Hakka dialects, minority languages
Literacy	definition: age 15 and over can read and write total population: 81.5% male: 89.9% female: 72.7% (1995 est.)
Legal system	a complex amalgam of custom and statute, largely criminal law; rudimentary civil code in effect since January 1, 1987; new legal codes in effect since January 1, 1980; continuing efforts are being made to improve civil, administrative, criminal, and commercial law
Population below poverty line	10% (2001 est.)
Labor force	706 million (2000 est.)
Labor force—by occupation	agriculture 50%, industry 23%, services 27% (2001 est.)
Telephones—main lines in use	135 million (2000)
Telephones—mobile cellular	65 million (January 2001)
Radio broadcast stations	AM 369, FM 259, shortwave 45 (1998)
Radios	417 million (1997)
Television broadcast stations	3,240 (of which 209 are operated by China Central Television, 31 are provincial TV stations and nearly 3,000 are local city stations) (1997)
Televisions	400 million (1997)
Internet service providers (ISPs)	3 (2000)
Internet users	45.8 million (2002)

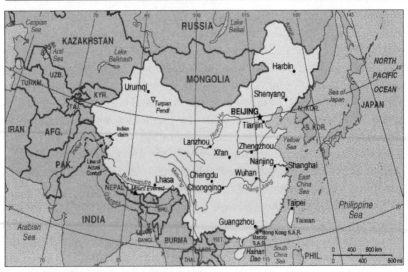

Source: The CIA World Factbook, 2003.

In terms of commercialization, however, the Chinese government strictly bans private and foreign ownership of the news media and only allows foreign nations to enter certain sections of the media industry. For example, they may engage only in the distribution of print media and TV drama programming, and only large state-owned enterprises may enter the broadcasting industry, engaging only in infrastructure construction with a share ceiling of 49 percent.

Corporatization of the Broadcasting Industry

Broadcasting System

Television is the dominant medium in China. The government has formed a four-tiered television system, with the China Central Television (CCTV) providing national broadcasting and the provincial, municipal, and county TV stations broadcasting at the local level. The local stations must unconditionally carry some signals, primarily news broadcasting, of the CCTV. So far, all of the provincial TV stations have their programs transmitted by satellite beyond their provinces, including twenty-two with over 100 million viewers each. A survey by SARFT showed that by the end of August 2001, 1.195 billion people in China had access to TV; 57.5 percent of the households received programs through cable networks, 36.3 percent via antenna, and 3.1 percent through localized or work unit network. Radio stations operate in a similar system as television.

TV, Radio, and Film Conglomerates

The Chinese government has promoted merging of TV, radio, and film since 2000 and built eight state-owned radio, television, and film groups by 2001. The largest group, the China Radio, Film and Television Group (CRFTG), established in December 2001, brought the CCTV, China National Radio, China Radio International, China Film Group Corp., China Radio and Television Transmission Network Cooperation Ltd., and China Radio and Television Web site under one umbrella. The giant media group is operated by governmental officials and has about 20,000 employees and an annual revenue of about 11 billion yuan (US$1.4 billion). The China Cable, also under SARFT, is piecing together the country's fragmented cable TV industry through the national fiber optic backbone, and a cable giant is expected soon. These mergers came when

China entered the World Trade Organization (WTO) and reflected China's attempt to grip its lucrative media market and strengthen its control of its propaganda machine before the country fully opens its huge domestic media market to the world.

TV Programming

China has adopted a licensing policy that strictly monitors TV programming. Programs have to be "politically correct," and content considered subversive, seditious, obscene, pornographic, superstitious, discriminatory, libelous, or insulting is banned. In general, the TV programming industry is not mature. According to a memo by SARFT in 2001, TV program demand in China was high, but its quality and producing capacity were low and not effective in satisfying the audience demands. In the past two decades, many programs, mainly series drama, have been imported by authorized state-run companies from Hong Kong, Taiwan, Korea, and Japan and quickly become popular. Now domestic entertainment programming is booming and becoming popular with the growth of private investment and the advertising industry. According to China's pledge to the WTO, nonnews foreign programs will eventually be allowed to broadcast in the whole country and the percentage of foreign programs is expected to increase sharply. This will inevitably pose great challenges to the CPC and the TV industry, but will enrich the consumption of the Chinese audience.

Foreign TV Channels

Currently, foreign TV channels are legally allowed only in luxurious hotels in most of China, except for Guangdong, the richest province. In 2001, the Chinese government allowed three entertainment channels—China Entertainment Television (CETV) owned by Time Warner, the Phoenix-Chinese Channel, and a cable TV channel owned by Rupert Murdoch's News Corporation—to broadcast in Guangdong province as an exchange for their broadcasting the CCTV-9 Channel in the United States. However, these imported channels must contain "no sex, no violence, no news."[2] The foreign satellite television operators have to beam their signals to a single centralized platform run by China's International TV Corporation, which is the only body responsible for importing foreign programs and monitoring foreign channels, with an annual fee of US$400,000. Before these three channels were legally accessible, millions of Chinese households could only semilegally watch foreign channels with satellite dishes that were subject to frequent crackdowns by the police.

Film

China's studio system is also experiencing tremendous commercialization. Before 1978, all of the film studios were owned and financed by the state to produce propaganda films, but now many studios have to raise funds by themselves and through box office receipts, though some still get financed by the state for producing propagandistic movies. Recently, the government has formed film groups to salvage the deteriorating state-owned studio system. Privately owned companies have to apply for a license to produce films and until 2002 could only release their films by purchasing official banners from state-owned studios. Foreign companies are allowed in TV programming, movie theater construction, and renovation and may collaborate with state-owned studios to produce films, but are banned from establishing joint-venture studios. Meanwhile, the Chinese government has allowed a state-owned company to import ten Hollywood blockbusters every year since 1995, and this number doubled after China joined the WTO.

Grouping the Print Media

Press and Periodicals

There are approximately 2,000 newspapers and 7,000 to 8,000 periodicals in China. All of the major newspapers are the mouthpieces of the Communist Party, with the *People's Daily* as the flagship under direct control of the CPC Central Propaganda Department. The party's propaganda departments at provincial, municipal, and prefectural levels have their mouthpieces as well. Besides the party press, there are also many trade newspapers and tabloids affiliated to the party newspapers.

Since 1996, with the party mouthpieces as the core, the Chinese government has actively promoted corporatization of the press and by 2001 had formed twenty-six press groups, which in some cases bring a dozen newspapers and magazines into one group. To attract readers and advertisers, many newspapers have turned from dry broadsheets devoted to the government's line into daring and lively newspapers, carrying fashion, Internet, and news articles that expose the negative side of the society, though they still refrain from sensitive political topics.

The Chinese government has banned private and foreign investment in news media for fear of losing ideological control and only allows it in the distribution industry. However, nonstate funding has been permeating into the media industry through various channels and some press groups have gone to the public through listed enterprises associated with them. It is reported that the government will eliminate these privately owned companies soon.

In order to tighten its ideological control and streamline the press, the government has clamped down on more than 820 periodicals and newspapers since 1997[3] and, in 1999, ordered that all local trade newspapers be affiliated with the party mouthpiece of the same level. In August 2001, the State Press and Publications Agency announced new rules for small newspapers and magazines that banned six categories of content, including material contradicting state ideology or official lines and policies; discriminating and endangering national unity; spreading rumors and false news; revealing state secrets and damaging national interests; spreading murder, violence, lewdness, superstition, and pseudo-science; and other content that violates the party propaganda discipline or government regulations on publishing or advertising. The government also warned that regions where two publications are closed down within one year for violating the guidelines would not be allowed to approve any new newspapers or magazines for another twelve months. The press and periodicals are monitored through a three-level postpublishing punishment, including internal criticism and warning, changing the staff and suspending license, and closedown.

Publishing Industry

China's publishing industry is booming but ideologically highly controlled. Before 1978, the industry was divided into three state-owned, autonomously operating sectors: publishing, printing, and distribution. The state allocated publication quotas to central/ministerial and local publishing houses and distribution was monopolized by the state-owned Xinhua bookstores. Since 1978, the publishing industry has become market-oriented, and the available book titles have increased ninefold, so that readers are enjoying more choices.

Privately owned companies have entered the publishing industry by buying the allowable quota of books from the state-owned publishing houses, and competing with the state distributing system. Periodical publishers must apply for a license and periodical numbers. Since the late 1990s, the government has promoted conglomeration, teaming the fragmented publishing, printing, and distributing organizations into publishing groups to cope with the pending international media companies. However, the publishing market as a whole is far from mature, and the quality of the books still needs improvement. China did not pledge to open its publishing industry to WTO members but will gradually open its distribution industry. In fact, the German publishing superpower Bertelsmann has already built up a 1.5 million "readers club" by circumventing China's regulations.

The Regulated Booming Internet

The Internet as a new medium is booming in China. According to the official statistics, by January 2002, there were about 12.5 million computer hosts for 33.7 million Internet users in China, and the Internet user population and its infrastructure capacity are doubling each year.[4]

The government has actively promoted the Internet for its lucrative commercial value, meanwhile formulating a four-tiered system to regulate the Internet. The government monopolizes the industry by screening the gateways to the global Internet, and only several authorized state-run companies are allowed to operate the networks connecting to the global Internet. The Internet service provider (ISP) must apply for a license to subscribe to these state-run networks, and individual users must register with authorities to subscribe to the ISPs.[5] The government also attempts to control the Internet by promoting filtering software, monopolizing domain name registration, and outlawing content deemed seditious, subversive, discriminatory, libelous, and insulting, as well as content judged to be spreading superstition, "evil cults," obscenity, pornography, gambling, violence, homicide, horror, and enticing crimes.[6]

Only news organizations that are directly affiliated with the various levels of governments are permitted to have news Web sites. Nonnews organizations must apply for licenses to run news Web sites; they can carry news only from officially approved domestic news organizations and are banned from carrying any news items based on their own sources. At the same time, many Western news Web sites are blocked with firewalls. News Web sites are currently not allowed to be listed in stock exchanges, and private and foreign companies are also banned from investing in these Web sites.[7]

However, Internet regulations are rarely enforced to the letter. Although a number of dissidents were put in jail for posting "subversive" messages, the government is not pursuing violators very actively, and nobody really cares or can control what you are doing at home as long as you don't take things into the public. The Internet has become an important source that allows traditional media to break blocked news, thus stepping beyond the governmental guidelines that only the official Xinhua News Agency can break sensitive political news and that local press can use only Xinhua's stories. Many traditional media also download and edit foreign news from the Internet, a practice banned by the government. The flagship mouthpiece of the CPC, the *People's Daily,* has opened its censored electronic bulletin boards and draws millions of visitors. Internet cafés are popular in cities, although they are ordered to install firewalls by the police and subject to frequent cleanup campaigns that clamp down on illegal operations.

Summary

In summary, China's media industry is in gradual transition from dry propaganda machine and ideological vehicle to lively, daring, market-oriented corporations. Although this process is still under the strict control of the CPC, the mass media have been fundamentally transformed from primarily serving the CPC propaganda to serving the audiences and advertisers. The CPC has reformed the mass media under the pressure of the information revolution and economic considerations, but the Chinese people have benefited from the transformation, although whether or not the transformation will bring to China political liberalization, as many expected, is still unclear.

Egyptian Media: Into a New Millennium
Shahira S. Fahmy

It was March 1999 when I spent five hours climbing a mountain in the Sinai Peninsula, Egypt. Before reaching the summit, I encountered a Bedouin serving hot tea. It was his job. The Bedouin spent two weeks isolated on top of the mountain and two weeks down at the village. In his house, the man owned a satellite dish, offering him access to al-Jazeera, CNN International,

Figure 7.2   **Egypt**

Population	70,712,345 (July 2002 est.)
Ethnic groups	Eastern Hamitic stock (Egyptians, Bedouins, and Berbers) 99%, Greek, Nubian, Armenian, other European (primarily Italian and French) 1%
Religions	Muslim (mostly Sunni) 94%, Coptic Christian and other 6%
Languages	Arabic (official), English and French widely understood by educated classes
Literacy	definition: age 15 and over can read and write total population: 51.4% male: 63.6% female: 38.8% (1995 est.)
Legal system	based on English common law, Islamic law, and Napoleonic codes; judicial review by Supreme Court and Council of State (oversees validity of administrative decisions); accepts compulsory International Court of Justice (ICJ) jurisdiction, with reservations
Population below poverty line	23% (FY95/96 est.)
Labor force	20.6 million (2001 est.)
Labor force—by occupation	agriculture 29%, industry 22%, services 49% (2000 est.)
Telephones—main lines in use	3,971,500 (December 1998)
Telephones—mobile cellular	380,000 (1999)
Radio broadcast stations	AM 42 (plus 15 repeaters), FM 14, shortwave 3 (1999)
Radios	20.5 million (1997)
Television broadcast stations	98 (September 1995)
Televisions	7.7 million (1997)
Internet service providers (ISPs)	50 (2000)
Internet users	600,000 (2002)

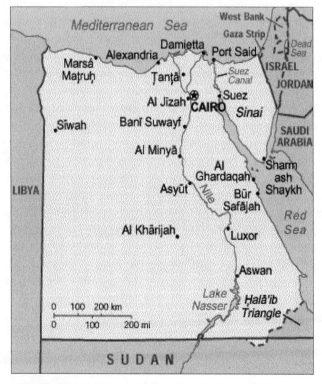

Source: The CIA World Factbook, 2003.

Radiotelevisione Italiana (RAI), and TV5 (a television consortium run by the governments of France, Belgium, Switzerland, and Canada).

Although one cannot claim this encounter represents a typical trend in Egypt, it makes clear that new developments are emerging. In the last century, the history of the Egyptian media has largely been influenced by the interaction of several political, economic, social, religious, and technological factors. These factors, such as Egypt's independence from the Ottoman and the British empires, the creation of the state of Israel and its ensuing wars, the change from a socialist system under President Nasser to a capitalist system under President Sadat and President Mubarak, the Gulf War, and the development of a politicized Islam, have affected the Egyptian media system in general and the press freedom in particular. Currently, the Egyptian media are confronted with a dual dilemma. One is produced by the technological change; the other is the result of the economic recession that has hit the country in recent years.

The independent Egyptian press appeared in the 1860s and 1870s during the country's cultural and intellectual renaissance under the Ottoman rule. Under the British rule, in 1947, restrictive laws and censorship regulations were imposed on Egyptian media. These regulations included prohibitions that dealt with social comportment, security, and national order. The censorship authority had complete power in imposing censorship regulations and issuing licenses. The inability to get rid of the strict regulations and censorship imposed by colonialism, combined with local values and traditions, affected the media system in Egypt. The censorship that was imposed during colonialism remained firm until 1976.[1] And although censorship laws have been modified, they still include numerous prohibitions concerning religious, sexual, and political taboos. Sensitive issues include corruption and the activities of militant Muslim groups.

That said, Egypt still maintains one of the most lenient media censorship policies in the Middle East. At least one news organization in every other Arab nation subscribes to Egypt's Middle East News Agency.[2] Currently, the Egyptian media have the right to criticize and discuss political, economic, and social events and any aspect of the government except some news concerning the president. However, within the next decade, the current situation of freedom of access to information and freedom of expression is expected to move toward full democracy.[3] With the increasing amount of information available in the new millennium, censorship regulations may well be altered.

Information and communication technologies have affected all countries worldwide and Egypt has been no exception. The information revolution in Egypt, while initially limited to the elite, is transforming political and social discourse. Beginning with the spread of satellite television, the steps toward privatization, and the increase in Internet access, these changes are creating a new type of political and social debate.

Egypt was one of the first Arab countries to have Internet connectivity. The Internet, while just beginning to have an impact, has great potential. However, the Internet is most likely to influence primarily the elite for three main reasons: the high access costs of a computer and Internet connection, the Internet's largely English content, and the need for computer literacy.[4] Although computer penetration is still low in Egypt, there is a steady increase. In the year 2000, Egypt had fifty Internet service providers and 300,000 Internet users, representing a 50 percent increase in Internet users from the previous year.[5] What is more, new regulations are facilitating Internet access. When Internet access first started in Egypt, users needed to pay a monthly fee to get the service, but in January 2002, a new policy allowed users Internet connection without subscription. Currently, users pay only for the cost of a local telephone call.

Literacy rates have been steadily increasing as well. Cairo has the largest publishing center in the Arab world and in Africa. Currently, there are eighteen main newspapers in Egypt, thirty weeklies, and many magazines, of which ten are online and two are in English.[6] In recent years, technical advances have enabled the press to give more emphasis to photographs in relation to text, especially in tabloids, which are filled with colorful pictures but contain no details of sexual encounters. One of the current overriding features of the newspaper market in Egypt is the intense concentration of the publicly owned press group, Dar Al-Ahram. The newspaper *Al-Ahram,* which has a circulation of nearly 1 million, is by far the most influential daily newspaper in the country. The online version and the international daily edition of *Al-Ahram*—distributed in Europe and North America—aim at reaching the Egyptian community abroad. Other important newspapers include *Al-Akhbar, Al-Gomhoreya,* and *Al-Wafd.* Egypt also imports a number of magazines and newspapers from abroad, although their distribution is limited to large cities, such as Cairo and Alexandria. The imports include cross-border, pan-Arab newspapers and magazines such as the major dailies *Al-Hayat* and *Al-Shark Al-Awsat,* which are published out of London.

Despite the increase in the literacy rate in Egypt that has led to an increase in readership in recent years, radio and television still remain the most widespread media.[7] In Egypt, radio has the highest penetration rates. The country has a strong oral tradition and more people listen to the radio in Egypt than in any other part of the world.[8] According to an almanac report, in 1997, there were an estimated 20.5 million radios in Egypt, with AM broadcasting from forty-two stations, FM broadcasting from fourteen stations, and shortwave broadcasting from three stations.[9] Radio Cairo is an external radio service that broadcasts in thirty-three languages in shortwave. Sot El-Arab (Voice of the Arabs), a station that until 1967 was heard by Arabs from Morocco to the Arabian Gulf, broadcasts to Europe and the Middle East. Hungry for diverse analyses, objective information, and nonmainstream media, many Egyptians have traditionally turned to outside radio outlets such as Radio Monte Carlo and the BBC.

While best known for its pyramids and ancient civilizations, Egypt, the most populated country in the region—with a population of 70 million—has played a central role in Arab media in modern times. Egyptian soap operas and movies have established the standard for broadcasting throughout the Arab world. The Egyptian cinema is the biggest and oldest cinema industry in the Arab world. Best known as the "Hollywood of the Arab World," the Egyptian film industry has supplied much of the Arab-speaking population with movies and recently with television shows from its newly established Media Production City in Cairo. It has produced over 3,000 films since the 1930s: Arab states have been almost entirely dependent on Egypt for their supply of films. However, the dissemination of television, satellite channels, the Internet, and high living costs drove people away from movie theaters, and the Egyptian cinema—like most cinemas worldwide—has been suffering from a crisis. Nevertheless, Egyptian film critics believe that the Egyptian cinema will transcend the difficulty. According to many, the industry still has a future. Privatization policies and new economic changes are being implemented. New movie theaters, which will provide revenue and more exposure for Egyptian films, are being built.

The state-owned Egypt Radio and Television Union (ERTU) is Egypt's national broadcaster and the Middle East's largest television and radio producer and broadcaster.[10] ERTU produces one-third of all Arab television drama just for the holy month of Ramadan.[11] With facilities throughout the country, ERTU transmits seventeen satellite channels via Nilesat and nine terrestrial channels of local programming, with a total viewing audience that exceeds 60 million people. Recently, new, private Egyptian television channels have been established: Al-Mehwar (The

Axis), Dream 1, and Dream 2. These privately owned satellite channels operate so as not to transgress guidelines related to the major taboos of politicizing religion and explicit sex.[12] The private channels broadcast from the free media zone at Sixth of October City, which is projected to be the base of the Arab media in the new millennium. The media city is owned by the Egyptian Company for Media Production (ECMP). ERTU owns 81 percent and private investors own the remaining 19 percent of ECMP. The country plans to attract more media companies to its free media zone, from Egyptian private media investors as well as Europe-based satellite television like MBC, ART, Orbit, and ANN, by offering existing media infrastructure and government economic support.

The Gulf War opened a new chapter in the history of the media in Egypt and the Arab world. CNN's international impact and its success in attracting a wide regional audience proved the strategic importance of satellite television in times of conflict. Several countries, including Saudi Arabia, Qatar, and Egypt, encouraged the installation of satellite television channels. Egypt was the first Arab nation to have its own satellite and an Arab satellite channel. Egypt has a share in Arabsat, owns Nilesat 101 and Nilesat 102, and rents space on Eutelsat and Intelsat. Nilesat transmits 32 radio channels and 134 satellite television channels. Egypt broadcasts several channels to the Middle East, Europe, and North America. Satellite television channels are both free and scrambled. Nile TV broadcasts in English and French as well as two hours of daily broadcast in Hebrew. The Egyptian satellite channel (ESC), the first Arab satellite channel, offers a combination of news, movies, and entertainment shows. It is one of the most popular satellite channels in the region.

Satellite broadcasting is changing the way information and entertainment are being received in Egypt. Although satellite penetration in Egypt is only 8 percent, more viewers are expected.[13] Many watch satellite TV at friends' or relatives' homes, clubs, and coffee shops. Satellite channels compete for audiences, and the Lebanese satellite stations, known for dance videos and classic movies, have very high ratings in Egypt. In the current political situation, al-Jazeera, although not free from criticism, is the first specialized news channel.[14] The Qatar-based channel, established in 1996, claims 35 million viewers worldwide and has become Egypt's most watched news satellite channel in prime time. Its talk shows on hot topics of religion and politics have attracted significant audiences. Covering the conflict in the Middle East and the recent conflict in Afghanistan, the channel broadcasts much footage of Palestinians' deaths in the intifada uprising and Afghan civilian casualties, inflaming public opinion to levels never expressed before.

Transnational media, such as al-Jazeera, encourage Arab nationalism, create cultural unity, increasingly shape public opinion in the region, and reduce the ability of governments to control the flow of information. The information revolution is having an increasing impact not only in Egypt but also in the whole Arab region. A growing dissatisfaction with both Western and governmental media coverage of the Middle East and its issues and a yearning for alternatives to the limited choices previously available have led to the rise of new pan-Arab satellite television channels and radio stations, as well as newspapers and magazines that operate in accordance with Western journalistic standards. These media are now influencing local broadcasting and forming public opinion from the bottom up.[15] For example, in terrestrial Egyptian channels such as Nile News, Channel One, and Channel Two, new political programs, such as *Rais al-tahrir* (Editor in Chief), include relatively controversial content. Another new political program available on satellite channels is *Al-Zel Al-Ahmar* (The Red Shadow).

Whereas one must not exaggerate the impact of the new media development in Egypt, because only the well-to-do can afford the high price of the pan-Arab daily newspapers, satellite TV, or Internet connections, this may soon be changing. Satellite television needs no subscription fees and the one-time cost of a locally manufactured antenna has become less than $200. The decrease in technology costs, coupled with the government's desire to use new technological innovations, will make media programming more available to the masses.

In conclusion, the principle of free flow of information seems to be widening to cover all forms of information, contributing to the progress of Egyptian society and its path toward democracy. The new media technologies represent an open window to the outside world. One thing is certain. In the short run, the new media developments—establishing an infrastructure, increasing access to satellite channels, developing media productions, privatizing media outlets, and facilitating Internet access—are likely to pave the way for change in the political culture in Egypt. In other words, the government's ability to take potentially unpopular positions will most likely be undercut. In the long run, however, it is impossible to predict the precise course of the information revolution. The long-term political impact and the effect of these current changes on the country in general and the Egyptian media in particular are yet to be seen.

Media in India
Dharma N. Adhikari

The ancient Indian tale of six blind men touching an elephant and then arguing about what it looks like is an apt metaphor about the media system in India. The sheer diversity that is India prevents any hasty analysis of its social and cultural practices. As part of this diverse social milieu, the media are characterized by a wide array of variations in their structure, values, and practices. At the risk of generalization, what follows is a brief overview of the Indian media.

With a population exceeding a billion people, scores of ethnic communities, five major religions, and a history that dates back to antiquity, India's present is as complex as its past. Charged with making sense of this complexity in the world's largest democracy is a vibrant free press, a relatively controlled but rapidly expanding broadcast and electronic media, and a surging Internet.

India's print media industry, which continues to grow amid the global trend of declining readership, ranks fifth in the world.[1] There are now 44,000 publications in 100 different languages and dialects catering to 127 million readers. The vernacular papers account for 85 percent of these publications. Although the English-speaking community constitutes only a small minority, the English press, historically more influential than the vernaculars, is the third largest in the world, directed at readers among the urban elite and upper echelon of the society. The vernacular papers in Hindi and regional languages have emerged as more influential and popular in the last few decades. The press and the radio reach 33 percent of the population, television reaches 47 percent, cinema 18 percent, and cable and satellite television 9 percent. There are now 22 terrestrial and 100 satellite channels, with 8 devoted to news, reaching 70 million households, and 70,000 cable operators catering to 35 million subscribers, making India the third largest cable market after the United States and China. Television in India remains largely an entertainment medium, and its popularity among the population, almost half of whom are illiterate, continues to soar. As in many other developing countries with high illiteracy rates and poor technological infrastructure, the Internet is not as ubiquitous as television, but Internet users in large metropolises are projected to reach 100 million by 2008. Private ISPs continue to proliferate since the government ended state monopoly in the sector in 1998. But as of 2001, the Internet reaches

Figure 7.3   **India**

Population	1,045,845,226 (July 2002 est.)
Ethnic groups	Indo-Aryan 72%, Dravidian 25%, Mongoloid and other 3% (2000)
Religions	Hindu 81.3%, Muslim 12%, Christian 2.3%, Sikh 1.9%, other groups including Buddhist, Jain, Parsi 2.5% (2000)
Languages	English enjoys associate status but is the most important language for national, political, and commercial communication; Hindi is the national language and primary tongue of 30% of the people; there are 14 other official languages: Bengali, Telugu, Marathi, Tamil, Urdu, Gujarati, Malayalam, Kannada, Oriya, Punjabi, Assamese, Kashmiri, Sindhi, and Sanskrit; Hindustani is a popular variant of Hindi/Urdu spoken widely throughout northern India but is not an official language
Literacy	definition: age 15 and over, can read and write total population: 52% male: 65.5% female: 37.7% (1995 est.)
Legal system	based on English common law; limited judicial review of legislative acts; accepts compulsory International Court of Justice (ICJ) jurisdiction, with reservations
Population below poverty line	25% (2002 est.)
Labor force	406 million (1999)
Labor force—by occupation	agriculture 60%, services 23%, industry 17% (1999)
Telephones—main lines in use	27.7 million (October 2000)
Telephones—mobile cellular	2.93 million (November 2000)
Radio broadcast stations	AM 153, FM 91, shortwave 68 (1998)
Radios	116 million (1997)
Television broadcast stations	562 (of which 82 stations have 1 kW or greater power and 480 stations have less than 1 kW of power) (1997)
Televisions	63 million (1997)
Internet service providers (ISPs)	43 (2000)
Internet users	7 million (2002)

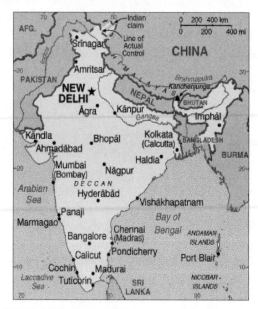

Source: The CIA World Factbook, 2003.

only 0.37 percent of the population despite India's rising stature as a software power.

The vibrant press enjoys extensive political freedom, although Freedom House's combined scores for both print and broadcast have often been "partly free."[2] With the exception of a state of emergency from 1975 to 1977, India's press has not come under direct state control since the country became independent in 1947 after 300 years of British rule. In the early years following independence, the media regarded their job as a public mission and voluntarily remained subservient to the government. However, in the subsequent decades, the symbiotic relationship between politics and the press has taken several turns, from close allies to ferocious foes. Television and the new media have further democratized communication, but only the print media have contributed to political participation and exchange of ideas.[3] Principally, the press is at par with most developed nations, and it faces many of the same problems, such as an increasing trend toward conglomeration, concentration, commercialization, and sensationalism and the challenges of balancing the long-held responsibility of sustaining the national unity of a culturally and linguistically diverse country with the expanding business interests. What distinguishes the Indian mediascape is the digital divide between the urban haves and the rural have-nots. More than 35 percent of the population lives under the poverty line. The reforms initiated in 1991 by the government have brought a sea change in the Indian media as they have in other businesses. The media's known subservience to state socialism rooted in Gandhian and Nehruvian autarky is fast eroding. Breaking away from its long-held tradition of austerity, India has entered the global market of competition and consumerism.

A liberalization policy, though inconsistent, has resulted in the opening of the media sector to private and foreign investments. The government still owns Doordarshan, the Pan-Indian Terrestrial TV, and All India Radio (AIR). They serve its propaganda purposes. AIR held exclusive monopoly on the country's airwaves since it was founded in 1936. But in March 2001 the Ministry of Information and Broadcasting finally began to loosen its hold on the country's airwaves and auctioned full-fledged commercial radio broadcasting licenses to private operators.[4] Across the country, 180 frequencies were offered in forty cities. But these frequencies are barred from airing news. Private businesses and family groups have long owned the print media, and the Internet remains a Wild West.

Television and the cable industry have already been opened to foreign investment, mainly from Rupert Murdoch's News Corporation. Other global conglomerates, like Time Warner and Yahoo!, have entered the field or are in the process of negotiating deals. Targeting the Indian market, CNN has launched a South Asia channel. But nowhere has there been so much debate about foreign ownership as in the print media. The government is determined to open nondaily print media to foreign investors, despite heated resistance in the print sector from large monopolistic conglomerates like the *Times of India* and *Hindustan Times,* ironically, the champions of liberalization.[5] Lacking financial resources to consolidate its operations, the vernacular press has been generally supportive of foreign direct investment (FDI), but critics continue to insist that FDI in print, a time-tested stable medium of communication and opinion, could have adverse effects on India's culture and national interest. The government's approach has been cautious. To appease the major newspapers, FDI is limited just to 26 percent. The equity limit on foreign ownership in satellite broadcasting is relatively high, at 49 percent.

The government appears to be convinced that partial foreign ownership will have little effect on programming and content of the media in India. Indeed, according to a UNESCO report, in 1990 only 8 percent of the content in Indian media was imported from abroad, one of the lowest figures in the world.[6] However, Indian channels are quick to copy Western genres and programs and adapt them to local tastes. For instance, Star TV's *Kaun Banega Karorpati* which shattered rating records in 2001, is the Indian version of *Who Wants to Be a Millionaire.* Star's main rivals, Sony and Zee, have taken on other American themes such as reality shows. Even MTV India, one of the most popular channels, has adapted to local tastes, with more than 85 percent of its content drawn from popular Hindi soundtracks and local pop.[7] The bottom line is that Indian media programming is mostly restricted by the mass appeal of genuinely local tastes. Television programs are mostly reruns or copycats of popular local dramas, Hindi soundtracks, and formulaic, sentimental, and stereotypical Indian films. Indeed, Bollywood, the world's largest film industry, in the southern city of Mumbai, has reason to be alarmed by nationally popular television programs.

India appears to be defying the America-centric idea of globalization or cultural imperialism. To its own surprise, the effects of foreign investment and technological innovations in the media have been just the reverse. The consolidation of Indian channels such as Zee and the expansion of state-owned Doordarshan have not only forced foreign channels to adapt to local programming, but also given rise to a new idea of Indian media imperialism in the region.[8] The Indian media, especially the satellite channels, reach the global Indian diasporas of 20 million and the Hindi-speaking populations in the subcontinent. The neighboring countries of Pakistan, Nepal, Bangladesh, Sri Lanka, and Bhutan routinely confront images and sound bites that their big neighbor would hardly welcome from the West. Especially, every escalation in the continuing India-Pakistan tensions spurs Pakistani charges of Indian info-war, media jingoism, distortion, and bias.

Parallel to "Indianization" is a strong trend of localization. Particularly, in the southern states, regional language channels such as Eenadu, Sun, Udaya, and Surya TV are more popular than any national or foreign channel. To target these niche markets and to tap huge business potential, foreign channels such as Star, BBC, and others are strategizing to launch regional channels.[9]

But with political freedom and the rapid growth of the media industry, there has also been an increase in the concern for quality and media ethics.[10] Critics have noted a disproportionate representation of minorities, unfair professional practices, proliferating obscenity, and upper-caste and -class bias in both print and broadcast media. Print media content, though largely mediocre, is moving toward shallow commercialism. Market imperatives have taken precedence over editorial independence, and even the venerable *The Hindu,* which resembled the unadorned *Wall Street Journal,* is turning gaudy in the race for "tabloidization." The media are increasingly thought of as a commercial product, segmenting communities into diversified niches. In recent years, cases of plagiarism, deception, and fabrication have come to the fore. In September 1999, V.N. Narayanan, a well-respected editor of the *Hindustan Times,* shocked media professionals when rival *Pioneer* exposed his verbatim plagiarism from a British columnist. The editor resigned. In mid-2001, Tehelka.com, a muckraking site, created controversy when it revealed it had used prostitutes and a hidden camera in its exposé of corruption in defense procurement.[11]

Unlike in the United States, the Indian government possesses vast regulatory apparatus, consisting of the Ministry of Information and Broadcasting; Prasar Bharati, a broadcast monitoring institution; and the Press Council. However, given the political appointments, private media find these institutions unethical. Yet the government has the power to censor security-related information through the Official Secrecy Act. Materials inciting communal, ethnic, and religious hatred or depicting pornography or obscenity are also subject to governmental censorship, though without prior restraint. However, there is a jurisdictional hurdle in controlling content in hundreds of freely available satellite channels linked up from abroad. Self-instituted codes of ethics in the postliberalization, profit-driven media may make it difficult to balance industry interests with those of mass consumers.

In sum, India's vast, heterogeneous media are in a state of transition. The liberalization of the economy has enabled the media to consolidate in distinct clusters—local, national, and marginally global. Affluent consumers have a wide array of choices for information and entertainment. Yet average Indian citizens are out of touch with most of these modern media and continue to live in the acoustic, oral environment, struggling to make sense of the world around them, analogous to the six blind men with the proverbial elephant.

Media in Jamaica
Berle Francis

The audiovisual media dominate Jamaica's media landscape, partly because Jamaica is essentially an oral society by tradition and partly because of a relatively high rate of illiteracy. It is estimated that some 30 percent of Jamaicans are functionally illiterate. Hence, in a country of just under 3 million people, there are thirteen radio stations and three television stations. Conversely, there are only two national daily newspapers, the *Daily Gleaner* and the *Jamaica Observer*. The *Sunday Herald* is a national weekly newspaper. In addition, there is an afternoon tabloid, aimed down-market, that is published six days a week. Several weekly and monthly specialist publications serve a variety of interests and sectors. Community newspapers, generally published biweekly or fortnightly, have emerged strongly.

Any attempt at understanding media in Jamaica must take cognizance of three salient factors: the sociopolitical history of the country, ownership and control, and the structure of the society itself.

Jamaica is a former colony of Great Britain, and it developed as what one may term a plantation economy. The island was one of Britain's major sugar-producing outposts, and, in order to ensure efficient and plentiful production of the crop, Africans were brought to the island in

Figure 7.4 **Jamaica**

Population	2,680,029 (July 2002 est.)
Ethnic groups	black 90.9%, East Indian 1.3%, white 0.2%, Chinese 0.2%, mixed 7.3%, other 0.1%
Religions	Protestant 61.3% (Church of God 21.2%, Baptist 8.8%, Anglican 5.5%, Seventh-Day Adventist 9%, Pentecostal 7.6%, Methodist 2.7%, United Church 2.7%, Brethren 1.1%, Jehovah's Witness 1.6%, Moravian 1.1%), Roman Catholic 4%, other, including some spiritual cults 34.7%
Languages	English, patois English
Literacy	definition: age 15 and over, has ever attended school total population: 85% male: 80.8% female: 89.1% (1995 est.)
Legal system	based on English common law; has not accepted compulsory ICJ jurisdiction
Population below poverty line	34% (1992 est.)
Labor force	1.13 million (1998)
Labor force—by occupation	services 60%, agriculture 21%, industry 19% (1998)
Telephones—main lines in use	353,000 (1996)
Telephones—mobile cellular	54,640 (1996)
Radio broadcast stations	AM 10, FM 13, shortwave 0 (1998)
Radios	1.215 million (1997)
Television broadcast stations	7 (1997)
Televisions	460,000 (1997)
Internet service providers (ISPs)	21 (2000)
Internet users	100,000 (2002)

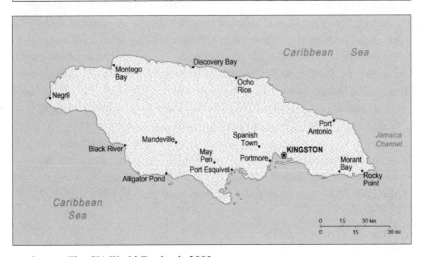

Source: The CIA World Factbook, 2003.

the eighteenth century as slaves to work the plantations. The slave owners saw no reason to educate the slaves, so they were all illiterate. Upon emancipation in 1834, the authorities felt that education would make the ex-slaves unfit for manual work, so they discouraged it.

It is against this background that the *Daily Gleaner* was born in 1834.

At 170 years old, it is one of the oldest media houses in the hemisphere. Set up to cater to the elite, it grew out of a slave-owning background and, over years, was run by the descendants of the owners of plantations. The ownership of the newspaper today is still of that philosophical bent. Hence, the *Daily Gleaner* makes very little effort to be part of the infrastructure of a developing country. But in the 1960s, when many former colonies were becoming independent, it focused heavily on news about independence efforts in Africa and southeast Asia. Today, its news is largely international. The more recent *Jamaica Observer* (founded in 1993), likewise, is owned by a businessman of the elite class, and the emphasis in its coverage of news and local events reflects the interests of this class. The British tradition of the country's mainstream print media has resulted in emphasis being placed on output for the elite rather than for the masses.

Because of the proximity of Jamaica to the United States and the proliferation of television and cable, the electronic media in Jamaica are dominated by output from the United States. This dominance has had a significant impact on Jamaican culture, particularly among the young. It is manifested in their clothes, their expressions, and their value systems.

One of the significant ways in which American cultural influence continues to shape the worldviews of Jamaican people is through the cinema, which, since the 1920s, has been an important form of entertainment for local people. However, this genre is experiencing some diminution through the competition posed by video and cable. The local response has been to produce full-length movies that speak to Jamaican culture and values. For example, the movie *Cool Runnings,* although not produced by Jamaicans, conveys many of the traditional values of lower-class Jamaican culture. *Cool Runnings* is the story of the first Jamaican bobsled team and the courage it took to be the first black team from a tropical country to participate in this winter sport.

Media in Small Societies

The impact of the mass media on public opinion is severely limited because, in small societies such as Jamaica, with their close face-to-face contact and strong interpersonal, direct communication network, many of the messages that are delivered by media are actually reinterpreted, modified, and thereafter passed through these informal channels. These channels operate through street-corner gatherings and groups, rum shops and barbershops, markets, workplaces and neighborhood friendship networks.

ernment. The broadcasting media contribute to making programs frivolous by playing up to the youth culture, broadcasting popular programs for the young generation in order to attract a higher audience rating.

It is easy to see the influence of the media on culture, politics, and the economy. This is the very beginning of media politics (politics by means of media) in Japan. Moreover, the election campaign for the leader of the Liberal-Democratic Party has occupied the television news programs since the spring of 2001. As a result, the political phenomenon called the Koizumi Reformation (named after Prime Minister Junichiro Koizumi) has occurred with the Japanese media. And the approval rate for the Koizumi cabinet exceeded 80 percent at first and then every day personal information about Makiko Tanaka, the minister of foreign affairs was broadcast by the media. In addition, the ideology of globalization rules the media of Japan simultaneously with Japan's recession after 1990. This economic principle has been called the "supremacy principle of market mechanism" since then, and the storm of competition and deregulation blows hard in the economic society of Japan.

Media in Moldova
Natalia Angheli

The media in Moldova in southeastern Europe are in a state of flux, facing a host of economic, political, cultural, and professional challenges. Almost twelve years after the breakup of the USSR, this former Soviet Republic, a country the size of Maryland, is still coping with the side effects of the transition period.

Emancipation from the Soviet rule brought with it a veritable media explosion. A plethora of new publications, radio stations, and TV channels appeared. According to the estimates of the Independent Journalism Center–Moldova, eighty-four national newspapers and magazines, thirty local print outlets, forty-eight local TV channels, nineteen local radio stations, nine news agencies, and four national broadcasters were operating in Moldova as of January 2003.

However, growing numbers have not translated into a free and balanced media. Excessive government control and harassment by authorities and inadequate regulating and self-regulating mechanisms seriously hinder the development of media in Moldova. These problems are augmented by a grave economic crisis (according to major development indices, Moldova is among the poorest countries in Europe).

Figure 7.6 **Moldova**

Population	4,434,547 (July 2002 est.)
Ethnic groups	Moldovan/Romanian 64.5%, Ukrainian 13.8%, Russian 13%, Jewish 1.5%, Bulgarian 2%, Gagauz and other 5.2% (1989 est.)
Religions	Eastern Orthodox 98%, Jewish 1.5%, Baptist and other 0.5% (2000)
Languages	Moldovan (official, virtually the same as the Romanian language), Russian (official), Gagauz (a Turkish dialect)
Literacy	definition: age 15 and over can read and write total population: 96% male: 99% female: 94% (1989 est.)
Legal system	based on civil law system; Constitutional Court reviews legality of legislative acts and governmental decisions of resolution; it is unclear if Moldova accepts compulsory ICJ jurisdiction but accepts many UN and Organization for Security and Cooperation in Europe (OSCE) documents
Population below poverty line	80% (2001 est.)
Labor force	1.7 million (1998)
Labor force—by occupation	agriculture 40%, industry 14%, services 46% (1998)
Telephones—main lines in use	627,000 (1997)
Telephones—mobile cellular	2,200 (1997)
Radio broadcast stations	AM 7, FM 50, shortwave 3 (1998)
Radios	3.22 million (1997)
Television broadcast stations	1 (plus 30 repeaters) (1995)
Televisions	1.26 million (1997)
Internet service providers (ISPs)	2 (1999)
Internet users	15,000 (2000)

Source: The CIA World Factbook, 2003.

Since Moldova gained independence in 1991, most media outlets have been financed by political parties and groups, and they reflect the opinions of their patrons on the major developments in the country. The government has maintained control over the national broadcaster TeleRadio Moldova, as well as several national and regional newspapers. Most newspapers are printed in state-owned printing facilities, and the state has largely maintained its monopoly over the distribution of print media.

Several media outlets operate as nongovernmental organizations, but most have been registered as private companies. Few of the latter, however, are run as real businesses.

The Moldovan media scene is extremely volatile. Due to the low purchasing capacity of the population, an advertising market of just US$1.2 million, and fickle political interests, the life span of many outlets has been fairly short. This is especially true of newspapers, many of which appeared in the run-up to the local or general elections and disappeared shortly afterward when their sponsors failed to get elected.

Radio and television are the most popular media. Seventy-four percent of Moldovan homes have at least one TV set, and 55 percent own a radio. According to a November 2002 opinion poll, 66 percent of respondents said they watched television every day, while 54 percent indicated they listened to the radio daily. By comparison, only 11 percent of poll participants said they read newspapers every day.

This is hardly surprising, because the price of newspapers is prohibitively high for most Moldovans, and the print run of most newspapers seldom exceeds 10,000 copies. There are no dailies in Moldova—most newspapers are published once a week, and a few come out three or four times a week.

Due to poor economic conditions, just 60,000 persons (less than 1.5 percent of the country's population) regularly use the Internet. Still, the number of Internet versions of major print publications is growing, and there are also several "online-only" outlets.

The media activity in Moldova is regulated by the laws on the press, on broadcasting, on advertising, on access to information, and on the national public broadcaster. Several other laws and ordinances contain media-related provisions. Media watchdogs have criticized many of these acts for hampering rather than fostering the development of the Moldovan media.

Implementation of the media legislation is another problem. Despite the fairly democratic provisions of the access to information law, a cult of secrecy pervades all Moldovan government institutions. Economic development indices and salaries of public officials, government ordinances and decisions of local bodies—all are considered highly sensitive material.

In addition to inadequate access to information, restrictive libel legislation also serves as a sad reality check for many journalists. Libel is a criminal offence, punishable by up to five years in prison. Public figures frequently sue reporters for even the most inoffensive materials, and the burden of proof lies solely with the defendant. These lawsuits usually last for months, and very few journalists win them. Tax inspection is another means used by the authorities to muzzle nongovernment media.

Censorship of state-owned media is widely spread, especially after Communists came to power in February 2001. Journalists are openly ordered what and how to write, and "disloyal" media managers are routinely sacked. The most vivid example of this censorship is seen in the national TV channel Moldova 1, whose newscasts are sadly reminiscent of the old Soviet "talking-head" news about the comings and goings of the Communist elite. In protest against censorship on that channel, its journalists went on a months-long strike in 2002, which generated wide international support but resulted in little change in the editorial policy.

Legal, financial, and administrative pressures often result in considerable self-censorship and frequent breach of ethical norms. Thus, 85 percent of journalists who participated in a nationwide survey in November 2002, noted that the country's reporters practice considerable partisanship in violation of the principles of free journalism, while 76 percent indicated that Moldovan journalists insufficiently respect the provisions of the ethics code.

Moldovan journalists are poorly paid (their monthly salaries usually do not exceed an equivalent of US$100) and frequently sell their services to the highest bidder. Hidden advertising, acceptance of money and gifts, recycling of stories—these are just some of the most common journalistic offences in Moldova.

Media managers frequently prefer to save money on staff salaries by hiring young, inexperienced reporters, who are paid a pittance. Even though many of these reporters do not have journalism degrees, they receive practically no in-house training. Niche reporting is underdeveloped, and journalists seldom have the possibility of establishing long-term contacts, compiling proper databases, and developing personal expertise—essential elements of quality journalism. Instead, Moldovan media abound in allegations, gossip, sensationalism, and trivialities. Few outlets provide analysis of important issues or reflect the spectrum of opinions on major developments in the country.

Western publications are too expensive for an average Moldovan reader, but broadcasts of major stations are available through cable TV and AM radio (CNN, Euronews, BBC, Voice of America, Radio Free Europe, Deutsche Welle, etc.). Few homes are equipped with satellite dishes.

There are several local affiliates of Russian and Romanian broadcasters, which are registered as local companies and enjoy a wide popularity among local news consumers (ORT Moldova, PRO TV Chisinau). Similarly, several affiliates of major Russian newspapers are registered locally, and their circulation by far exceeds that of Moldovan publications (*Komsomol'skaya Pravda v Moldove, Argumenty i Fakty v Moldove, Trud v Moldove*).

In the absence of adequate financial means and professional expertise, reliance on foreign content is a way for many Moldovan media outlets to stay alive. For example, Moldovan news in the local editions of Russian newspapers is usually no more than a few pages, and other publications also are full of reprints from foreign papers. The listings of many Moldovan broadcasters are based primarily on retransmission of programs from Russia.

Moldova is signatory to major international acts regulating copyright issues, and yet illegal retransmission and reprinting of foreign content are quite common. According to some estimates, as many as 90 percent of local TV and radio stations are engaged in unauthorized rebroadcasts from Russia.

Lack of professional solidarity and a deep cultural rift among journalists are another problem. The Moldovan media are generally divided along language lines. Sixty-five percent of the population are ethnic Moldovans, whose mother tongue is Romanian, and the rest are Ukrainians, Russians, Bulgarians, and representatives of several other groups for whom Russian is the first language. Perspectives on the major developments in the country in minority and majority language media differ significantly. This division has found its way into journalists' professional associations, some of which have been created to promote the interests of certain ethnic groups. Lack of unity has made the task of attaining professional goals and establishing a free and balanced media in Moldova even more difficult.

Even though the public's trust of the media stands at 52 percent (according to a November 2002 opinion poll), it is but a skewed and incomplete picture of events that Moldovan citizens get from them. At the moment, the nation's media do not set the public agenda or serve as public watchdogs over the interests of those in power. They are frail and offer but a feeble resistance to the ills of the transition period.

New Zealand and Global Media: The Shire to the Western World's Middle-Earth
Geoff Lealand

In the last few weeks of 2001, New Zealand was swept by a wave of pride in advance of the release of *The Fellowship of the Ring*, the first film of *The Lord of the Rings* trilogy. The director (Wellington-based Peter Jackson) was hailed as a national hero: his home city was renamed "Middle-Earth" for two weeks, the Labour government appointed a minister in charge of the *Lord of the Rings*, and tourists began to arrive, searching for traces of Hobbiton or Mordor in the landscapes of New Zealand.

As one anonymous commentator noted, it was further evidence that "New Zealand has always served as the Shire to the western world's Middle-Earth." The most ambitious film venture ever now looks like it will also be one of the most profitable and prize-winning film ventures ever. With a generous injection of foreign (U.S.) cash and a local talent base, New Zealand can give the rest of the world reason to pause and gaze on the remarkable cultural achievements of a tiny Pacific nation of 3.9 million souls, sited at the very ends of the earth.

As in all things New Zealanders say and do, there is deep irony and ambiguity. Jackson's trilogy is the biggest film ever made in New Zealand and has energized what would be regarded as a cottage film industry by Hollywood standards. In terms of the conventions of national cinema, however, it is not a New Zealand film. The leading actors are American, British, and Australian; the stories draw on the myths and tales of ancient Europe; and at the end of the food chain is the giant U.S. media conglomerate Time Warner.

This has always been the contradictory space New Zealand inhabits, ever open to the world but also struggling to find its own, unique place.

Figure 7.7 **New Zealand**

Population	3,908,037 (July 2002 est.)
Ethnic groups	New Zealand European 74.5%, Maori 9.7%, other European 4.6%, Pacific Islander 3.8%, Asian and others 7.4%
Religions	Anglican 24%, Presbyterian 18%, Roman Catholic 15%, Methodist 5%, Baptist 2%, other Protestant 3%, unspecified or none 33% (1986)
Languages	English (official), Maori (official)
Literacy	definition: age 15 and over can read and write total population: 99% (1980 est.)
Legal system	based on English law, with special land legislation and land courts for Maoris; accepts compulsory ICJ jurisdiction, with reservations
Population below poverty line	NA
Labor force	1.92 million (2001 est.)
Labor force—by occupation	services 65%, industry 25%, agriculture 10% (1995)
Telephones—main lines in use	1.92 million (2000)
Telephones—mobile cellular	2.2 million (2000)
Radio broadcast stations	AM 124, FM 290, shortwave 4 (1998)
Radios	3.75 million (1997)
Television broadcast stations	41 (plus 52 medium-power repeaters and over 650 low-power repeaters) (1997)
Televisions	1.926 million (1997)
Internet service providers (ISPs)	36 (2000)
Internet users	2.06 million (2002)

Source: The CIA World Factbook, 2003.

It has, in recent decades, led the world in removing all impediments in the way of free markets and unfettered membership in a deregulated global media environment. There have been no public input into broadcast frequency allocation, no obligations on broadcasters in respect to quality thresholds or local content, no restraints on advertising and sponsorship, and no limits on foreign investment in the media. This has meant that, for example, media giant Newscorp Ltd owns 49 percent of the New Zealand newspaper chain Independent News Limited (INL) and has a major interest in pay-TV, through INL's 66 percent share of the dominant supplier Sky. The other large newspaper company, Wilson and Horton (publisher of the leading-circulation daily *New Zealand Herald*), is owned by the Irish company Independent News and Media. The Canadian company Canwest owns TV3 and TV4 and radio networks, and the television network Prime is Australian-owned.

Nevertheless, more than 70 percent of the national television audience still turn to the two-channel, state-owned Television New Zealand. Through the 1990s, these channels followed commercial imperatives, maximizing profits and delivering healthy dividends to the government. The funding agency New Zealand on Air filled a residual public service television role. With the certainty that a change of government in New Zealand usually brings a change in broadcasting policy, the Labour government (elected in November 1999) is now redirecting Television New Zealand back to a clearer public service broadcasting role. It has a charter to subscribe to and there is talk of local content quotas.

In the same decades that New Zealand has taken the best and the worst from international media producers, it has been much engaged with finding and fostering a distinctive national identity, which will distinguish it from the homogenizing forces of globalization and give due regard to the bicultural (Maori and Pakeha) face of contemporary New Zealand. In this regard, New Zealand is little different from other small, developed nations living on the periphery of large countries and global media conglomerates.

However, the consequences of this struggle between the local and the global seem more dramatic and visible in New Zealand because it is a thoroughly media-saturated society, geographically distant from the major land masses but bound to the world by cables, wavelengths, and satellite signals.

New Zealanders are media-rich. There are, for example, 414 radio stations for a population of 3.9 million people. With further availability on the FM frequency band, there could be another 200 to 300 stations in the near future. In the largest city of Auckland, there are now more radio stations than the much larger market of Sydney, Australia. New Zealand has the fourth-highest cinema attendance per head of population, with close to 300 cinema screens. Newspaper readership surveys in 2002 showed that every day 1.6 million New Zealanders read a daily newspaper, with that number growing to 2.3 million over a week. The largest daily (the *New Zealand Herald*) had a daily readership of 552,000 in February 2002. Close to 97 percent of New Zealand homes receive color TV, with the average home owning two sets. Over 80 percent of homes also own VCRs, while 42.8 percent owned a computer in March 2000. New Zealanders are currently the fifth-highest Internet users, after Finland, the United States, Norway, and Iceland. Over half (52 percent) of New Zealanders aged over ten years identify themselves as regular Internet users and close to 99 percent of New Zealand schools are Internet-connected.

New Zealand has a relatively free press, constrained only by libel laws, a light self-regulation through the Press Council, and commercial imperatives. Television receives some attention from the Broadcasting Standards Authority, and there are structures of film and video censorship. The media, in all their forms, are integral to social, political, and cultural life and are demonstrably used and valued by the great majority of New Zealanders. Locally made media (such as the long-running nightly television soap *Shortland Street*) are very popular, but so are imported films, music, and television programs. Many older New Zealanders favor British programming, while younger New Zealanders favor American or local media. Across generations, there does seem to be a strong demand for more New Zealand-made films, music, and television programs. There does not seem to be a shortage of creative talent; the major constraint is the comparative costs of "making your own" as against importing films and television programs. It has been estimated, for example, that the average return from a New Zealand film ranges between one and twenty-five cents in the New Zealand dollar. This means that, in many cases, financial considerations have to come second to cultural and citizenship imperatives as New Zealand strives to tell its own stories. In all their cultural endeavors, New Zealanders will continue to play out a role as a small nation on the margin of the world's media producers, with all the opportunities, constraints, and contradictions that such a position entails, despite the extraordinary phenomenon of *The Lord of the Rings*.

Figure 7.8 **Russia**

Population	144,978,573 (July 2002 est.)
Ethnic groups	Russian 81.5%, Tatar 3.8%, Ukrainian 3%, Chuvash 1.2%, Bashkir 0.9%, Belarusian 0.8%, Moldavian 0.7%, other 8.1%
Religions	Russian Orthodox, Muslim, other
Languages	Russian, other
Literacy	definition: age 15 and over can read and write total population: 98% male: 100% female: 97% (1989 est.)
Legal system	based on civil law system; judicial review of legislative acts
Population below poverty line	40% (1999 est.)
Labor force	71.3 million (2001 est.)
Labor force—by occupation	agriculture 11%, industry 28%, services 61% (2001 est.)
Telephones—main lines in use	30 million (1998)
Telephones—mobile cellular	2.5 million (October 2000)
Radio broadcast stations	AM 420, FM 447, shortwave 56 (1998)
Radios	61.5 million (1997)
Television broadcast stations	7,306 (1998)
Televisions	60.5 million (1997)
Internet service providers (ISPs)	35 (2000)
Internet users	18 million (2002)

Source: The CIA World Factbook, 2003.

Russia: The Media and the Unfreedom of the Press
Aleksander Grigoryev

The Russian media were rigorously controlled by the state until Russia received its independence in 1990. After that point, the media were taken out from under state control and granted an opportunity to develop under free market conditions.

Until The Law on Print and Other Media of the USSR (which served as a basis for the analogous law accepted in the Russian Federation in

December 1991) was passed in June 1990, no legislative basis had existed in Russia for regulating the media. The absence of legislation was compensated for by Communist Party norms. Glasnost was not considered a right but a privilege. During the twelve-year evolution of the media in Russia, there have been many attempts to make freedom of the press a privilege again. These attempts have been increasingly successful over the last few years, and one cannot say that there has been a general opposition to these attempts from Russia's journalistic community. This is due to a number of shifts in the Russian media.

In the early 1990s, many media enterprises became independent of the organs that controlled them before. In the age of the USSR, all media sources were subdivisions of one or another state organ: for example, the Soviet information agency, Pravda, belonged to the Central Committee (CC) of the Communist Party of the Soviet Union (CPSU); primary television channels were subdivisions of the State Committee for Television and Radio Broadcasting. At the same time, however, the newly independent enterprises could not support themselves. The advertising market in Russia was in its infancy; the population's standard of living had dropped. Media organizations had no managers who could successfully direct them as business ventures. As a result, they were forced to seek support (in the form of direct or indirect grants) either from the new government organs or from the business sector.

A unique media business structure formed in Russia as a result of this shift in relationships among the government, the public, and the media, and as a response to the general economic environment. Almost all of Russia's major businesses developed their own media holdings. Businesses used the media as bargaining chips in establishing relations with different levels of government and as weapons in political and economic rivalries.

The term "media wars" became popular in Russia in the mid-1990s, when media outlets controlled by opposing corporations began publishing stories about unethical or illegal activities on the part of other companies. A fight for the Sviaznest Group between Boris Berezovsky and Vladimir Gusinsky, famous media magnates, was a particularly outstanding example.

Many of the media were focused on "political money"—subsidies and bribes from representatives of political parties or movements. To illustrate, a number of media projects, like the NTV television channel, which later became one of the symbols of freedom of speech in Russia, were originally created as instruments for earning political money, and the media magnates Vladimir Gusinsky and Boris Berezovsky, currently in opposition to President Putin, created their wealth primarily by using their media holdings to solidify their political connections.

Unfortunately, such events seriously undermined the reputation of journalists, lowered the quality of materials, and caused a sharp drop in domestic opinion of the media. In addition, the authorities no longer saw information published by the media on crimes and misdemeanors of government officials as signals for taking action. Many media outlets began to depend on constant financial support of the government or their owners. The practice of taking money from "newsmakers" for publishing positive, or even informative, reports became widespread. Since this kind of income often exceeds the annual salaries of journalists, reporters have become, in effect, copywriters who serve the interests of the advertisers instead of the public. In fact, advertising and public relations agencies publish lists detailing how much they will pay to have their information placed in the media. These tendencies have developed both nationally, and in the regions.

This kind of activity contradicts the professional code of ethics of the Russian journalists (accepted at the Congress of Russian Journalists in 1994), which states that "the malicious exploitation of facts, libel, receiving compensation for publishing false information or hiding true information are serious professional offenses; a journalist should never accept any reward or fee from a third party for publishing materials of any kind." However, the low prestige of journalism and the absence of social and other protective measures for media employees have made this statement an empty declaration.

Another disparity has been created at the level of relations between Russia's capital and the outlying regions. Since 70 to 80 percent of all Russian finances are centered in Moscow and not in the regions, there is a major difference between urban and regional media outlets. The former are generally better off financially, have more modern technology, and have access to international information. The latter lag significantly in technology and professionalism. The standard of living is better in Moscow than elsewhere in Russia, and Moscow media organizations prosper by selling advertising space in the capital's advertising market. In the outlying regions, however, the advertising market is not developed and the people can not afford subscription costs or access to paid cable television.

As a result, none of the provincial media organizations were able to make themselves known outside of their areas, not to mention on a national or international level. On the other hand, Moscow media outlets are expanding into the regions or even into other countries with high percentages of Russian speakers (the newspaper *Moskovsky Komsomoletz,* for example, has created daughter publications in the United States and in Israel), creating local departments, affiliates, and daughter companies. Polls conducted by Russia's largest institute for the study of public opinion, VTsIOM, show that information consumers have gradually switched from central to local periodicals (with a pragmatic-informative and commercial-entertainment content), but even more so from print to television, which is watched by the entire family and associated with leisure time at home.

The functions of the media have shifted toward news and entertainment. The most popular programs are news shows (watched several times a day), feature films (Soviet and Russian films are becoming increasingly popular, especially old, nostalgic films), comedy shows, concerts, sporting events, and crime shows. A similar pattern appears on the Internet—a record number of Russian Internet users like entertainment sites.

The insufficient number of foreign investors on the Russian market further complicates the Russian media market. Foreign media organizations had been interested in the Russian media in the early 1990s. In particular, American investors developed an interest in the Russian Internet. In January 1990, a public organization Glasnet was created (www.glas.apc.org, and later glasnet.ru) and funded by the Association for Progressive Communications, a Russian-based organization. The word *glasnet* was also invented by Americans, who combined the words *glasnost* and *network.*

Some of the most commercially successful international media investments into the Russian market have been the projects of the Dutch firm Independent Media, which has been active in Russia since 1992 and owns the rights to the Russian editions of magazines like *Cosmopolitan,* and *Men's Health* and publishes many of Russia's major English-language newspapers—the *Moscow Times* and the *St. Petersburg Times* and the nationwide business newspaper *Vedomosti* (jointly with the *Wall Street Journal* and the *Financial Times*). The German Group Burda publishes a number of popular entertainment magazines. There are a number of other more or less successful regional projects from Scandinavian and American media groups.

A number of media projects were stopped for political reasons. For example, the popular *Itogi* magazine, originally run by the out-of-favor media magnate Vladimir Gusinsky, was forced out from under his control. As a result, *Newsweek* magazine refused to cooperate with *Itogi*. It is necessary to note that foreign investors generally are reluctant to invest in the capital-intensive spheres of the media market, like the development of a publishing house.

Foreign investors lost interest after a number of scandals and stopped investing almost completely after the major financial crisis that rocked the country in 1998. The situation became even worse after Vladimir Putin came to power and began a campaign against the press of the opposition. As a result of this campaign, the Committee for the Protection of Journalists named Vladimir Putin as one of the top ten enemies of the press.

At the same time, the presence of foreign investors in the Russian media market has created dissatisfaction at the local level. Media outlets controlled by foreign investors are generally more successful than their Russian counterparts. Government officials become very irritated if these outlets attempt to take political action in addition to conducting business. For example, Russian officials interpreted Radio Liberty's introduction of Chechen-language broadcasts in March 2002 as an unfriendly act by the United States.

This has been a significant loss. Foreign investors brought not only money, technology, and management to the Russian market, but also a modern, democratic attitude toward the relationship between the media and power or between the media and the public. Most media projects introduced by Western investors were fairly successful, but there are still very few major investors developing media projects in Russia.

Periodically, Russian authorities at different government levels introduce measures limiting foreign media organizations on the Russian market. At times, these attempts have been made retroactively—for example, the Russian State Duma speedily accepted amendments to the Law on Mass Media, which would limit the share foreign investors could hold in Russian media organizations to 50 percent. Duma deputies did not try to hide the fact that this action was taken to prevent American media magnate Ted Turner from acquiring a controlling packet of shares in the NTV television channel. Some suggested that foreign shareholders of Russian television stations should be required to sell to their Russian partners any shares exceeding the proscribed amount.

These steps are completely in line with Russia's policy in the information sphere. In September 2000, the Russian Security Council passed the Russian Information Security Doctrine. The doctrine characterized the primary threats and challenges in the information sphere. The document was published at the height of the conflict between the state organs against the Media Most company, privately owned by Vladimir Gusinsky. Despite the document's declarative nature, it was single-minded in defining as a threat the activity of Western media organizations critical of the actions of Russian authorities. For example, the section on threats to Russian national security in the information sphere listed "the activity of foreign political, economic, military, intelligence and informational structures aimed against the interests of the Russian Federation in the information sphere."

Viktor Ozerov, the deputy chairman of the Security and Defense Committee of the Federation Council, raged: "In 1991, the Soviet Union—a mighty state, a superpower—collapsed as a result of informational-psychological warfare. The nation was dismembered and placed under the control of the West, and above all, the US. Russia is subject to large-scale, direct, ideological influence from the West, which can be characterized as cultural-spiritual aggression." Such views stem, in part, from the fact that, according to many Russian experts, Russia lost the first Chechen War (1996) because of the successful propaganda of Chechen separatists supported by most of the Russian media.

Instead of introducing a locally based economic framework, the Russian government accepted federal laws On State Support of the Media and Publishing of the Russian Federation and On the Economic Support of Regional (city) Newspapers. The two laws technically provided for various benefits to the media; however, financial support for regional and city newspapers has never been provided for in Russia's national budget. In reality, both of the laws extend the traditional relationship between the government and the media that has existed since the time of the Soviet Union.

In this way, the state created a system that provided economic support to ineffective, but loyal media organizations and obstructed honest competition. For example, only 100 percent Russian-owned media organizations qualify for certain benefits. Government organs that use no market mechanisms to select beneficiaries distribute these benefits and allowances: the benefits and grants are given exclusively to media outlets that are loyal to the government.

This is only one of the methods used by the state to control the media.

Although the Constitution formally guarantees Russian citizens the right to freedom of information, there are obstacles to the actual realization of that right. The state controls all major media outlets either directly (with the aid of the Ministry of the Press, Television Broadcasting and Sources of Mass Communication, which controls media licenses) or through subsidiaries.

There are several hundred television companies in Russia, about 30,000 newspapers, over 1,500 radio stations, and more than 400 information agencies. According to various sources, between 70 and 90 percent of Russian residents regularly read newspapers or other periodicals. The total circulation of Russian publications in 1994 (more recent data are not available) was about 61 million copies. According to research conducted by the MASMI Research Group and by ProActive International, an international business development company, in December 2001, 14 percent of Russia's urban population had access to the Internet. The Russian Department of Government Information reports that there are 8 million Internet users in Russia, slightly more than half of whom are regular Internet users.

At the moment, the state directly controls the largest national television channels (ORT, RTR, Kultura) and a number of regional companies, as well as the largest national radio stations (Mayak, Radio Russia) and the main information agencies (ITAR-TASS and RIA News). The state also owns and controls almost all of Russia's major political and news Internet sites through their supporting structures. Until very recently, Vladimir Putin's personal spin-doctor, Gleb Pavlovsky, and his Foundation for Effective Policy directly administered this process. It should be noted that Pavlovsky first attempted to enter the international market through government Internet projects—the sites he controls are foreign-language intensive and pursue international visitors.

Companies that are totally controlled by the state—the natural gas monopoly RAO Gazprom and the energy monopoly RAO UES—are used to manage media companies: national television companies (NTV, TNT, and Ren-TV), the Prometheus network of regional television companies, popular radio stations (Ekho Moskvy and Otkrytoe Radio), a number of prominent newspapers (*Trud, Tribuna*), and the like.

Oligarchs loyal to Vladimir Putin control the rest of the major players on the media market. The Lukoil oil company owns a controlling number of shares of the TV-6 television channel. The Interros group owns the *Izvestia* newspaper and the country's largest FM radio station, Europe

Plus. Alfa Group owns the nation's leading business magazine, *Expert,* the *Komsomolskaya Pravda* newspaper (right now one Norwegian media company is preparing to buy some shares of *Komsomolskaya Pravda*), a network of STS television companies, and other outlets. Regional barons have their own media holdings, the largest belonging to Moscow's highly influential mayor, Yuri Luzhkov. Only minor nonpolitical media outlets are able to maintain their independence. At the same time, almost all news coming into Russia from abroad passes through the filter of state-controlled media, which present the news in a certain light.

Although there is no official censorship, the security services have a semiofficial system of controlling the Internet—SORM-2 (System of Operative-Investigative Measures). Every Internet provider must install equipment (at its own expense) allowing the Russian Federal Security Service to control all Web sites and electronic mail. Providers refusing to do so promptly lose their licenses, which are distributed by a special service organ, Federal Agency for Government Communications and Information, which was formerly a part of the Committee for State Security (KGB). Television and radio stations are controlled in a similar manner: Broadcasting licenses are granted for fairly short terms, and if the government is dissatisfied with a media outlet's political outlook, it will simply refuse to reissue its license. The state controls almost all broadcasting systems and all television towers in Russia. The Russian Television and Radio Broadcasting Network (RTRS), formed recently, placed all of the nation's broadcasting frequencies under the jurisdiction of one state organization.

Control over journalists is equally severe. Their access to information is limited. There is an unspoken list of closed topics—such as the national ecological situation, military bases, events in Chechnya, and the actions of the president and his entourage. The whole world has heard about the trials of journalists who tried to write about the real state of affairs in these spheres. Ecologist Grigory Pasko, for example, received a long prison term for giving information on the ecological problems in Russia's Pacific Fleet to Japanese journalists.

In addition, journalists are forced to practice self-censorship. Russian journalists can maintain their freedom of speech only so long as they stay away from taboo subjects and navigate among power clans. The range of forbidden topics is rather limited, given the public's low interest in politics and the effective efforts of government services to create a positive image for Russia's current government.

Government and government-related organs closely follow all publications and clandestinely monitor journalists. According to the Glasnost Defense Foundation, in the Republic of Tatarstan, this task is carried out by the Press Ministry's State Inspection for the Protection of the Freedom of the Press. This organization follows all criticism of local authorities, immediately issues warnings, and initiates lawsuits against media organizations, forcing them to pay large fines. The state controls public associations of journalists, either through their supporting structures or by creating its own organizations.

Positive changes will definitely come with the development of the free market economy, the institutions of civil society, and the like. However, the current regime is highly disinterested in such changes. Russia's society and authorities see the media primarily as a means of earning political capital, which can be traded for power and money.

The Media System of South Africa
Maretha de Waal

Historical and Legislative Background of the Media System of South Africa

Charting the media system in South Africa inevitably requires understanding the sociopolitical dynamics of the society over a period of time and tracking how deep-cutting societal changes continue to affect the current media situation. Driven by the national priorities of democracy and nation building since the new government took office after the 1994 elections, the values of freedom, equality, and order are specifically articulated in media policies. These values are in sharp contrast to apartheid values.

The laws that restricted freedom of the press during the apartheid era "were the ones that most effectively curtailed the activities of anti-government black groups" and closed off "from public scrutiny and criticism the widespread imposition of official control over the black population and the increasing activities of the police and military forces."[1] These media restrictions effectively excluded large parts of the South African reality from becoming news, making invisible to the public eye the experience and existence of large numbers of people, as well as denying specific social groups a public voice, both inside and outside of South Africa.

Figure 7.9 **South Africa**

Population	43,647,658
Ethnic groups	black 75.2%, white 13.6%, Colored 8.6%, Indian 2.6%
Religions	Christian 68% (includes most whites and Coloreds, about 60% of blacks and about 40% of Indians), Muslim 2%, Hindu 1.5% (60% of Indians), indigenous beliefs and animist 28.5%
Languages	11 official languages: Afrikaans, English, Ndebele, Pedi, Sotho, Swazi, Tsonga, Tswana, Venda, Xhosa, Zulu
Literacy	definition: age 15 and over can read and write total population: 85% male: 86% female: 85% (2000 est.)
Legal system	based on Roman-Dutch law and English common law; accepts compulsory ICJ jurisdiction, with reservations
Population below poverty line	50% (2000 est.)
Labor force	17 million economically active (2000)
Labor force—by occupation	agriculture 30%, industry 25%, services 45% (1999 est.)
Telephones—main lines in use	more than 5 million (2001)
Telephones—mobile cellular	7.06 million (2001)
Radio broadcast stations	AM 14, FM 347 (plus 243 repeaters), shortwave 1 (1998)
Radios	17 million (2001)
Television broadcast stations	556 (plus 144 network repeaters) (1997)
Televisions	6 million (2000)
Internet service providers (ISPs)	150 (2001)
Internet users	3.068 million (2002)

Source: The CIA World Factbook, 2003.

The media operated in a very restrictive legal environment during the apartheid era, with more than 100 laws that restricted the conduct of both journalists and media content. These laws included a total ban on the presence of journalists at scenes of unrest or security action, as well as the prohibition of the publication of any material falling within the definition of "subversive statements."[2]

The dismantling of apartheid included, among other provisions, the relaxation of restrictions on organizations and individuals, the lifting of certain restrictions imposed under the Internal Security Act 74 of 1982, and the repeal of the 1989 Media Emergency Regulations. Restoring freedom of speech and freedom of expression to the media and the general populace not only transformed the media's place and role in society, it also redefined the media as an instrument of civil society and participatory democracy. This involved both legislative and structural transformation.

Transforming the Media According to a New Media Policy Framework

The new Constitution of South Africa, Act no. 108 of 1996—specifically the Bill of Rights, section 16(1)—guarantees the right to freedom of expression, freedom of the press and other media, freedom to receive or impart information or ideas, and freedom of artistic creativity. The right to freedom of expression does not extend to propaganda for war, incitement of imminent violence, or advocacy of hatred that is based on race, ethnicity, gender, or religion and that constitutes incitement to cause harm (section 32[2]). The Constitution lays down guidelines to determine what is permissible in the reporting of accidents and disasters, crime, civil unrest, judicial proceedings, official corruption and abuse of power, politics, consumer affairs, sex offenses and scandals, security, and national security. Very little legislation relates specifically to the press and the work of reporters. Journalists are subject to the same laws as ordinary citizens with their rights of acquiring and disseminating information.[3] Current laws tend to regulate, rather than restrict the media.

Media freedom is, however, not an absolute right, in the sense that any law of general application could limit it (section 36[1]). For example, section 205 of the Criminal Procedures Act (no. 51 of 1977) still compels journalists to divulge their sources or other information in a court case if that is deemed to be relevant to solve an alleged offense.[4]

The Bill of Rights also protects people's right to privacy (section 14) and makes provision for the right of citizens to any information held by the state or by other persons that is deemed necessary for the exercising or protection of those citizens' rights (article 32[1]). This gave impetus to the Protection of Access to Information Act (no. 2 of 2000), which compels government to divulge information to the citizenry.[5]

Because the government, like its predecessor, has historically equated ownership with control, the democratization, differentiation, and demonopolization of the media system in South Africa involved the separation of the policy-making, regulatory, and operational functions of the media sector. This was accomplished by means of a set of four acts, which have to be read in conjunction with each other: the Independent Broadcasting Authority Act, no. 153 of 1993; the Telecommunications Act, no. 103 of 1996; the Broadcasting Act, no. 4 of 1999; and the Independent Communications Authority of South Africa Act, no. 13 of 2000.

The first two acts brought about the establishment of two independent bodies to enable the transformation and to control the telecommunication sector. The South African Telecommunications Regulatory Authority (SATRA) was given the responsibility of licensing and the allocation of the frequency spectrum, and the Independent Broadcasting Authority (IBA) was charged with the regulation of broadcasting in the country. Recognizing that technologies in the field of communications are causing rapid convergence, IBA and SATRA merged to form the Independent Communications Authority of South Africa (ICASA) as of July 1, 2000. The core responsibility of ICASA is to regulate broadcasting and telecommunications in the public interest.

Based on the values of freedom, equality, and order, the media are now exercising mostly self-control and are accountable to society. They must therefore avoid anything that could cause crime, violence, or public disorder.[6] The content of the media is also expected to reflect the pluralistic diversity of the society. An ombudsman regulates the press, while the Broadcasting Complaints Commission of South Africa (housed within ICASA) regulates broadcasting. Both of these institutions regulate media conduct through the application of voluntary codes of conduct.

Broadcasting

The early development of broadcasting in South Africa followed a pattern similar to Europe and North America. Established as a statutory body in

1936, the South African Broadcasting Corporation (SABC) was modeled largely on the British Broadcasting Corporation (BBC), with the exception that the SABC was not subject to regular commissions of inquiry.[7]

Financial constraints forced the public broadcaster to establish commercial broadcasting alongside that of the SABC (up to this point, broadcasting was limited to shortwave and medium-wave radio broadcasts in English and Afrikaans only). Starting in 1949, a half-hour program was transmitted daily on the English and Afrikaans medium-wave services in IsiZulu, IsiXhosa and Sesotho. The first full-scale radio stations aimed at black listeners came into being in 1962 with the introduction of FM (frequency modulation) transmissions. News was "patronizingly insular,"[8] in that content emphasized local news almost to the exclusion of international events.[9] Programming consisted primarily of traditional choir and jazz music, as well as jive. Discussions were limited to topics lacking overt political content.

The previous government had established the so-called independent national states of Transkei, Bophutatswana, Venda, and Ciskei, where South African legislation did not apply. Consequently, protective laws granting a monopoly to the SABC were not binding in these states.[10] Independent radio stations in these independent "homelands" made major inroads into the political thinking and consciousness of the day.

Until 1993, the SABC was the only public broadcaster, controlling three television channels and twenty-two radio services. The activity of the corporation was limited largely to radio services until May 5, 1975, when the SABC introduced the country's first television service, with the official launch on January 5, 1976.

Bop-TV came on the air on December 31, 1983, as an initiative of the government of Bophutatswana, airing popular international programs and avoiding a progovernment approach to its news. Bop-TV was eventually formally incorporated into the SABC on March 1, 1998.[11]

South Africa saw its first privately owned subscription television service, called M-Net (commercially owned by newspaper groups), in October 1986. M-Net was listed on the Johannesburg Stock Exchange in 1990, introducing a large number of individuals as shareholders. However, the major press groups still retain the majority of shares. In addition to their global acquisitions, M-Net launched its international service into Africa, via satellite, in 1995. The company has since launched the DStv platform, offering twenty-eight TV and forty-six audio channels, using direct broadcast satellite technology.

The IBA issued a new terrestrial free-to-air license service to allow for the entry of e-tv, a new player into the TV market in general and the terrestrial free-to-air market in particular. E-tv became the fourth free-to-air service on October 1, 1998, funded solely through advertising revenue; it is thus not encrypted. The promulgated Local Content Regulations in the Government Gazette allowed a two-year phase-in period, after which broadcasters were required to meet minimum weekly averages of South African production, broken down into specific categories such as drama, current affairs, and children's programs. The regulations required the SABC to dedicate 50 percent of airtime to locally made programs on all three channels; the free-to-air channel was required to dedicate 20 percent and M-Net 5 percent in encoded time and 20 percent in open time.

The Broadcasting Act, no. 4 of 1999, the dominant piece of legislation within the broadcasting environment, provides a charter for the SABC as a public service broadcaster with a public commercial broadcasting component as a separate entity. The public broadcasting component is charged with providing services in all of the eleven official languages, as circumstances permit. In addition, the SABC is required to cater to the cultural and multilingual diversity of South Africa and provide impartial, balanced, and fair journalism; formal and informal educational programming; and national and minority sports programs. The public commercial services are required to subsidize the public service component.[12]

SABC radio still remains the dominant force in the South African broadcasting environment, commanding 81 percent of the total adult radio listenership. The public service portfolio contains the stations with the largest listenership—some 63 percent of the SABC's total listenership.[13]

The SABC's television service, consisting of three channels, broadcasts in eleven languages, reaching a daily audience of 12 million viewers. SABC1 focuses on nation-building projects based in the community, aimed at younger viewers. SABC2 presents programming that addresses the needs of four separate language groups, namely Sesotho, Xitsonga, TshiVenda, and Afrikaans. Additional programming is in English or is multilingual. SABC3 changed from mainly educational programming to family entertainment and more specialized and niche programming. Programs shown on this channel originate from Britain, the United States, Canada, and Australia. SABC3 is predominantly in English and carries the main flagship English news bulletin of the day at 8 P.M.[14]

The Print Media

Prior to 1994, South Africa's print media were dominated by four media institutions—Argus Holdings, Times Media, Perskor, and Nasionale Pers Beperk (later called Naspers)—which controlled 90 percent of the daily circulation of newspapers in the country. Between the four of them, they also owned or controlled a third of the registered papers in the rural areas, an estimated 70 percent of the knock-and-drops, and half of the registered magazines.

Argus Newspapers was sold to Independent Newspapers, owned by Irish businessman Tony O'Reilly, in 1995, to become by far the biggest of the newspaper groups. In 1999 the company delisted to become a private company. Trading as Independent Newspapers and Media (SA), the company controls fourteen daily and weekly newspaper titles in South Africa as well as local newspapers in the Cape. By the company's own estimates, it reached about 2.8 million readers per week in the year 2000, took up close to 50 percent of the advertising expenditure of paid-for newspapers in the country, and reached 63 percent of the English newspaper readers with its publications.[15]

Historically, the Argus group controlled the afternoon newspaper market, and the Bailey group, which founded South African Associated Newspapers (SAAN) in 1906, controlled the morning market. This agreement stood for sixty years. In a politically volatile situation, however, SAAN was restructured in 1987 and renamed to become Times Media Limited (TML). By 1996, TML was part of the Omni Media Corporation, controlled by the mining giant Anglo-American through the Johnnic Commission, a media and entertainment empowerment group. In the same year, the National Empowerment Consortium (NEC), a black empowerment coalition of about forty black businesses and trade unions, took over control of Johnnic. Since then it has started to unbundle from a broad industrial company to an infotainment group with primary interests in media, entertainment, and information technology. This takeover coincided with the internationalization of media interests in the group. United Kingdom–based Pearson's has majority say in Johnnic's running of *Business Day* and *Financial Mail.* Pearson's also set up the large Internet publishing operation I-Net Bridge with TML.[16]

Naspers controls the Afrikaans press and dominates the magazine market. It has significant stakes in, among others, M-Net, the subscription television provider. M-Net serves 1.2 million subscribers in forty-one countries across Africa and on adjacent islands. The control of Naspers is still effectively in the hands of the directors.[17]

Another significant printing company was Perskor, established in 1935, which merged with Caxton in 1998. The new company is known as Caxton Publishers and Printers. Control lies with CTP Holdings, in which Johnnic's Omni Media Corporation is the major shareholder. Caxton Publishers' interests include an English daily, about thirty regional and community newspapers, and fifteen magazine titles.

Independent, TML, Naspers, and Caxton are by no means the only printing companies in the country. During the time of the struggle for political liberation, the mainstream press—usually considered to be the publications of the four major press groups—ignored the struggle against apartheid. As a result, an "alternative press" became active when the political, social, economic, and cultural views of certain social groups were excluded from the popular media market. After the reform initiatives were launched in 1990, the mainstream press started to cover news of the recently unbanned political parties and trade unions. The alternative press therefore lost its exclusivity in respect of certain news events. Withdrawal of overseas funding after the dismantling of apartheid made it even more difficult for alternative newspapers to survive. Those who did not make some adjustments eventually had to close down.

Film

South Africa has more than 100 film, television, and video production companies. These companies mainly specialize in advertising, educational, documentary, news, journal, sport, children's, and other television programming for the SABC, M-Net, e-tv, government institutions, and private companies. Following an artificially induced boom in the local film industry during the 1970s and 1980s, feature film production has declined to a few titles per year. Despite numerous efforts on the part of government to stimulate the industry, it is best described as "stagnant."[18]

Current Trends and Media Convergence

When the merger of AOL and Time Warner was announced in January 2000, the Johannesburg Stock Exchange media index rose by 8 percent. The market viewed the merger as a significant step, indicating that the Internet would play an important role in the future of the media industry. The biggest local beneficiaries at the time were Naspers, Johnnic, and Primedia. Naspers's media convergence strategy is proving to be of benefit to a number of subsidiaries at the operational level. M-Web and MultiChoice, the company that operates pay-TV platform DSTV, recently entered into a joint venture to create South Africa's first interactive television. Interactive television enables MultiChoice subscribers —for the first time in South Africa—to send and receive e-mail by using their television sets. South Africa has also recently seen its first locally produced reality television programs. The popularity of the reality TV genre has opened up a new dimension of the media system in South Africa. While reality TV is no longer a television phenomenon internationally, it is still a solid ratings driver in South Africa, with interactivity— partly by cellular technologies—as a key feature.

III

Applications of
International Media
Communications

8

International Advertising

Advertising is an industry focused on attracting public attention to a product or service, using the channels of mass communications. In recent years, advertising has emerged as a major form of global communication:

- Advertising throughout Latin America increased by more than 14 percent, to $21.3 billion, in 2000.[1]
- More than $11 billion was spent on advertising in the People's Republic of China in 2001.[2]
- Spending in the emerging markets of China, Hong Kong, Indonesia, Malaysia, Singapore, South Africa, and Thailand grew by approximately 15 percent in 2001.[3]
- Procter & Gamble Company spent $3.82 million on advertising worldwide in 2001.[4]
- Prominent U.S. brands are now running more commercials and print ads around the world. In 2002, Colgate-Palmolive Company spent just 19.4 percent of its global total in the United States, 49 percent in Europe, 17.9 percent in Asia, and 11 percent in Latin America.[5]
- There was a 6 percent growth rate worldwide in advertising in 2002.[6]

International advertising now extends beyond products and services. For instance, countries now use advertising to promote their image abroad. In 2002, the government of Poland hired DDB Corporate Profiles, an advertising agency in Warsaw, to promote tourism and trade. Szymon Gutkowski, managing director of DDB Corporate Profiles, comments, "Politicians now realize that a country is a brand." However, Sarah Boxer cautions, "As with any other brand, people have associations, good or bad, with the nations they know. But can you change people's minds by repackaging, rebranding a nation?"[7] Indeed, advertising often serves political functions in authoritarian countries. China's "Regulations for Advertising Management" declares that advertising in China should be used for "the promotion of socialist construction."[8] International advertising serves two main manifest functions. The first is to provide information. International advertisers are often faced with the difficult task of introducing their product to a global audience. In many cases, advertisers must start from the beginning, providing a simple description of the product before explaining why this particular brand is beneficial. The second manifest function is to create a recognizable identity for a product. A successful ad enables consumers to differentiate one brand from its competition.

In addition, advertising fulfills the following latent functions:

Values Formation

The International Advertising Association considers values formation as part of its mission: "Today, the International Advertising Association believes brand building communications is a force that can contribute meaning and values necessary and useful to individuals as they choose how to live their lives and shape their social and economic relationships."[9] Advertising conveys cumulative messages about what is important in life. Through transnational advertising, a culture's traditional values are often challenged by Western values. For instance, Hong Cheng and John C. Schweitzer found that the Western cultural values of individualism, modernity, and sex were the most frequently portrayed cultural values in international ads presented on Chinese television (see Table 8.1).[10] At the same time, advertising can *regate* a country's traditional values—particularly those that do not benefit the advertisers. To illustrate, commenting on Chinese television commercials, Cheng and Schweitzer observe:

> Some traditional values do exist and even continue to be widely held by the Chinese. Such a list at least includes "diligence," "face-saving," "frugality," and "tolerance." But based on our study, none of these values is found in contemporary Chinese advertising. We believe that this is due to the nature of these cultural values—they do not help sell products.[11]

Indeed, advertising featuring Western ideology sometimes blends into a national programming, sending conflicting messages to the audience. Fouad Ajami provides the following example from programming that appeared on the Arab television station al-Jazeera:

One of most heavily promoted talk shows right now is called "The First of the Century's Wars," in homage to the battle in Afghanistan. . . . The show paused for a commercial break. One ad offered a striking counterpoint to the furious anti-Westernism of the call-in program. It was for Hugo Boss "Deep Red" perfume. A willowy Western woman in leather pants strode toward a half-naked young man sprawled on a bed. "Your fragrance, your rules, Hugo Deep Red," the Arabic voiceover intoned. I imagined the young men in Arab-Muslim cities watching this.

In the culture where the commercial was made, it was nothing unusual. But on those other shores, this ad threw into the air insinuations about the liberties of the West—the kind of liberties that can never be had by the thwarted youths of the Islamic world.[12]

Creating Needs

The intention of advertising is to persuade people that they need to purchase the product. This can create consumption patterns inconsistent with their traditional values and lifestyles as well as societal problems such as the impact of the disposal of waste on the environment.

Shaping Lifestyle

Advertising encourages its target audience to incorporate the use of the advertised products into their lifestyles. To illustrate, until recently, fast food was not considered an option by the inhabitants of many countries. However, restaurants like McDonald's and Burger King have played a role in changing eating habits throughout Europe and Asia.

Audience

The success of a company depends on the relationship that it develops with its target audience. To illustrate, Sears has estimated that it costs $114 to acquire a new customer, but only $3 to increase business from its best customers by 15 to 20 percent.[13] As a result, its advertising messages are personal in tone, to engender brand loyalty among consumers.

Some international advertisers employ a *standardization* approach, in which advertisements are virtually unchanged from country to country. The rationale behind this "broadcasting" ad approach is that universal needs create common markets for goods. George Murdock has identified a series of "cultural universals," including athletic sports, bodily adornments, calendars, cooking, courtship, education, etiquette, family, folklore, funeral rites, gestures, gift giving, incest taboos, joking, kin groups, law, magic, marriage, mealtimes, mourning, mythology, property rights, religious rituals, tool making, and weather control.[14] Standardized ads that address these universal needs can be very effective for a global audience.

However, many international advertisers have adopted a *localization* approach, in which they modify their ad strategy to appeal to audiences in different countries. This strategy is an extension of the principle of "narrowcasting," as advertisers construct culturally specific messages for audience members within a country. (For further discussion, see Chapter 2, Process.)

To illustrate, the New York advertising firm of Saatchi and Saatchi mounted an ad campaign in Thailand for Pampers Disposable Diapers, stressing the convenience of the product. But to the surprise of the company, the ads were ineffective. Focus groups revealed that Thai women were worried that using disposable diapers would brand them as bad mothers, interested more in their own convenience than the comfort of their babies. In response, Saatchi developed a subsequent ad campaign stressing that because disposable diapers stay drier than cloth ones, using Pampers was a sign of being a responsible parent. Sales for Pampers in Thailand soared.

Localized advertisements are directed at the lifestyles of a country. For instance, beer is always served cold in the United States. As a result, their commercials emphasize how cold and crisp the taste is by displaying mountain settings or showing the beer on ice. However, in Germany, where certain beers are served warm, this appeal would be counterproductive. Advertising can be particularly challenging when the product is not part of the country's lifestyle at all. For instance, although iced tea is a common beverage in the United States, it is uncommon in Europe, where tea is always served hot. Consequently, ads promoting iced tea would not be effective in Europe. Localizing an ad campaign is generally more expensive than a standardized ad promotion. As a result, smaller companies (i.e., those with less than $25 million in annual sales) generally opt for a standardized approach. Because of the expense, advertisers are less likely to invest time and money in adapting an ad campaign in less affluent global markets (i.e., less than $6,000 per capita yearly income).[15]

Some companies have begun to employ a "glocal" ad strategy, in which ad agencies develop localized ad campaigns based on a standardized concept. For instance, the McDonald's Corporation introduced a new world-wide ad campaign strategy in 2003, based on the common theme "I'm lovin' it." In this campaign, television commercials, print ads, billboards, interactive ads, and promotions based on the "I'm lovin' it" theme have been developed by local ad agencies to suit local markets.

Patterns of Ownership

Advertising is a by-product of the capitalistic system, in which profit-driven companies rely on ads to promote their products. In contrast, countries with state-owned or socialist economies have little need for this type of service. To illustrate, advertising appeared in the former Soviet Union during the 1960s for Aeroflot airline. The slogan, "Fly Aeroflot," was a source of amusement: The airline company was state-owned, and people could not fly by anything else; it was a commercial they did not need.

However, as many countries have moved toward a market-based economy, even countries such as China are seeing an influx of advertising. By 2001, China had moved into a virtual tie (with Germany and the United Kingdom) as the world's third largest advertising economy, behind the United States and Japan.[16]

Roughly 80 percent of all advertising is produced by four transnational conglomerates: the Omnicom Group (United States), the Interpublic Group of Companies (United States), the WPP Group (England), and Publicis (France).[17] The emergence of the transnational advertising conglomerate is consistent with the trend toward globalization. Stuart Elliott explains:

> Driving this concentration of power is an assumption that ad agencies must have a global presence, enormous size and a full range of marketing services simply to survive. Clients themselves have become bigger and more global. Many have changed their marketing strategies to rely less on television and print ads and more on other avenues like coupons, direct mail, sports sponsorships, in-store promotions and product placements in movies and on television shows. Media companies, meanwhile, have ballooned in size and range, and now package print and television with the Internet and other paths to consumers.[18]

The United States is the home of the world's largest and most influential advertising industry. As of 2001, 43 percent of the advertising produced in the world originates in the United States.[19] Indeed, half of the top 100 global marketers—and six of the top ten—are U.S. companies.[20] However, the global dominance of transnational advertising agencies introduces the possibility that they may face conflicts of interest among their stable of clients. Elliot provides the following example:

> In 2001, PepsiCo switched $350 million of its ad business from an agency acquired by Interpublic to an Omnicom shop because Interpublic also represents Pepsi's archrival, Coca-Cola. A short while later, Coca-Cola shifted work on its Sprite brand from Interpublic to a WPP-owned agency, saying it didn't want to rely on a single advertising conglomerate.[21]

Regulations

Generally speaking, the advertising industry regulates itself. However, individual countries may impose their own sets of restrictions on product claims. Some countries impose regulations on advertisements based upon cultural taboos. In Bahrain, Iceland, Nigeria, Norway, Portugal, and Thailand, the law forbids or restricts the display of women in ads unless the product is relevant for women as consumers.[22] In China, regulations stipulate that "an advertisement shall not be released if it is reactionary, obscene, superstitious, or absurd in content."[23] Ads for certain products, such as undergarments, are prohibited.

There have also been some efforts to regulate advertising on a regional basis. In 2002, health ministers for the European Union banned tobacco ads in the member nations' magazines and newspapers, on radio, and on the Internet, as well as prohibiting cigarette companies from sponsoring events like Formula One motor racing. The fifteen members of the Union are obliged to incorporate the pan-European law into their national statutes by July 2005.

International Advertising and the Internet

The Internet has contributed to the dramatic growth of international advertising. Advertising is inexpensive to produce and distribute globally on the Internet. The Internet also enables advertisers to move to a microcasting communications strategy, in which advertising messages are personalized to meet an individual's specific interests, buying habits, and financial capacity. As a result, marketers are able to send e-mail ads directly to individuals, alerting them about promotions tailored to their particular consumer preferences. Instant messages have also emerged as an effective avenue for delivering advertising. For instance, Vans, a sneaker company, developed an Instant Messaging Alert system to keep Vans customers informed about upcoming skateboard tours.

The fluid nature of the Internet makes it easy to camouflage the advertising function, so that advertising is often difficult to detect. For instance, ads are incorporated into online computer games, such as Dodge Speedway. The race car is adorned with the automobile maker's name and logo, and the track's walls and billboards contain ads for Dodge cars. Some of these "advergames" permit marketers to monitor players without their knowledge, providing information about the models and colors of cars the players prefer.[24] Advertising links may also be inserted into editorial copy without being labeled accordingly, so that individuals seeking additional information on a topic instead find themselves in an advertiser's Web site.

Eventually, advertising will adapt to the next generation of hybrid media: the Internet on television. As television evolves into an "information appliance," the world on-screen will become a virtual display window; if you like a pair of shoes that an actor is wearing on a situation comedy, you will be able to click on the image and order the item.

Cultural Context

Many countries have their own distinctive advertising styles, which are extensions of their cultural and artistic traditions (Table 8.1, pp. 231–233). For instance, Japan's literary tradition emphasizes imagery and symbolism, sometimes without "metaphorical or allegorical meaning"—that is, symbolism for its own sake, without underlying persuasive intent. In like fashion, Japanese ads are typically subtle and indirect.[25] In contrast, German ads emphasize technical and factual information, reflecting its tradition of craftsmanship. John L. Graham and Michael A. Kamins explain:

> Germans, in business, downplay imagination; expansive presentations tend to be written off as Phantasie. Orderly, logical presentations, on the contrary, deserve respect. The differences in advertising style (between Germany and Japan) may be illustrated by advertisements of Lufthansa and

of Japan Airlines. In a series of advertisements, Lufthansa gives priority to technical information, and places the technical quality of its fleet and the maintenance of equipment in the foreground. For Lufthansa, an essential advertising claim is the punctuality of its services. It does not advertise flying with comfort but advertises safety, dependability. In advertisements of Japan Airlines, stress is put on comfort on board, and on the experience of flying, in accordance with the old Zen tradition that the way is as important as the goal.[26]

Worldview

In advertising, what is frequently being sold is the worldview of the ad. For instance, a Coors beer commercial takes place on a beach, where young people are partying. The beer assumes a prominent position in the center of the ad—suggesting that beer is central to having a good time. However, if you mentally airbrush out the product, it is clear that what is being advertised is the worldview of the ad—young people having fun in a social setting—as a way of promoting the product.

National ads can provide clues about the lifestyles that characterize a country. For instance, in a study comparing Swedish and American advertising, Swedish advertisements were much more likely to portray models in outdoor activities than United States ads.[27]

Western advertisements send cumulative messages about acquisition as the solution to problems, ranging from cleaning one's carpet to being accepted by the popular crowd. In a larger sense, ads encourage the audience to think of themselves and others in terms of their consumer behavior.

Another theme found in Western advertising is that consumerism is the way to move beyond provincial, traditional culture and join the global community. In a Budweiser Beer ad targeted at an international audience, the slogan "One world, one Bud" is accompanied by a visual montage: a shot of Japanese people, a cityscape of Venice, Italy, and a group of monks at a Buddhist temple. The voice-over declares, "One feeling, one spirit, one product, one feeling of pride." Thus, the ad offers the product as a means by which a person can become a member of the global community. High-tech items such as cameras and computers are often positioned as symbols of modern global culture. And Chevy trucks and Dr. Pepper soft drinks are brands that are presented as symbols of the "Western" way of life.

Table 8.1

Cultural Values Examined in Chinese and U.S. Television Commercials

Value	Description
Adventure	This value suggests bravery, courage, boldness, daring, or thrill. Skydiving is a typical example.
Beauty	This value suggests that the use of a product will enhance the loveliness, attractiveness, elegance, or handsomeness of an individual.
Collectivism	The emphasis here is on the individual in relation to others typically in the reference group. Individuals are depicted as integral parts of the group.
Competition	The emphasis here is on distinguishing a product from its counterparts by aggressive comparisons. While explicit comparisons may mention the competitor's name, implicit comparisons may use such words as "number one" or "leader."
Convenience	A product is suggested to be handy and easy to use.
Courtesy	Politeness and friendship toward the consumer are shown through the use of polished and affable language in the commercial.
Economy	The inexpensive, affordable, and cost-saving nature of a product is emphasized in the commercial.
Effectiveness	A product is suggested to be powerful and capable of achieving certain ends.
Enjoyment	This value suggests that a product will make its user wild with joy. Typical examples include the capital fun that beer or soda drinkers demonstrate in some commercials.
Family	The emphasis here is on the family life and family members. The commercial stresses family scenes: getting married, companionship of siblings, kinship, being at home, and suggests that a certain product is good for the whole family.
Health	This value recommends that the use of a product will enhance or improve the vitality, soundness, strength, and robustness of the body.
Individualism	The emphasis here is on the self-sufficiency and self-reliance of an individual or on the individual as being distinct and unlike others.
Leisure	This value suggests that the use of a product will bring comfort or relaxation.

Table 8.1 *(continued)*

Magic	The emphasis here is on the miraculous effect and nature of a product, e.g., "Bewitch your man…"; "Heals like magic."
Modernity	The notion of being new, contemporary, up-to-date, and ahead of time is emphasized in a commercial.
Natural	This value suggests spiritual harmony between man and nature by making references to the elements, animals, vegetables, or minerals.
Neatness	The notion of being clean and tidy is stressed in a commercial.
Nurturance	This value stresses giving charity, help, protection, support, or sympathy to the weak, disabled, young, or elderly.
Patriotism	The love of and the loyalty to one's own nation inherent in the nature or in the use of a product are suggested here.
Popularity	The focus here is on the universal recognition and acceptance of a certain product by consumers, e.g., "Best seller"; "Well-known nationwide or worldwide."
Quality	The emphasis here is on the excellence and durability of a product, which is usually claimed to be a winner of medals or certificates awarded by a government department for its high grade or is demonstrated by the product's excellent performance.
Respect for the elderly	The commercial displays a respect for older people by using a model of old age or asking for the opinions, recommendations, and advice of the elders.
Safety	The reliable and secure nature of a product is emphasized.
Sex	The commercial uses glamorous and sensual models or has a background of lovers holding hands, embracing, or kissing to promote a product.
Social status	The use of a product is claimed to be able to elevate the position or rank of the user in the eyes of others. The feeling of prestige, trend setting, and pride in the use of a product is conveyed. The promotion of a company manager's status or fame by quoting his words or showing his picture in the commercial is also included.
Technology	Here, the advanced and sophisticated technical skills to engineer and manufacture a particular product are emphasized.

Tradition	The experience of the past, customs, and conventions are respected. The qualities of being historical, time-honored, and legendary are venerated, e.g., "With eighty years of manufacturing experience"; "It's adapted from ancient Chinese prescriptions."
Uniqueness	The unrivaled, incomparable, and unparalleled nature of a product is emphasized, e.g., "We're the only one that offers you the product."
Wealth	This value conveys the idea that being affluent, prosperous, and rich should be encouraged and suggests that a certain product or service will make the user well off.
Wisdom	This value shows respect for knowledge, education, intelligence, expertise, or experience.
Work	This value shows respect for one's labor and skills. A typical example is that a medication has regained a desperate patient his or her ability to work.
Youth	The worship of the younger generation is shown through the depiction of younger models. The rejuvenating benefits of the product are stressed, e.g., "Feel young again!"

Source: Hong Chen and John C. Schweitzer, "Cultural Values Reflected in Chinese and U.S. Television Commercials." *Journal of Advertising Research* 36, no. 3 (May/June): p. 27.

Affective Response

Advertisers recognize that products are purchased for psychological as well as product satisfaction. Consequently, ads are often directed at the primal emotions of the audience. To illustrate, an American advertising campaign for Budweiser Beer, produced for an international market, consists of a series of ads directed at the primal emotions of the various audiences. One of the ads, produced for a Canadian market, sends the message that people can satisfy their primal need for acceptance by purchasing the product. The ad centers on the complex relationship between siblings. The visuals of the ad show a boxing match. A voice-over makes the following pronouncement (accompanied by the following on-screen graphics): "fierce competitors; lifelong bout; losses; rematch; thirst to win." The ad then cuts to a close-up of the older of the two boxers, who looks like he has taken a bit of a beating. He turns to the younger man and says, "Pretty good." The next shot is a close-up of the young man, who is beaming. The voice-over and accompanying graphics complete the equation: "= Kid Brother." The affective appeal of the ad resonates with all audience members (regardless of culture) who have had to struggle to gain the acceptance of an older sibling. Somehow, the implication is that the product has played a role in this very important rite of passage.

Another advertising appeal capitalizes on an individual's attachment to traditional culture. A Budweiser ad, produced for a Japanese audience, begins with a geisha, dressed in her traditional garb. She appears to be bowing in a subservient posture but is, in fact, hiding a Budweiser in her kimono. Thus, in a humorous way, the ad presents the product as a bridge between traditional and modern cultures.

Humor is an appeal that spans different cultures. Humor is a positive emotional response among all people; we are grateful to people who make us laugh. As a result, the advertiser hopes that the consumer will transfer these positive feelings to the product. For instance, in a Budweiser ad, produced for a Chinese market, a band of determined ants carries a bottle of Budweiser en masse to an anthill. However, the bottle becomes stuck upside down in the entrance to the anthill. After a moment's pause, we hear the sound of the bottle being opened. Music starts blaring, and the anthill begins shaking—evidence of an instant party. No words are necessary; in a humorous way, the ad conveys the message that the product is the central ingredient for a good time.

Some countries are more likely to employ affective advertising strategies than others are. For instance, Japan makes greater use of emotional appeals to elicit a positive emotional response through image than U.S. ads.[28] According to Hans Meissner, the primary purpose of advertising in Japan is to create a mood for consumption. Once the proper mood is set via advertising, aggressive pricing policies are used to precipitate purchase.[29] In addition, some emotional appeals are particularly effective in a particular country, since inhabitants may be uncomfortable with certain emotions. *The Economist* provides this example:

> Procter and Gamble's "all-in-one" shampoo with conditioner, Wash & Go, had been positioned globally as a time saver in a busy world. In the United States and Europe, this was signified by a woman rushing into a gym locker room and slamming the locker door, but in Thailand, the creative content was toned down, though it still communicated convenience in a hectic world.[30]

In this case, the emotional outburst in the ad was edited out of the Thai version, since members of the Thai culture are uncomfortable with overt expressions of anger.

Although primal emotions are universal, the circumstances that trigger a particular affective response may vary from country to country. For instance, a person's sense of humor is often rooted in his or her culture. As a result, an ad that is intended to be funny may be considered insulting in another culture.

Production Values

Although production elements can have a universal meaning, the selection of certain production elements may convey a distinctive cultural meaning as well. As a result, advertising styles vary, depending on the culture. For example, Asians ads are characterized by complexity and decoration, balance and harmony, and naturalism.[31]

Word Choice

Advertisers must consider word choice carefully when constructing messages for an international market. For example, when Diet Coke was introduced in Europe, consumers did not purchase the product, in part because the connotation of the word "diet" suggests a medical condition. The implication was that the product was a form of medicine. Consequently, the name of the cola was changed in Europe to "Lite" Coke. In contrast, while Americans are comfortable with the notion of a "lite" beer, they would be less enthusiastic about purchasing a "diet" beer.

In some cases, language assumes a symbolic meaning. For instance, the use of the English language in international advertising represents modernity and globalization to an international audience. English is often used in packaging in Japan because it associates the product with social mobility and an internationalized outlook.[32] However, some words suffer from an unflattering translation. For example:

- When the American Dairy Association entered the South American market with its "Got milk?" campaign, the Spanish translation read, "Are you lactating?"
- "Come alive with Pepsi" was translated in Thailand to "Bring your ancestors back from the dead with Pepsi."
- Kentucky Fried Chicken's "Finger-lickin' good" slogan is translated in Chinese as "Eat your fingers off." And in Iran, the KFC slogan is translated as "So good you'll eat your fingers"—a traditional Farsi compliment.
- The Spanish translation of the Coors Beer slogan, "Turn it loose," is "Suffer from Diarrhea."
- Clairol introduced the Mist Stick, a curling iron, in Germany, only to find out that *mist* is slang for manure.

Some advertisers have learned to alter their word choice for its global audience. For instance, in China *Coca-Cola* was initially translated as *Kekoukela,* meaning "Bite the wax tadpole" or "female horse stuffed with wax," depending on the dialect. Coke's ad agency then researched 40,000 Chinese characters, finding a phonetic equivalent *Kkokou Kole,* which is translated as "happiness in the mouth."

Because of translation problems, the strongest trademarks are often *neologisms*—words that are invented for products. To illustrate, in 1999, Amtrak unveiled its new high-speed train, the Acela Express, to serve the Northeast. Amtrak president George D. Warrington explained that this neologism was selected to represent a new conceptual orientation for the railroad:

"Acela" is more than just a name for Amtrak's new high-speed trains, Acela is a brand representing a whole new way of doing business. A combination of acceleration and excellence, Acela means high speed and high quality—we are changing the journey for every customer on every train with faster trip times, comfortable amenities and highly personalized service.[33]

Connotative Image

The use of images assumes major importance in an advertiser's ability to reach an international audience. While many images employed in international advertising have a universal meaning, some ads use images with culture-specific meanings. For instance, Russian ads frequently feature images of bears (the national symbol of Russia), which inform the local audience that the product is made in Russia.

At times, images used in global advertisements send unintended messages to other cultures. For instance, the ad campaign for Chevy trucks, with its slogan "Like a Rock," features photographs of the product in the mountains or in rocky terrain. In the United States, rocks suggest durability, toughness, solidness, and dependability. However, to a global audience, this image suggests heaviness and lack of mobility: in short, a vehicle which is undrivable.[34]

In response, some international ad campaigns use "neologistic images" that are not meant to be associated with any particular culture. An article in *The Economist* provides this explanation:

> A three-minute ad for Chivas Regal whisky may be a taste of things to come. Created by Ogilvy & Mather in Thailand (but also aired in Hong Kong, Taiwan and Singapore), the advertisement is shot in western locations—such as jazz clubs—and uses Eurasian actors who look western and therefore glamorous, but are also eastern and therefore familiar. Above all, Eurasians are not immediately identifiable as Thai or Chinese or Malay, so they are acceptable in many countries rather than restricted to one.[35]

Lines of Inquiry: International Advertising

I. Analyze a sample of international ads from around the world.
   A. What do these ads reveal about differences in cultural values, attitudes, and preoccupations?

B. Compare the affective appeals used in the ads. What does this comparison reveal about cultural differences?

C. Compare cumulative messages as reflected in advertising, focusing on:

1. Success
2. Gender roles
3. Sex

II. Examine a sample of ads produced for an international audience.

A. Do the ads reflect a standardized or localized approach? If an ad is localized, analyze how the communications strategy, style, and content have been adapted to the culture of the country.

B. Identify the values, attitudes, and preoccupations that are reflected in the ads. Do they conflict with the values, attitudes, and preoccupations of the country in which the ad appears? Explain.

III. What messages are conveyed about these products in different countries?

A. How are the following products advertised?

1. Alcohol
2. Tobacco
3. Computers

B. Compare ads from different countries that promote the same brand (e.g., Budweiser or IBM). What do the differences reveal about these countries?

IV. Examine a sample of ads produced in one country.

A. Who is the target audience?

B. Identify affective appeals used in these ads.

C. What is the worldview suggested by the advertisements?

D. What do the ads reveal about the country's cultural preoccupations, attitudes, values, behaviors, and myths?

E. Can you identify a national style characteristic of ads produced within the country?

F. Is there evidence of the influence of Western cultural values in the ads?

G. In what ways do the following elements provide perspective on the cultural sensibility of the country?

1. Advertising theme
2. Slogan
3. Product attributes

    4. Product packaging
    5. Product name
V. Analyze a sample of national ads, focusing on the use of the following production elements.
    A. Nonverbal elements
       1. Do any nonverbal elements (e.g., gesture, posture, and facial expression) convey messages?
       2. Do any nonverbal elements appear incongruous? Could they have a cultural significance?
    B. Models or Performers
       1. Describe the people who are being used to promote the product in the ad. What messages do these people convey with regard to images of success?
       2. Do the models or performers provide insight into the target market? Explain.
       3. Are celebrities used to promote the product? What messages are conveyed by the selection and presentation of these celebrities?
    C. Editing
    D. Color
    E. Connotative words
    F. Connotative image
    G. Music
    H. Headlines
VI. Select a country and conduct research on its advertising.
    A. How much advertising appears in the country?
       1. What proportion of its advertising is produced within the country?
       2. What proportion of its advertising is produced outside of the country?
    B. What kinds of products are advertised in the country?
    C. Are there national regulations on advertising?

9

Applications
Media Literacy Analysis

The following essays are samples of media literacy analysis by students at Webster University, St. Louis, Missouri.

Media Literacy Analysis: Process

Monica Wallin conducted the following media literacy analysis, applying the keys of process.

The Internet has reduced the distance between people, countries, and cultures. Groups that once were marginalized and isolated now have a window to the world. Alternative political parties, social movements, and even individuals have freedom to create a Web site and express their ideas.

In my case study, I have analyzed the Web site of the Colombian guerrilla organization Revolutionary Armed Forces of Colombia (FARC). The FARC is a Marxist guerrilla organization that has existed in Colombia for around thirty years. As an average Colombian who knows only what the media portray about the guerrillas, I was motivated to go to their Web site and analyze what their message is from the point of view of media literacy. I will analyze the communication process, the context in which it is developed, and the framework that supports the FARC Web site.

The FARC's Web site has multiple communicative functions. First of all, the Web site is a channel of expression. The main objective of the Web site is to express the FARC's ideology and present a rationale for its violent actions. A mass medium has never existed before that would allow marginal or revolutionary groups to express their ideas with such autonomy, control, and anonymity. The reader who launches into the FARC's Web site is going to find out what it is about, its thinking and ideology. Through the Web site, the guerrilla organization can reach thousands of people and express its ideology without the intervention of the government. The FARC controls the words, the images, and, consequently, the message.

A second function is information. A person who is unfamiliar with the FARC can access its Web site to find information about its ideology, history, and opinions. The Web site has sixteen different main sections, including articles, correspondence, and interviews. These articles state the FARC's position about its revolutionary fight against neoliberalism, privatization of natural resources, and social injustice. Some articles do not have a specific author but are clearly compatible with the FARC's ideology. Others are signed by the known leaders of the FARC, such as Raul Reyes and Manuel Marulanda (Tirofijo).

The FARC's Web site also contains a history section that provides background on the formation and development of this armed group. In most Web sites, the About Us section provides information about the geographic location of the media communicator. However, for the FARC's Web site, the geographic location is generally presented as "the Colombian Mountains." A section called *Pleno* (complete) takes the audience to the pictures of the leaders of the group. What is interesting about this is that the word *pleno* would not mean anything to an average audience. It does not say much about what is going to be seen, but in fact the pictures of the leaders are information that anybody would be interested to see.

At the same time, a latent function for this Web site is persuasion. The FARC's Web site is its window to the world to justify its acts of violence. The Web site is its tool to persuade audiences that it is a legitimate social group, not drug dealers, delinquents, or terrorists. The FARC's articles present the group as concerned with the social needs and welfare of the country. The language is patriotic and, in some respects, poetic. The site also includes a section, *Musica Fariana,* with links to songs that guerrilla members have composed. The lyrics are another way to express their ideology and to protest against the system. This part of the Web site presents the FARC as a group that cares for the cultural expression of its members.

After analyzing the media communicator and the function of the Web site, it is time to identify the audience. Who visits the FARC's Web site? Whom does the FARC want to inform or persuade? One way to analyze the audience is to identify the languages that the Web site offers. At the bottom of the screen are different flags that take the audiences to different versions of the Web site in German, Italian, English, Portuguese, and Russian. The FARC clearly realizes that it has international interest, so the links to language options reach a worldwide audience.

In addition, an important part of the Web site is the magazine *Resistencia* (Resistance), which appears to be published for two different audiences: a national audience and an international audience. Each foreign-language version of the Web site has a link that would take the audience to the home page of the magazine. The international versions of the Web site have also a subscription form for the magazine, which I found interesting considering that the national version does not offer that option.

The FARC Web site also has sections targeting women, university students, and people interested in ecological issues.

Using the keys of process allowed me to go deeply into the ideology and point of view of the FARC. I am aware that the material on the Web site expresses the point of view only of the FARC, but it was interesting to find out about that viewpoint directly, without the mediation of the news or other people's opinions. I am aware that to obtain a more critical and objective opinion about the FARC movement in Colombia, I would need to consult different sources and explore different points of view. But for now I would say that the FARC Web site opens doors to different expressions, and it is important for audiences to be able to explore sites without the mediation of the traditional media channels.

Media Literacy Analysis: Media Ownership and Cross-Promotion

Melissa Waugh conducted an analysis of the impact of media ownership on content through cross-promotion.

In the age of media giants, a handful of large, multinational conglomerates controls almost all formats of media, including newspapers, magazines, books, films, and television programming. An industry once consisting of independent, family-owned businesses has changed dramatically during the last two decades.

This study examines prime-time shows airing during the week of February 26, 2001, investigating cross-promotion on Time Warner's television programming.

Promotion of Warner Brothers Music

According to the company Web site, "The WB television network has established itself as a branded network targeted to young adults and teens. The WB's goal of being the destination network for the 12–34 demographic coincides with the network's fourth consecutive season of being number one with female teens" (Time Warner Web site). Not only are female teens the favored demographic for the WB network, they are also among the largest consumers of pop and alternative music. This presents a prime opportunity for Warner Brothers to cross-promote its musical wares.

Several of the WB's prime-time shows routinely include music by Warner Brothers artists, accenting a particular moment of teen drama. For example, a relationship dispute between the romantically involved lead characters on *Jack & Jill* featured a song by Paula Cole (WEA/ Warner Brothers Records) about the emotional trauma of ending a relationship.

At the end of shows like *Jack & Jill,* another interesting promotional tactic occurs—a minicommercial for Warner Brothers CDs. Just before the show's closing credits, an announcer says something like: "Tonight's episode of *Jack & Jill* featured music by Paula Cole." Accompanying the narrative is a still shot of the CD cover, with the artist's name and CD title appearing below it. To draw viewer attention, the CD cover appears on the right side of the screen, with the WB logo on the left side to balance the shot. This relative positioning of the CD cover on the right side is significant because audiences are drawn to objects placed on the right side of the screen.

During the week of February 26, 2001, the network promoted six CDs produced by Warner Brothers on four of the network's prime-time shows.

Warner Brothers has also discovered additional ways to promote its artists on the WB network. One tactic is the "live" appearance of its musicians. For example, the sisters on *Charmed* (a science fiction drama about witchcraft) own a nightclub where Warner Brothers artists routinely perform at the end of an action-packed episode. The formula goes something like this: During the first fifty minutes of the episode, the witch sisters confront mental and physical challenges to overcome or vanquish an evil demon that threatens their existence. After their triumph, the sisters return to the nightclub to celebrate with live music and dancing, accompanied by attractive males who frequent the club. This restoration of order prompts an affective response in the viewers, who watch the sisters dance in celebration. It is also a positive reinforcement of the Warner Brothers musicians who perform at the club. The Marvelous 3 appeared during the week's episode, and the group's CD was promoted during the end-of-show CD pitch.

WB musical promotions also extend beyond the "live" performances and CD advertisements. The shows' writers regularly incorporate references to WB musicians into the characters' dialogue. Like the kind of car a person drives, the music a character chooses defines his or her personality. This presents a latent message that musical preference is an important choice for the impressionable teen viewer, who, of course, should consider a Warner Brothers artist the acceptable selection.

On the freshman drama *Gilmore Girls,* Lorelei (a main character) debates musical taste with her ex-boyfriend (a guest star). He prefers Offspring (Columbia Records); she likes Metallica (Elektra, a WB subsidiary). Not coincidentally, the show's protagonist asserts her alliance with a WB artist, while the nonrecurring character states his preference for the competition. Their romance was doomed for several other reasons, but this musical rift is a sure sign that the couple would part ways. Their musical identities, a reflection of their personalities, are in conflict. The ex-boyfriend, wallowing in his poor musical taste, eventually leaves Lorelei and her small town behind. This show also presents an instance of antipromotion: Warner Brothers uses its programming to shed negative light on the competition. This time, the focus is on a competitor's record label.

So upon close inspection, the viewer can detect two distinct messages at work in the WB network's programming. The manifest message is teenage entertainment through melodramatic programming. The latent message is less obvious—the promotion and ultimate sale of Warner Brothers–produced artists. While the latent message is generally quite subtle on most WB programs, it is far more obvious on another show—*Popstars.*

This thirty-minute program chronicles the creation of yet another teen pop group. At the beginning of the fall television season, *Popstars* followed the audition of hundreds of teenage girls looking for their big break. Eventually, executives from Warner Brothers Music selected five teens to form the new female supergroup. Ensuing episodes revolved around recording sessions at Warner Brothers studios, live performances coordinated by Warner Brothers Music, and the promotion of the group's CD for 143 Records (a subsidiary of Warner Brothers Music). As if the latent sales message was not already obvious, the show embraces the practice of name-dropping for Warner Brothers artists. For example, the March 2 episode introduced two studio producers by describing their work with "megastars like Mandy Moore and Monica." Of course, both artists have signed with Warner Brothers, and many critics would question their status as "megastars." This label is an attempt to build the popularity of existing Warner Brothers artists.

In yet another cross-promotion effort, the *Popstars* episode closed with the announcement of an Internet contest whose winner would receive a free makeover. How should the typical teenage girl, insecure about her appearance during the awkward years, enter the contest? Try the *Popstars* keyword on AOL. There are truly no missed opportunities to target the company's media products for the teen audience.

Promotion of Warner Brothers Films

Warner Brothers continues its cross-promotion tactics by marketing films that appeal to the teenage and young adult audience through programming on the WB network. Typically, this involves using Warner Brothers films as pop-culture references throughout the characters' dialogue.

In the opening scene of *Jack & Jill,* Beno (a supporting character) reveals that his current love interest is dating other men. Beno's friend responds:

> MIKE: Wait until the green-eyed monster comes breathing down your door.
> (Mike exits.)
> JILL: What's with Mike?
> BENO: He's been reading too much Harry Potter.

Not coincidentally, Warner Brothers produced the Harry Potter movies.

Home video and DVD sales have also become an integral part of a movie's total profit for both the film producers and distributors. *Dawson's Creek* featured a subtle plug for another Warner Brothers film, which is currently available in video stores. Jack and Jen, two of the show's teen characters, attempt to learn more about the town psychiatrist by following him into a local store. When they spot him looking at the video jacket of *Interview with the Vampire,* they speculate on his sexual orientation. Most viewers (myself included) would not immediately make the connection between the movie and homosexuality. This could potentially cause an underlying desire to watch the movie and investigate the reference. Magazine advertisers hope for a second glance at their ads and subsequent recognition of the product on the shelf. The same tactic appears to be at work on *Dawson's Creek*.

While the network's prime-time programming presents an opportunity for promotion of Warner Brothers films, it is also an opportunity for antipromotion of competitors' works. This may include spotlighting movie failures. On *Jack & Jill,* the main characters gather in the tavern owned by Jill. When a karaoke-machine salesman enters the bar and presents his pitch for the product, Jill responds, "Sorry, we're not interested; karaoke is dead. Thank you, Gwyneth." This is a very subtle reference to *Duets,* a September 2000 movie starring Gwyneth Paltrow as an aspiring singer with a fondness for karaoke. The film was an utter failure for Hollywood Pictures (the film's production company), mainly because it spotlighted a dying 1990s fad. Walt Disney owns Hollywood Pictures and is a long-time Warner Brothers competitor, not only in films, but also on network television, since Disney owns the ABC network.

Promotion of Other Television Shows Produced by Warner Brothers

Uncovering the subtleties of film promotion on the WB network requires a critical investigation of passing references within character dialogue, and the same awareness is necessary to detect a different kind of cross-promotion. The characters on the WB routinely mention programs appearing on other Warner Brothers–owned television networks. At times, they'll even mention a particular network by name. On *Dawson's Creek*, a teenage couple (Joey and Pacey) awake early on a Saturday morning. A grumpy Pacey declares, "You know, ever since they invented the Cartoon Network, there's really no need to get up this early on a Saturday." Through this passing reference, Pacey plugs the Cartoon Network—a subsidiary of Turner Entertainment, owned by Warner Brothers—which, unlike other networks, shows cartoons in the afternoon. Pacey cites the convenience of watching cartoons in the afternoon, perhaps a key selling point for the typical teenager who likes cartoons and prefers to sleep in on a Saturday.

Another reference to Turner programming occurs on the drama *Popular.* As a group of high school boys discusses its plans to crash a fraternity party at a local college, one character declares himself an expert because he has "seen *Animal House* on TBS a million times." What seems like a straightforward reference to repeat programming on Turner

Broadcasting System (TBS) warrants careful consideration. Is it necessary for the character to specifically mention the TBS superstation? He could convey the same meaning by instead stating, "I've seen *Animal House* a million times on cable." Once the relationship between Warner Brothers and Turner Entertainment is examined, it is apparent that the inclusion of TBS is a plug for the superstation. The reference also promotes "binge viewing" of whatever programming the superstation may offer, and the WB's target teenage audience certainly has more leisure time for such a practice.

The final instance of crossover program promotion occurs on *Dawson's Creek,* which should be nominated for "Promoter of the Week," considering the ample material it has supplied for this essay. As Jack and Jen continue to stalk the town psychologist, Jack (a homosexual character) provides a level of perspective that usually comes only from Jen, his heterosexual counterpart. Here's the dialogue:

> JEN: When did you surpass me as an alternate link to gay?
> JACK: Sex and the City.

The implication here is clear. As a fan of HBO's megahit, Jack has gained insight into the heterosexual world. By watching a television show, Jack can relate to his friend on a level he was previously unable to attain. Of course, HBO is a subsidiary of Warner Brothers Television.

Conclusion

Ironically, local commercials for the WB network feature a musician singing this refrain: "The night is young . . . And free . . . on the WB." While there is little doubt about the youth factor, one could certainly argue that teens and young adults pay for the programming each time they are prompted to purchase a CD or movie produced by Warner Brothers through cross-promotion.

Media Literacy Analysis: Comparative Analysis of *Ringu* and *The Ring*

Patsy Zettler conducted a comparative analysis of the Japanese film Ringu *(1998) and its American remake,* The Ring *(2002), focusing on how these films reveal cultural differences.*

At first glance there does not seem to be much difference between the Japanese film *Ringu* (1998) and its American remake *The Ring* (2002). Both are horror films based on an urban legend about a videotape that causes those who watch it to die in seven days. In both films, a young female journalist uncovers the mystery behind the video. And both films share one of the most terrifying climaxes in horror film history, as the revengeful ghost-like image of a murdered girl crawls out of a television screen into the home of an innocent victim, literally scaring him to death.

Though there are many similarities between the two films, the American filmmakers made some significant revisions in the Japanese original in order to accommodate the cultural tastes of the American moviegoing audience.

The most obvious changes can be seen when comparing the production elements in *Ringu* to those in *The Ring*. *Ringu* was made with a much smaller budget than *The Ring,* which was produced by DreamWorks SKG. *Ringu,* therefore, has fewer special effects than *The Ring*. This is especially noticeable in the death scenes. While *Ringu*'s actors simply mimic the faces of dead people, *The Ring* shows faces created with engorged veins, bluish skin, popping eyes, and large, gaping, twisted mouths. American audiences have come to expect such effects, especially in the horror film genre.

In addition, the sets in *The Ring* are more detailed and stylized than those in its Japanese counterpart. Since the title of the film represents the ring of light above the well where the murdered girl's body is hidden, circular shapes are seen throughout the American version—for instance, in clocks, oval mirrors, the moon, and even on clothing, as in the circles on a doctor's sweater. In contrast, the minimalist set designs in *Ringu* seem to show that Japanese audiences prefer to concentrate more on the characters than on what is going on in the background.

This emphasis on the characterization can also be found in *Ringu*'s narrative style. The Japanese version tends to tell the story at a slower pace using less action, more conversation, slower editing, and longer camera shots that seem to linger on the characters. The story unfolds through the conversation of the characters. In contrast, the American version uses more action, less conversation, faster editing, and shorter shots. The American story, therefore, unfolds more through its imagery. A comparison of two similar scenes from both films demonstrates the differences between the Japanese way of telling versus the American way of showing.

In *Ringu,* the main character, Reiko Asakawa, a journalist who has been investigating the mystery behind the video, receives a telephone call from her ex-husband, Ryuji Takayama, who tells her that he has discovered that the mother of the murdered girl committed suicide by throwing herself into a volcano. The Japanese audience does not see the suicide. Instead, they receive the information through conversation, while watching alternating shots of Reiko and Ryuji with phone receivers pressed to their ears. In contrast, the journalist in *The Ring*, Rachel Keller, watches a video in which the mother of the murdered girl is shown committing suicide. Along with Rachel, American audiences watch the mother as she stands on the edge of a cliff and then throws herself into the ocean.

Not only do American audiences see the suicide instead of just hearing about it, they also see this image from the murdered girl's point of view. This subjective camera technique has created an additional narrative possibility inferring that the murdered girl may have used her psychic powers to cause her mother's suicide. By using this point of view in the narrative, the American filmmakers made the girl more evil than the murdered girl in the Japanese film.

Although the production elements and the narrative styles are the most obvious differences between the two films, another subtler difference involves the relative ages of the characters in each film. *Ringu* shows members of Reiko's extended family, including her aging parents, the grandparents of Yoichi, Reiko's young son. The grandparents play important roles as they help Reiko by taking care of Yoichi. Ultimately, the grandfather is willing to sacrifice his life in order to save Yoichi.

In *The Ring,* most of the characters are young adults and teenagers. There are no grandparents for Aidan, Rachel's young son. This seems to suggest that Japanese culture, as reflected in the movie, accepts and respects all ages, while American audiences are youth-oriented, ignoring older people.

When it comes to gender and the relationship between the female lead character and her male counterpart, the two films are also very dissimilar. In *Ringu,* Reiko is a journalist investigating the story behind the strange video. But once she asks her ex-husband, Ryuji, a college professor and psychic, to help her solve the video's mystery, he takes over the investigation and sends her and her young son, Yoichi, to the safety of her parents' home. Later, with the curse of the video upon them, Reiko joins Ryuji in a race of time to find the well in which the murdered girl's body was dumped. Ryuji uses his psychic powers to find the well and climbs down in search of the body. He orders Reiko to remain above ground, pulling up bucket after bucket of water with a rope. Exhausted, Reiko collapses to the ground, giving up. Ryuji climbs from the well, strikes Reiko, and orders her to go down the well and search for the body.

In the American version of the film, Rachel is also a journalist, who investigates the mystery of the video with the help of her ex-husband Noah, a photographer. Rachel is more assertive than Reiko: she is the one who follows leads, makes decisions, and comes up with ideas. Instead of Noah taking over the investigation as Ryuji did, Noah accepts instructions from Rachel on what he can do to help. And then, in the same scene as in *Ringu* where the couple discovers the well, Rachel is not ordered into the well by her ex-husband, but instead is knocked into the well by the murdered girl's spirit. In response, Noah, acting more compassionately than Ryuji, desperately tries to save Rachel. The differences between these scenes indicate that, in the Japanese version, men are more dominant than the women are. However, in the American version, men and women share a more equal relationship.

One last cultural difference is revealed in the ways in which the lead characters solve their problems. In the final scenes of both films, the women have discovered the mystery to the video and how to lift the curse, which is to make a copy and show it to someone else. Each woman is then faced with a decision: In order to save her son, who has watched the video, she must choose someone for him to show the video to. In *Ringu*, Reiko decides to have Yoichi show it to his grandfather, who by becoming exposed to the cause, would die in seven days, making the ultimate sacrifice for his grandson. And if he is the last viewer of the video, the curse could end in Japan. Keeping the problem within the family, Reiko has made a noble choice that could save the rest of the world. However, in *The Ring*, Rachel decides to have Aidan show his copy of the video to strangers, who then could show it to others. So, in America, the curse could go on and on. Rachel's decision is less noble than Rieko's; she chooses only to save her son while bringing havoc to the rest of the world. This difference seems to signify that, culturally, Americans are more worried about themselves individually, while the Japanese consider everyone as part of a whole.

This comparative analysis of *Ringu* and *The Ring* has revealed some significant differences between the cultural sensibilities of Japanese and American moviegoing audiences. Japanese audiences seem to prefer the telling of a story (even a horror story) with fewer special effects and more concentration on the characters than American audiences do. They also appear to have stronger familial ties than Americans and to respect older persons more. And when it comes to gender differences, as reflected in *Ringu*, Japanese couples may share less equality than the men and women in American films.

As long as differences like these exist between cultures, there will be a need to remake original films from other countries in order to satisfy the cultural tastes of specific audiences. However, the more media-literate audiences become, the more likely they are to view foreign films in their original form and appreciate the cultural differences.

Media Literacy Analysis: Newspapers

Steven Schoen conducted an analysis of two newspapers that target the same audience.

Each day subscribers to the *Miami Herald* get two newspapers bundled together. Responding to the bilingual character of the Miami cultural and political scene, the *Miami Herald* and *El Nuevo Herald* are delivered together: two newspapers produced from the same Knight-Ridder resources for the same geographic area, yet clearly targeted at two culturally different audiences, one English-speaking, the other Spanish-speaking. (There is no French Creole edition for the less organized and less powerful Haitian community.) An examination of the layout and editorial decisions for the front pages of the two papers on Sunday, September 17, 2000, highlights the different cultural contexts of Spanish- and English-language readers and reflects an editorial strategy designed to appeal to the respective cultural perspectives and interests of each group—with the likely effect of reinforcing those perspectives and interests. The Spanish-language paper has a greater focus on family issues and other traditional values, while the English-language paper seems more in tune with general U.S. cultural tendencies, such as a sensitivity to issues of inclusion (i.e., women and gays). The line between the language groups, however, should not be drawn too sharply. Many English readers are of Hispanic origin and there are clear cultural differences between Cuban-American, Mexican-American, and various other Hispanic readers. Still, the front pages of the two newspapers reflect clear differences between their readers.

The most visually prominent above-the-fold element of the English-language edition is a picture featuring the U.S. women's gold medal Olympic swim team. The four women are embracing, obviously celebrating their win. Under the picture of the women is a smaller picture of Ian Thorpe, the Australian gold medal–winning swimmer. The Spanish-language paper also features an Olympics story at the top of the front page, but the picture and text are only about Thorpe. The U.S. women's swim team is not included on the front page at all. Whether the omission reflects a perception by editors that Spanish-language readers have less fervor about U.S. athletes, less interest in women's sports, or both is unclear. It is hard to imagine, however, the same editorial decision being made for (or tolerated by) English-language readers.

Also above the fold in the English-language paper is a story about Hurricane Gordon approaching the Florida gulf coast. *El Nuevo Herald* gives the story front-page exposure too, but at the bottom of the page. At press time, the hurricane was of little threat to the Miami metro area, but still menacing Florida farther north. Perhaps the more prominent placement of the story in the English-language paper reflects a perceived deeper sense of connection to the rest of Florida among English readers than among the more geographically concentrated Spanish-speaking community in the Miami area.

At the top of *El Nuevo Herald*'s front page, along with the Ian Thorpe story, are a picture and text featuring the plight of neglected elderly people. The article, not included in the *Miami Herald,* has the largest headline on the page. Although stories about old people might also be expected to appeal to the many English-speaking retirees in the area, *El Nuevo Herald*'s prominent above-the-fold, front-page placement seems culturally significant. In the Hispanic community, which prides itself on maintaining respect for older people as an important cultural value, a story about the abuse of the elderly might be expected to have particularly strong impact. The text of the article centers on the neglect of elderly Hispanic people by their own family members, which further conflicts with the community's sense of its own values—in this case, the cultural importance of strong family relationships. The Hispanic community might see its own concern about decaying cultural values reflected in the high-profile coverage in *El Nuevo Herald,* linking the paper in readers' minds with the values of their community.

A story given significant space on the *Miami Herald*'s front page, but not covered at all in the September 17, 2000, issue of *El Nuevo Herald,* follows the growing movement by local schools and governmental agencies to deny the use of their facilities to Boy Scouts because of the Scouts' ban on gay people. The article contrasts the Boy Scouts with a wide variety of other youth agencies, such as Girl Scouts, 4-H, and the YMCA, that do not discriminate against gays. A strong and visible South Florida gay community gives the controversial story a high enough profile to reach the front page of the English-language paper, but it is left out of the Spanish-language coverage. Again, this is consistent with the cultural perspective of the Hispanic community, which, rooted in Roman Catholicism and influenced by machismo, tends to ignore homosexuality.

Although the presence or placement of a particular story in a newspaper does not necessarily directly correspond to a particular cultural perspective, the editorial and layout decisions that went into the front pages of the *Miami Herald* and *El Nuevo Herald* on September 17, 2000, combine to suggest a strong link between each publication and the cultural perspectives of its readers. Knight-Ridder's responsiveness to its readers is in many ways beneficial, but English- and Spanish-speaking people in Miami must live together in the same community. If their respective newspapers only reinforce their current cultural perspectives, the two groups are not likely to understand their differences and find new ways to work together. Publishing newspapers for both the English- and Spanish-speaking people of Miami puts Knight-Ridder in a position to make the cultural diversity represented by the two language groups serve as an opportunity for enrichment. Unfortunately, the September 17, 2000, editions of the *Miami Herald* and *El Nuevo Herald* suggest this may not be happening.

Notes

Chapter 1. Introduction: International Media Literacy

1. Benedict Anderson, *Imagined Communities: Reflections on the Origin and Spread of Nationalism,* rev. ed. (London and New York: Verso, 1991), pp. 5–7.

2. Kofi Annan, speaking at a gala ceremony in the Norwegian capital of Oslo where he and the United Nations were jointly presented with the one hundredth Nobel Peace Prize, BBC World News, December 10, 2001, http://news.bbc.co.uk/1/hi/world/europe/1701605.stm.

3. Edward W. Said, interviewed by David Barsamian, *The Progressive,* April 1999.

4. Owen Gibson, "US Turns to British News," *The Guardian* (London), May 12, 2003.

5. "An International Right to Know," *New York Times,* January 25, 2003.

6. www.cdi.org/russia/johnson/default.cfm.

7. Thomas L. Friedman, "Global Village Idiocy," *New York Times,* May 12, 2002.

Chapter 2. Process

1. John Sawyer, "Soap Operas Are Proving Helpful in Informing Public," *St. Louis Post-Dispatch,* December 1, 2002.

2. Thomas L. Friedman, "Global Village Idiocy," *New York Times,* May 12, 2002.

3. Federal Trade Commission, Protecting Children's Privacy Under COPPA: A Survey on Compliance, www.ftc.gov/os/2002/04/coppasurvey.pdf.

4. Simon Romero, "When Villages Go Global," *New York Times,* April 23, 2000.

5. Ibid.

6. Editorials, *St. Louis Post-Dispatch,* May 31, 2002.

7. Ibid.

8. Caryn James, "British Take a Blunter Approach to War News," *New York Times,* November 9, 2001.

9. Rick Lyman, "China Is Warming to Hollywood's Glow; Before Big Profits, Hurdles Remain," *New York Times,* September 18, 2002.

10. Don Corrigan, telephone interview by research assistant Anne Bader, June 6, 2003.

11. Texas Press Association Confidential Bulletin, www.texaspress.com/AskAttorney/attorney0602.htm.

12. Patrick Tyler, "Arab Politics: Saudi to Warn Bush of Rupture Over Israel Policy," *New York Times,* April 25, 2002.

13. William Safire, "Walk Back the Cat," *New York Times,* April 29, 2002.

14. Craig S. Smith, "Beware of Cross-Cultural Faux Pas in China," *New York Times,* April 30, 2002.

15. United Nations *Human Development Report 2002,* chapter 3, "Deepening Democracy by Tackling Democratic Deficits," chart: "Who Owns the Media?" p. 78, http://hdr.undp.org/reports/global/2002/en/pdf/chapterthree.pdf.

16. Aleksander Grigoryev, interview by Art Silverblatt, Washington, DC, November 18, 2001.

17. Andrey Mikhailov, "What Do Russians Read," www.pravda.ru, translated by Maria Gousseva.

18. Benjamin Compaine, "Global Media," *Foreign Policy,* www.foreignpolicy.com/issue_novdec_2002/bio.

19. Frederic M. Sherer and David Ross, *Industrial Market Structure and Economic Performance,* 3rd ed. (Boston: Houghton Mifflin, 1990.)

20. David D. Kirkpatrick and Andrew Ross Sorkin, "AOL Is Trying to Find Buyer for Book Unit," *New York Times,* January 23, 2003.

21. Richard A. Gershon, *The Transnational Media Corporation* (Mahwah, NJ: Lawrence Erlbaum Associates, 1997), p. 30.

22. Rick Lyman and Laura M. Holson, "Holidays Turn Into Hollywood's Hot Season," *New York Times,* November 24, 2002.

23. Mark Balnaves, James Donald, and Stephanie Hemelryk Donald, *The Penguin Atlas of Media and Information* (New York: Penguin Putnam, 2001), p. 61.

24. Alan Riding, "Filmmakers Seek Protection From U.S. Dominance," *New York Times,* February 5, 2003.

25. Marwan M. Kraidy, "The Global, the Local, and the Hybrid: A Native Ethnography of Globalization," *Critical Studies in Mass Communication* 16, no. 4 (December 1999): 456.

26. Ben Bagdikian, *The Media Monopoly,* 5th ed. (Boston: Beacon Press, 1997), p. 36.

27. Peter Phillips, "The Importance of Independent News Sources for Freedom and Democracy," www.projectcensored.org/resources/complete.html.

28. Ibid.

29. David D. Kirkpatrick, "AOL Is Expected to Announce Big Policy Shift," *New York Times,* December 3, 2002.

30. General Electric Web site, www.ge.com/.

31. Ibid.

32. Phillips, "The Importance of Independent News Sources for Freedom and Democracy."

33. Scott cited in James Brooke, "As Tokyo Loses Luster, Foreign Media Move On," *New York Times,* August 12, 2002.

34. Patrick Murphy, unpublished paper, April 2003.

35. Kirkpatrick and Sorkin, "AOL Is Trying to Find Buyer for Book Unit."

36. Reshma Kapadia, "AOL TW Posts Loss of Nearly $100 Billion," Reuters, New York, January 29, 2003.

37. Steve Lohr and Saul Hansell, "The Stairmaster of Mergers," *New York Times,* July 21, 2002.

38. David D. Kirkpatrick and Jim Rutenberg, "AOL Reporting Further Losses; Turner Resigns," *New York Times,* January 30, 2003.

39. Agence France Presse, "News Corp. Loses 1.74 Billion Dollars in April–June Quarter," August 14, 2002.

40. Mark Landler, "Bertelsmann Encounters Some Turbulence," *New York Times,* September 4, 2003.

41. Laura M. Holson, "As Disney Loses Steam, Insider Loses Patience," *New York Times,* August 18, 2002.

42. Laura M. Holson, "Disney Net Is Down 42%, But Its Revenue Rises 6%," *New York Times,* January 31, 2003.

43. Bayan Rahman, "Moody's Downgrades Sony," *Financial Times* (London), June 26, 2003.

44. Bloomberg News, "Viacom, International Paper Lead Stocks South." *St. Louis Post-Dispatch,* October 25, 2002.

45. Suzanne Kapner, "Vivendi Chief Said to Weigh Overhaul of Canal Plus," *New York Times,* July 23, 2002.

46. John Tagliabue, "Vivendi Posts Higher Operating Profit and Smaller Net Loss," *New York Times*, September 25, 2003.

47. Case cited in Steve Lohr and Saul Hansell, "The Stairmaster of Mergers," *New York Times,* July 21, 2001.

48. Saul Hansell, "As Broadband Gains, The Internet's Snails, Like AOL, Fall Back," *New York Times,* February 3, 2003.

49. David D. Kirkpatrick, "A TV House Divided; A Debate on Skipping Ads at AOL Time Warner," *New York Times,* October 28, 2002.

50. Jim Rutenberg, "Israeli Cable Outlets Get Permission to Remove CNN," *New York Times,* August 2, 2002.

51. David D. Kirkpatrick, "Retreat Seems to Fit Mood of Media's Big Gathering," *New York Times,* July 13, 2002.

52. David D. Kirkpatrick and Andrew Ross Sorkin, "AOL Is Trying to Find Buyer for Book Unit," *New York Times,* January 23, 2003.

53. David D. Kirkpatrick, "2 Rival Houses Said to Consider Bids to Acquire AOL Book Unit," *New York Times,* February 25, 2003

54. David D. Kirkpatrick, "Short of Cash, Media Giants Are Selling Assets," *New York Times,* September 9, 2002.

55. Ibid.

56. Suzanne Kapner with Laura M. Holson, "Vivendi Chief to Discuss Options for U.S. Divisions," *New York Times,* September 11, 2002.

57. David D. Kirkpatrick and Bill Carter, "AOL Time Warner and Disney Revive Talks on News Venture," *New York Times,* September 25, 2002.

58. Stuart Klawans, "Glimpses of China on Film Never Seen in China," *New York Times,* February 18, 2001.

59. Balnaves, Donald, and Donald, *Penguin Atlas of Media and Information,* p. 49.

60. Riding, "Filmmakers Seek Protection from U.S. Dominance."

61. Tyler Cowen, "Myth of the Media Giants," *National Post,* January 6, 2003.

62. Smith, "Beware of Cross-Cultural Faux Pas in China."

63. Barbara Mueller, *International Advertising* (Belmont, CA: Wadsworth, 1996), p. 117.

64. Tina Wheeler, "La Femme Nikita or Point of No Return," unpublished paper, December 2003, Webster University, St. Louis, Missouri, p. 10.

65. Michele Willens, "Putting Films to the Test, Every Time," *New York Times,* June 25, 2000.

66. Timothy Havens, "The Biggest Show in the World: Race and the Global Popularity of The Cosby Show," *Media Culture & Society* 22 (July 2000): 373.

67. Ibid., p. 385.

68. Simon Jones, *Black Culture, White Youth: The Reggae Tradition, from JA to UK* (London: Macmillan, 1988), p. 373.

69. Linda K. Fuller, *The Cosby Show: Audiences, Impact, and Implications* (Westport, CT: Greenwood Press, 1992), p. 114.

70. Chart, "Channeling Our Energy," compiled by TV-Turnoff Network, quoted in *New York Times Magazine,* February 16, 2003, p. 9.

71. Marc Lacey, "Where 9/11 News Is Late, But Aid Is Swift," *New York Times,* June 3, 2002.

72. Central Intelligence Agency, *The World Factbook.* Estonia—Communications, 2003, www.cia.gov/cia/publications/factbook/geos/en.html.

73. Balnaves, Donald, and Donald, *Penguin Atlas of Media and Information,* p. 49.

74. Ciu Jian cited in Rick Lyman, "China Is Warming to Hollywood's Glow; Before Big Profits, Hurdles Remain," *New York Times,* September 18, 2002.

75. International Telecommunications Union, World Communication Indicators, 1999.

76. Balnaves, Donald, *Penguin Atlas of Media and Information,* p. 50.

77. "US Beats the World with Over 40% of Global Traffic" (Trends), *New Media Age,* August 8, 2002, p. 16.

78. "China Reports 45.8 Million Internet Users," *Deutsche Presse-Agentur,* July 23, 2002.

79. Steven Lee Meyers, "The World: Singing the Praises of Mr. Personality," *New York Times,* September 1, 2002.

80. David Rothkopf, "In Praise of Cultural Imperialism? Effects of Globalizationon Culture," *Foreign Policy,* June 23, 1997.

81. Thom Shanker and Eric Schmitt, "Threats and Responses: Hearts and Minds; Firing Leaflets and Electrons, U.S. Wages Information War," *New York Times*, February 24, 2003.

82. Tim Weiner, "C.I.A. Had Ability to Plant Bay of Pigs News, Document Shows," *New York Times,* March 24, 2001.

83. Laurance Zuckerman, "How the C.I.A. Played Dirty Tricks with Culture," *New York Times*, March 18, 2000.

84. Katharine Q. Seelye, "TV Drama, Pentagon-Style: A Fictional Terror Tribunal," *New York Times,* March 31, 2002.

85. Ibid.

86. Felicity Barringer, "U.S. Messages to Arab Youth, Wrapped in Song," *New York Times,* June 17, 2002.

87. Pattiz cited in Oliver Burkeman, "Arab World Now Faces Invasion by American TV," *The Guardian,* April 24, 2003.

88. Pratkanis cited in Daniel Golman, "Voters Assailed by Unfair Persuasion," *New York Times,* October 27, 1992.

89. Sarah Boxer, "Propaganda, the Sly Art That Makes Opposites Look Alike," *New York Times,* October 30, 1999.

90. Richard Leiby, "When Bombs Are Not Enough," *Washington Post,* December 10, 2001.

91. Ibid.

Chapter 3. Context

1. Kristin Hohenadel, "Paris for Real vs. Paris on Film: We'll Always Have the Movies," *New York Times,* November 25, 2001.

2. James W. Loewen, *Lies My Teacher Told Me* (New York: New Press, 1995), p. 14.

3. Daniel Woolls, "Spaniards Rave over Sitcom Based on Franco," Associated Press Worldstream, International News, August 1, 2002.

4. Bill Madosky, interview by Art Silverblatt, St. Louis, Missouri, March 2, 2000.

5. Julie Salamon, "Israeli-Palestinian Battles Intrude on 'Sesame Street,'" *New York Times,* July 30, 2002.

6. "Searching the Web, Searching the Mind," *New York Times* editorial, December 23, 2001.

7. Daniel J. Wakin, "Anti-Semitic 'Elders of Zion' Gets New Life on Egypt TV," *New York Times,* October 26, 2002.

8. Alan Cowell, "What Can the New Economy Do for Places Without an Old One?" *New York Times,* April 23, 2000.

9. Frank Rich, "The Best Years of Our Lives," *New York Times,* May 26, 2001.

10. Elaine Sciolino, "Iranian Cinema: Expressions of a Country's Soul," *New York Times,* March 11, 2001.

11. Steven Brill, "Rewind: Crack in Great Wall," *Brill's Content,* June 1999.

12. Suzanne Kapner, "Agencies Say British Regulators Are Too Quick to Ban Ads," *New York Times,* January 4, 2002.

13. John Sawyer, "Soap Operas Are Proving Helpful in Informing Public," *St. Louis Post-Dispatch,* December 1, 2002.

14. Rachael L. Swarns, "A Hit Song Puts Ethnic Tensions at Center Stage," *New York Times,* June 10, 2002.

15. Milton Rokeach, *Beliefs, Attitudes, and Values: A Theory of Organization and Change* (San Francisco: Jossey-Bass, 1968), p. 113.

16. Hong Cheng and John C. Schweitzer, "Cultural Values Reflected in Chinese and U.S. Television Commercials," *Journal of Advertising Research* 36, no. 3 (May/June 1996): 27.

17. Charles R. Wiles, Judith A. Wiles, and Anders Tjernlund, "The Ideology of Advertising: The United States and Sweden," *Journal of Advertising Research* 36, no. 3 (May/June 1996): 57.

18. "No Sex Please, We're British. Trends," *New Media Age,* December 6, 2001, p. 16.

19. Barbara Friedman, interview by Art Silverblatt, St. Louis, Missouri, February 8, 2003.

20. Marker cited in Hohenadel, "Paris for Real vs. Paris on Film.

21. Ed Stoddard, "South Africans Laugh at 'Survivors,'" *New York Times,* November 28, 2001.

22. Sciolino, "Iranian Cinema: Expressions of a Country's Soul."

23. Norimitsu Onishi, "Globalization of Beauty Makes Slimness Trendy," *New York Times,* October 3, 2002.

24. Berle Francis, interview by Art Silverblatt, St. Louis, Missouri, March 9, 2003.

25. Robert McChesney, address at Webster University, St. Louis, Missouri, February 2003.

26. Alan Riding, "Filmmakers Seek Protection from U.S. Dominance," *New York Times,* February 5, 2003.

27. Mark Balnaves, James Donald, and Stephanie Hemelryk Donald, *The Penguin Atlas of Media and Information* (New York: Penguin Putnam, 2001), p. 46.

28. Columbia Records—News, www.columbiarecords.com/news/pressreleases/0509b2001.html.

29. Edward Rothstein, "Why American Pop Culture Spreads," *New York Times,* June 2, 2001.

30. Sony A. Ross, "Survey Says: Foreigners Like U.S. Culture But Not Policies," Associated Press, Washington, December 4, 2002.

31. Alexis Bloom, "Television Comes to Bhutan," *New York Times,* May 13, 2001.

32. Simon Romero, "When Villages Go Global," *New York Times,* April 23, 2000.

33. Bloom, "Television Comes to Bhutan."

34. Cowell, "What Can the New Economy Do for Places Without an Old One?"

35. Neal Gabler, "The World Still Watches," *New York Times,* January 9, 2003.

36. Suzanne Kapner, "U.S. TV Shows Losing Potency Around World," *New York Times,* January 2, 2003.

37. www.weforum.org/site/homepublic.nsf/Content/Global+Digital+Divide+Initiative.

38. Romero, "When Villages Go Global."

39. Jane Perlez, "Boy Kisses Girl: That's Sweet, and Sensational!" *New York Times,* June 11, 2002.

40. Merle E. Ratner, "Winning Hearts and Minds: Combating Cultural Imperialism to Defend Independence," Summer Seminar, July 20–21, 2001, Université de Provence, Aix-en-Provence, France.

41. "Communism, Capitalism and Cocktails: Cuban Photographer Sues Over Smirnoff's Use of Che," *Toronto Star,* August 9, 2000.

42. Cheng and Schweitzer, "Cultural Values Reflected in Chinese and U.S. Television Commercials," 27.

43. Bloom, "Television Comes to Buhtan."

44. A.O. Scott, "Lifting the Veil on a Far-Off World," *New York Times,* November 23, 2001.

45. William B. Helmreich, *The Things They Say Behind Your Back: Stereotypes and the Myths Behind Them* (New Brunswick, NJ: Transaction, 1983), p. 44.

46. Akkad cited in Laurie Goodstein, "Hollywood Now Plays Cowboys and Arabs," *New York Times,* November 1, 1998.

Chapter 4. Framework

1. "Israeli Leader Accepts U.S. Peace Plan," *St. Louis Post-Dispatch,* May 24, 2003.

2. "Sharon Gives Plan for Mideast Peace Qualified Support," *New York Times,* May 24, 2003.

3. Daoud Kuttab, "The Arab TV Wars," *New York Times,* April 6, 2003.

4. Sharon Waxman, "Arab TV's Strong Signal: The al-Jazeera Network Offers News the Mideast Never Had Before, and Views That Are All Too Common," *Washington Post,* December 4, 2001.

5. Mumme cited in Erica Goode, "Babies Pick Up Emotional Clues From TV, Experts Find," *New York Times,* January 21, 2003.

6. Thomas L. Friedman, "Glasnost in the Gulf," *New York Times,* February 27, 2001.

7. Neal Gabler, "The Nation: The Illusion of Entertainment; Just Like a Movie, But It's Not," *New York Times,* August 4, 2002.

8. Sandra Basso, interview by research assistant Anne Bader, St. Louis, Missouri, May 16, 2003.

9. *Bowling for Columbine,* dir. Michael Moore, United Artists, 2002.

10. Nohr cited in Claire Murphy, "How British TV Is Winning a World," *Marketing,* June 22, 2000, p. 19.

11. Elaine Sciolino, "Iranian Cinema: Expressions of a Country's Soul," *New York Times,* March 11, 2001.

12. Rollo May, *The Cry for Myth* (New York: W.W. Norton, 1991), p. 54.

13. Daniel Chandler, "Semiotics for Beginners," www.aber.ac.uk/.

14. Rick Lyman, "Suddenly, It's Easier to Find a Hero Than a Villain," *New York Times,* December 22, 2002.

15. Alan Cowell, "Silliness as a Balm; Hogan! Germans Need You," *New York Times,* July 20, 1997.

16. Rick Lyman, "Job Openings in Hollywood: Heroes Wanted," *New York Times,* August 4, 2002.

17. Gardner cited in Ibid.

18. Andrews cited in John Sawyer, "Soap Operas Are Proving Helpful in Informing Public," *St. Louis Post-Dispatch,* December 1, 2002.

19. Murphy, "How British TV Is Winning a World," p. 19.

20. Sciolino, "Iranian Cinema: Expressions of a Country's Soul."

21. John Cawelti "Myth, Symbol, and Formula," *Journal of Popular Culture* 8 (1974): 13

22. Basinger cited in Lyman, "Job Openings in Hollywood: Heroes Wanted."

23. Gardner cited in Ibid.

24. Stuart Klawans, "Glimpses of China on Film Never Seen in China," *New York Times,* February 18, 2001.

Chapter 5. Production Elements

1. Kathy Corley, interviewed by Art Silverblatt, St. Louis, Missouri, March 8, 2003.

2. Bernard Weinraub, "Pioneer of a Beat Is Still Riffing for His Due," *New York Times,* February 16, 2003.

3. Corley, interview.

4. Elaine Sciolino, "Iranian Cinema: Expressions of a Country's Soul," *New York Times,* March 11, 2001.

5. George Gerbner, in *The Killing Screens: Media and the Culture of Violence*, dir. Sut Jhally, Media Education Foundation, 1994.

6. Wallace S. Baldinger, *The Visual Arts* (New York: Holt, Rinehart, and Winston, 1960), p. 16.

7. Craig S. Smith, "Beware of Cross-Cultural Faux Pas in China," *New York Times*, April 30, 2002.

8. Thomas Wolfe, *Look Homeward Angel*, London: Scribner & Sons, 1957, p. xiv.

9. Caryn James, "British Take a Blunter Approach to War News," *New York Times*, November 9, 2001.

10. "Most Underreported Humanitarian Stories," Doctors Without Borders/ Médecins Sans Frontières, www.doctorswithoutborders.org/publications/reports/ 2002/top10_2002.html.

11. Julian Borger and Alex Bellos, "US 'Gave the Nod' to Venezuelan Coup," *The Guardian* (London), April 17, 2002.

12. Ibid.; Katty Kay, "Bush Team Met Chavez Coup Leaders," *The Times* (London), April 17, 2002.

13. Agence France Presse, "US Military Attache Was with Venezuela Coup Planners Beforehand," April 18, 2002.

14. David Adams, "Venezuelan Coup Plotter 'in Miami,'" *The Times* (London), April 24, 2002.

15. Fouad Ajami, "What the Muslim World Is Watching," *New York Times*, November 18, 2001.

16. Greg Philo, "Television News and Audience Understanding of War, Conflict and Disaster," *Journalism Studies* 3, no. 2 (April 2002): 173.

17. Laura Stuhlman, unpublished paper, November 2002.

18. Ajami, "What the Muslim World Is Watching."

19. Ibid.

20. Theroux cited in Richard Critchfield, *An American Looks at Britain* (New York: Doubleday, 1990), p. 242.

21. Ivelisse DeJesus, "New Collegiate Dictionary Truly Reflects the Times," *Star-Ledger* (Newark, New Jersey), January 6, 2001.

22. Marc Lacey, "To the Beat of a Hit Song, the New Kenya Sends Spirits off the Charts," *New York Times*, February 16, 2003.

23. William Safire, "Movable Modifier," *New York Times Magazine*, November 18, 2001.

24. Patrick E. Tyler, "As Crisis Deepens, Mubarak Finds Himself on the Sidelines," *New York Times*, April 2, 2002.

25. William Safire, "Regime Changes," *New York Times Magazine*, March 10, 2002.

26. C.J. Chivers, "Islamists in Iraq Offer a Tour of 'Poison Factory' Cited by Powell," *New York Times*, February 9, 2003.

27. Carlotta Gall, "Marines at U.S. Embassy Kill 3 Afghan Soldiers in Incident Called Error," *New York Times*, May 22, 2003.

28. "Aussie Jets Clear Path to Baghdad," *Herald Sun* (Melbourne, Australia), April 5, 2003.

29. Eleanor and Michel Levieux, "No, Chirac Didn't Say 'Shut Up,'" *New York Times*, February 23, 2003.

30. Lacey, "To the Beat of a Hit Song."

31. Susan Sachs, "Anti-Semitism Is Deepening Among Muslims; Hateful Images of Jews Are Embedded in Islamic Popular Culture," *New York Times,* April 27, 2002.

32. Deirdre Shesgreen, "World Press Is Showing Different, More Graphic War," *St. Louis Post-Dispatch,* April 6, 2003.

33. Barbara Friedman, interview by Nikolai Zlobin, St. Louis, Missouri, April 22, 2003.

34. "International Conflex Re-brands for 2003 show," Exhibition Bulletin, www.e-bulletin.com/.

35. "Taiwan Bike Makers Drive Export Sales with New Logo," *Taiwan Economic News* (Taipei), October 2, 2002.

36. "Cher Selects Margo Chase to Create Identity for Farewell Tour," *Mark Business Wire,* August 28, 2002.

37. Sarah Boxer, "A New Poland, No Joke," *New York Times,* December 1, 2002.

38. Thomas Lee, "Schnucks Is the First in the Area to Offer Irradiated Meat," *St. Louis Post-Dispatch,* January 13, 2003.

39. Organic Consumers Association, www.organicconsumers.org/Irrad/EPA-radura.cfm.

40. "New Logo to Boost Malayawata Image," *The Star* (Malaysia), September 11, 2002.

41. Christina Michelmore, "Old Pictures in New Frames: Images of Islam and Muslims in Post World War II American Political Cartoons," *Journal of American and Comparative Cultures* 23, no. 4 (Winter 2000): 37.

42. David L. Paletz, "Post–September 11 Cartoons in Arab Media Skewer the United States, Article Says," AScribe Newswire, 2000.

43. JHB Live: Kultcha Uncut, www.jhblive.co.za/index.htm.

44. Michael Colton, "Newsbreak Sonata," *Brill's Content* (July/August 1999).

45. Ibid.

46. Philpott cited in Dale G. Leathers, *Successful Nonverbal Communication: Principles and Applications,* 3rd ed. (Boston: Allyn and Bacon, 1997), p. 6.

47. Paul Farhi, "Everybody Wins," *American Journalism Review* (April 2003), www.ajr.org.

48. Larry A. Samovar and Richard E. Porter, *Communication Between Cultures,* 2nd ed. (Belmont, CA: Wadsworth, 1995), p. 193.

49. Smith, "Beware of Cross-Cultural Faux Pas in China."

50. Ibid., p. 191.

51. Leathers, *Successful Nonverbal Communication,* p. 42.

52. Desmond Morris, *Bodytalk* (New York: Crown Trade Paperbacks, 1994), p. 189.

53. Li He, interview by research assistant Anne Bader, St. Louis, Missouri, May 16, 2003.

54. Leathers, *Successful Nonverbal Communication,* pp. 77–78.

55. William V. Ruch, *International Handbook of Corporate Communications* (Jefferson, NC: McFarland, 1989), p. 242.

56. Smith, "Beware of Cross-Cultural Faux Pas in China."

57. "Read or Listen, But Don't Look; Eyes Will Lie, Says TV Researcher," *St. Louis Post-Dispatch,* February 2, 1995.

58. Samovar and Porter, *Communication Between Cultures,* p. 200.

59. Seva Gunitsky, interview by Nikolai Zlobin, April 3, 2003, Washington, DC.

Chapter 6. Analysis of National Media Systems

1. "The Annual Survey of Press Freedom," Freedom House, www.freedomhouse. org/pfs2002/pfs2002.pdf.

2. "Press Freedom Index," Reporters Without Borders, www.rsf.fr/article. php3?id_article=4116.

3. Ibid.

4. Ibid.

5. Joseph Kahn, "China Has World's Tightest Internet Censorship, Study Finds," *New York Times,* December 4, 2002.

6. Erik Eckholm, "In China, So Many Liberties, So Little Freedom," *New York Times,* January 3, 1999.

7. Elisabeth Rosenthal, "China Struggles to Ride Herd on Ever More Errant Media," *New York Times,* March 17, 2001.

8. Marc Lacey, "Tanzania Sees AIDS Lurking Between the Lines," *New York Times,* August 22, 2002.

9. Jennifer S. Lee, "Twenty Journalists Slain in 2002, Fewest in 17 Years, Group Says," *New York Times,* April 1, 2003.

10. Ibid.

11. Nazila Fathi, "Taboo Surfing: Click Here for Iran," *New York Times,* August 4, 2002.

12. Rachel L. Swarns, "Zimbabwe Proposes Keeping Reporters Out," *New York Times,* December 1, 2001.

13. Rosenthal, "China Struggles to Ride Herd on Ever More Errant Media."

14. Eckholm, "In China, So Many Liberties, So Little Freedom."

15. Seth Mydans, "Burmese Editor's Code: Winks and Little Hints," *New York Times,* June 24, 2001.

16. Kirtley cited in "Critics Say New Rule Limits Access to Records," *New York Times,* Editorial, February 27, 2002.

17. "Press Freedom Index," Reporters Without Borders.

18. Barbara Friedman, e-mail to Art Silverblatt, April 28, 2002.

19. "Critics Say New Rule Limits Access to Records."

20. Aleksander Grigoryev, interview by Art Silverblatt, Washington, DC, November 17, 2001.

21. Michael Wines, "Last Private Russian TV Network Is Put Off Air, and Suspicions Fly," *New York Times,* January 23, 2002.

22. Bill Kovach and Tom Rosenstiel, "All News Media Inc.," *New York Times,* January 7, 2003.

23. "A New Media Law," *Russia Journal,* Editorial, April 20–26, 2001, p. 108.

24. Alan B. Albarran and Sylvia M. Chan-Olmstead, *Global Media Economics* (Ames: Iowa State University Press, 1998).

25. Rick Lyman, "China Is Warming to Hollywood's Glow; Before Big Profits, Hurdles Remain," *New York Times,* September 18, 2002.

26. Sabrina Ta Vernise, "Russia Battles Video Piracy; But the Pirates Shoot Back," *New York Times,* December 2, 2002.

27. Ibid.

28. "China Says 40 Million Discs Will Be Crushed in New Piracy Crackdown," *Agence France Presse*, August 13, 2002.

29. Elaine Sciolino, "Iranian Cinema: Expressions of a Country's Soul," *New York Times*, March 11, 2001.

30. Alison Langley, "World Health Meeting Approves Treaty to Discourage Smoking," *New York Times*, May 22, 2003.

31. Central Intelligence Agency, *The World Factbook: China—People*, www.cia.gov/cia/publications/factbook/geos/ch.html#People.

32. Roula Khalaf, "Religious Backlash Leads to Sacking of Saudi Editor," *Financial Times* (London), May 28, 2003, p. 13.

33. William Safire, "On Language: Words at War," *New York Times*, September 30, 2001.

34. Verlyn Klinkenborg, "Between the Lines of an Iraqi Letter," *New York Times*, November 16, 2002.

35. Berle Francis, interview by Art Silverblatt, St. Louis, Missouri, November 4, 2002.

36. "UN Commission on Population and Development to Meet from 31 March to 4 April; Theme—Population, Education and Development," Communications Ltd., PRESSWIRE, March 28, 2003, http://80–web.lexis-nexis.com.library3.webster.edu/universe/document?_m=361c5476ca98159157c4ff6d4aac3b28&_docnum=5&wchp=dGLbVlz-lSlzV&_md5=76932ae902aef47eac87e7b43d8feeae.

37. Mona Charen, "Who Are We?" *Jewish World Review*, December 24, 2002, www.jewishworldreview.com/cols.

38. Paul Recer, "Where in the World Are We? Young People Have No Clue," *Chicago Sun-Times*, November 21, 2002, p. 4.

39. Mark Balnaves, James Donald, and Stephanie Hemelryk Donald, *The Penguin Atlas of Media and Information* (New York: Penguin Putnam, 2001), p. 17.

40. *The Quill* (November/December 1991).

41. Paul Krugman, "Citizen Conrad's Friends," *New York Times*, December 23, 2003.

42. William E. François, *Mass Media Law and Regulation*, 2nd ed. (Columbus, OH: Grid, 1978), p. 137–38.

43. Suzanne Daley, "A New Book Offers French an Earful of Politics," *New York Times*, October 21, 2001.

Chapter 7. Case Studies: National Media Systems

China

1. Constitution of the People's Republic of China, Article 22.

2. "AOL Gains Cable Rights in China by Omitting News, Sex and Violence," *New York Times*, October 29, 2001.

3. "About 820 Newspapers and Periodicals Ceased Publication," *People's Daily* (Beijing), December 25, 2000.

4. See the official Web site of the Chinese Internet Network Information Center at www.cnnic.org.cn.

5. Ibid., "PRC Interim Regulation of the Computer Information Network and the Internet," Articles 3 to 12.

6. Ibid., "Regulation of Internet Information Service," Article 15.
7. Ibid., "Interim Regulation of Internet News," Article 6.

Egypt

1. Said Essoulami, "The Press in the Arab World: 100 Years of Suppressed Freedom," www.cmfmena.org/magazine/features/100 years.htm.
2. John Merrill, *Global Journalism,* 3rd ed. (New York: Longman, 1995), p. 140.
3. IFLA/FAIFE *World Report: Libraries and Intellectual Freedom— Egypt,* May 8, 1999, www.faife.dk/.
4. In fact, Arabization of the Internet has been a critical factor in developing information systems in Egypt. But with the increasing number of users, companies are responding. The Arabic version of Windows 98 was introduced only five months after the introduction of the English version.
5. *Information Please Almanac,* Egypt, www.infoplease.com/ipa/A0107484. html. See also Central Intelligence Agency, *The World Factbook, 2003,* Egypt, www.cia.gov/cia/publications/factbook/goes/eg.html.
6. BBC News, *World: Middle East: Country Profile: Egypt.* Online at http://news.bbc.co. See Merrill, *Global Journalism.* Also see Tina van der Heyden, *Egypt Media Report,* http://journ.ru.ac.za/amd/egypt.htm.
7. Based on 1995 circulation figures, for every 1,000 individuals, there are 312 radio receivers, 126 television receivers, and only 67 newspapers. See World Association of Newspapers, www.wan-press.org.
8. Douglas Boyd, "A New 'Line in the Sand' for the Media," *Media Studies Journal* 7, no. 4 (Fall 1993): 134–138.
9. *Information Please Almanac,* Egypt. See also A. Mokhtar Hallouda and Adeeb Ghonaimy, The Arab Countries: Economic and Social Context 2002, www.unesco. org/webworld/wcir/en/pdf_report/chap14.pdf.
10. Television was introduced in Egypt in 1960.
11. Heba Saleh, "Clouded View of Grand Design: The Company Aims to Maintain Egypt's Dominance of Arab Film Production, But Analysts Are Nervous of Its Public Sector Origins," *The Financial Times Limited,* May 9, 2001.
12. "First Egyptian Private Channel on Nilesat 102," November 4, 2000, www.arabicnews.com/ansub/Daily/Day/001104/2000110429.html. See also "Private Media Push and Pull," *Al-Ahram Weekly,* February 24–March 1, 2000.
13. Steve Negus, "Letter from Cairo," *The Nation,* November 19, 2001.
14. Rick Zednick, "Perspective on War: Inside Al-Jazeera," *Columbia Journalism Review* (March/April 2002), p. 47.
15. Edmund Ghareeb, "New Media and the Information Revolution in the Arab World: An Assessment," *Middle East Journal* 54, no. 3 (2000): 395. Also see Jon B. Alterman, "Counting Nodes and Counting Noses: Understanding New Media in the Middle East," *Middle East Journal* 54, no. 3 (2000): 355.

India

1. The constantly changing figures, cited throughout this monograph, are taken from various sources published recently. See the chapter on India in Shelton

Gunaratne, ed., *Handbook of Media in Asia* (London: Sage, 2000). Also see Gyanesh Kudaisya, "India's New Mantra: The Internet," *Current History* 100, no. 645 (April 2001): 162; Mark Landler, "A Glut of Cable TV in India," *New York Times,* March 23, 2001; and David Page, *Satellites Over South Asia: Broadcasting, Culture and the Public Interest* (New Delhi: Sage, 2001).

2. Kristen Guida, "Press Freedom in 2001," Freedom House, www. freedomhouse.org/.

3. Sunanda K. Dutta-Ray, "Country Report: India," *Media and Democracy in Asia: An AMIC Compilation* (Singapore: Asian Media Information and Communication Center, 2000), pp. 46–65.

4. "India Tunes In," *Asiaweek,* August 13, 2001, p. 183.

5. Sultan Shahin, "India's Print Media Make Their Own Headlines," *Asia Times,* January 19, 2002, www.atimes.com/ind-pak/DA19Df03.html.

6. UNESCO, "Television Transnationalization: Europe and Asia," UNESCO Reports and Papers No. 109, Paris: UNESCO, 1994.

7. "Most Asian Video Nets Focus on Music," *Billboard,* February 17, 2001, p. 1.

8. Prasun Sonwalkar, "India: The Makings of Little Cultural/Media Imperialism," *Gazette* 63, no. 6: (2001) 505–519.

9. Ramesh Sehgal, "Star TV Eyes Big Investment in India," *Multichannel,* 21, no. 40 (2000): 46. See also Ashok Nag, "BBC World Unspools Its Digital Service," *Variety,* January 7, 2002, p. 42.

10. Vivek Goenka, "Journalism in India: A Changing Perspective," *Editor and Publisher,* June 22, 1996, p. 68.

11. Manu Joseph, "A Sticky Wicket for Tehelka.com," *Wired,* May 12, 2001, www.wired.com/news/politics/0,1283,43677,00.html.

Jamaica

1. Ranganath H.K., *Using Folk Entertainment to Promote National Development.* UNESCO Population Communication Manual, 1980, p. 15.

South Africa

1. Kenyan G. Tomaselli, Ruth Tomaselli, and Johan Muller, *Narrating the Crisis: Hegemony and the South African Press: Addressing the Nation* (Johannesburg: Richard Lyon, 1987), p. 76.

2. William A. Hachten and C. Anthony Giffard, *Total Onslaught: The South African Press Under Attack* (Johannesburg: Macmillan, 1984), p. 113.

3. Paul Y. Burns, *Media Law* (Durban, South Africa: Butterworths, 1990), pp. vii–viii.

4. D. Wigston, "A South African Media Map," in *Media Studies,* vol. 1: *Institutions, Theories and Issues,* ed. P.J. Fourie (Lansdowne, South Africa: Juta, 2001), p. 70.

5. L.M. Oosthuizen, "Media Ownership and Control," in *Media Studies,* ibid., p. 176.

6. Ibid., p. 175.

7. Ibid., p. 178.

8. Wigston, "A South African Media Map," p. 8.

9. Tomaselli, Tomaselli, and Muller, *Narrating the Crisis,* p. 73.

10. Wigston, "A South African Media Map," p. 12.
11. Ibid., p. 12.
12. Ibid., p. 14.
13. Ibid., pp. 26–27.
14. Oosthuizen, "Media Ownership and Control," p. 140.
15. Ibid., pp. 141–142.
16. Ibid., p. 144.
17. Wigston, "A South African Media Map," p. 98.

Chapter 8. International Advertising

1. Patricia Thorp, "Growth of Latin American Economies Exceeds World Average," International Advertising Association, Thorp & Company, 2000, www.iaaglobal.org.

2. "Nielsen Media Research—International—Predicts Second-Half Rebound in Global Ad Sales, Expects Full-Year Growth of 2%," *Business Wire*, May 31, 2002.

3. Ibid.

4. Laurel Wentz, "P&G and GM Lead Global Ad Spending; Annual Ranking Shows Top 100 Marketers' Outlays Declined by 2.6% in 2001," *Advertising Age*, November 11, 2002, p. 28.

5. Ibid.

6. Thorp, "Growth of Latin American Economies Exceeds World Average."

7. Sarah Boxer, "A New Poland, No Joke," *New York Times*, December 1, 2002.

8. Baiyi Xu, "The Role of Advertising in China," working paper, Department of Advertising, University of Illinois at Urbana-Champaign, 1989.

9. The International Advertising Association, www.iaaglobal.org/about_iaa.asp? articleID=15&openNav=1.

10. Hong Cheng and John C. Schweitzer, "Cultural Values Reflected in Chinese and U.S. Television Commercials," *Journal of Advertising Research* 36, no. 3 (May/June 1996): 27.

11. Ibid.

12. Fouad Ajami, "What the Muslim World Is Watching," *New York Times*, November 18, 2001.

13. Morgan Anderson Consulting, "How Marketers Are Refocusing to Protect and Enhance Their Companies' Brand Assets," 2000, www.morgananderson.com

14. George P. Murdock, "The Common Denominator of Cultures," in *Science of Man in the World Crisis*, ed. Ralph Linton (New York: Columbia University Press, 1945), pp. 125–42.

15. W.L. James and J.S. Hill, "International Advertising Messages: To Adapt or Not to Adapt," *Journal of Advertising Research* 3, no. 3 (June/July 1991): 65.

16. Nielson Media Research, International www.nielsenmedia.com.

17. Patricia Winters Lauro, "In an Industry Where Conglomerates Roam, the Small Agency Has a Good Shot, Some Say," *New York Times*, December 23, 2002.

18. Stuart Elliott, "Ready or Not, the Future Is Big and Bundled," *New York Times*, November 13, 2000.

19. Nielson Media Research International.

20. Wentz, "P&G and GM Lead Global Ad Spending," p. 28.

21. Elliott, "Ready or Not, the Future Is Big and Bundled."

22. Mark Balnaves, James Donald, and Stephanie Hemelryk Donald, *The Penguin Atlas of Media and Information* (New York: Penguin Putnam, 2001), p. 70.

23. Cheng and Schweitzer, "Cultural Values Reflected in Chinese and U.S. Television Commercials."

24. Michel Marriott, "Playing with Consumers," *New York Times,* August 30, 2001.

25. John L. Graham and Michael A. Kamins, "Content Analysis of German and Japanese Advertising in Print Media from Indonesia, Spain, and the United States Print Media," *Journal of Advertising* 2, no. 2 (June 1993): 5.

26. John F. Sherry Jr. and Eduardo G. Camargo, "May Your Life Be Marvelous: English Language Labelling and the Semiotics of Japanese Promotion," *Journal of Consumer Research,* September 14, 1987, pp. 174–88.

27. Charles R. Wiles, Judith A. Wiles, and Anders Tjernlund, "The Ideology of Advertising: The United States and Sweden," *Journal of Advertising Research* 36, no. 3 (May/June 1996): 57.

28. Barbara Mueller, *International Advertising* (Belmont, CA: Wadsworth, 1996), p. 117.

29. Hans G. Meissner, "A Structural Comparison of Japanese and German Marketing Strategies," *Irish Marketing Review* 1 (Spring 1986): 21–31.

30. "Full of Western Promise," *The Economist,* November 14, 1992, pp. 83–84.

31. Bernd H. Schmitt and Yigand Pan, "Managing Corporate and Brand Identities in the Asia-Pacific Region," *California Management Review* (Summer 1994): 32–48.

32. John F. Sherry Jr. and Eduardo G. Camargo, "May Your Life Be Marvelous: English Language Labelling and the Semiotics of Japanese Promotion."

33. John H. Grizzell, unpublished paper, October 2000.

34. "And What Does It Mean in Farsi," *Time Magazine,* November 26, 2001.

35. "Full of Western Promise," pp. 83–84.

About the Authors
and Contributors

Art Silverblatt is professor of communications and journalism at Webster University, St. Louis, Missouri. He earned his PhD in 1980 from Michigan State University. He is the author of *Media Literacy: Keys to Interpreting Media Messages* (1995, 2001), and coauthor of *The Dictionary of Media Literacy* (1997) and *Approaches to Media Literacy: A Handbook* (1999).

Nikolai Zlobin is a former professor of history at Moscow State University and is currently director and senior fellow of the Russia Program at the International Center in Washington, D.C. He earned an MA and PhD from Moscow State University, and is the author of ten books and more than 200 academic articles. He writes a regular column for the Russian daily *Izvestia* and has been a special correspondent for a number of other Russian periodicals. His opinion pieces have appeared in the *New York Times*, the *Los Angeles Times*, the *International Herald Tribune*, and the *Chicago Tribune*, among other publications.

Contributors to Chapter 7

Dharma N. Adhikari is working on his PhD at the Missouri School of Journalism, specializing in Asian media. He has worked as a journalist in Nepal for over a decade.

Natalia Angheli is senior consultant for the Independent Journalism Center, a leading Moldovan media development nongovernmental organization. She has a PhD in linguistics from the University of Bucharest in Romania and an MA in journalism from the University of Missouri. Dr. Angheli has lectured at Moldovan universities and has reported for the Associated Press and other Western media organizations.

Maretha de Waal, DLitt et Phil, is director of the Centre for Gender Studies at the University of Pretoria in South Africa.

Shahira S. Fahmy, PhD, has worked for seven years in communications in the Middle East and in Western Europe and currently is a faculty member at Southern Illinois University at Carbondale, specializing in international and visual communication.

Berle Francis is a business communication specialist who has worked as a journalist in Jamaica and in Montreal, Canada. She has held various positions, including director of public relations for Jamaica's Urban Development Corporation and vice president of Peter Martin Associates, and is the founder of Berl Francis and Company, Ltd. Jamaica's marketing and communication fraternity has twice named her Public Relations Personality of the Year.

Aleksander Grigoryev was a journalist in Russia and currently is editor of Washington ProFile International Information Agency in Washington, D.C.

Geoff Lealand is senior lecturer in screen and media studies at the University of Waikato in Hamilton, New Zealand.

Takashi Yasuda earned a PhD in sociology at Touhoku University in Japan. He is author of *The Reading of P. Bourdieu's Sociology: The Restoration to Reality of Social Action and Subjectivity* (1998).

Juyan Zhang, earned a PhD from the Missouri School of Journalism and is an assistant professor in the communications department of Monmouth University. He is a former reporter and editor of Guangzhou Daily Press Group, China's first and largest press group. He received his ML and BL in international relations respectively from Beijing University and Renmin University of China.

Index

ABC, 30, 31, 37
Accessibility, media. *See* Media access
Ada Apa Dnegan Cinta? (Indonesia),
    73
Adelphia Communications, 36
Advertisement
    "advergames," 229
    affective response, 234–35
    audience relations, 225–27
    Canada, 234
    China, 67, 168, 223–24, 227, 228,
        231–33*t*, 234
    connotative image, 237
    consumerism, 225, 230, 235
    cultural context, 65, 67, 74, 229–30
    cultural universals, 225–26
    culture-specific meanings, 234–37
    cumulative message, 230
    defined, 223
    framework, 82
    geographical elements, 154
    Germany, 226, 229–30
    global growth, 223
    "global" strategy, 226–27
    government regulation, 228
    Great Britain, 65, 67
    humor utilization, 234, 235
    image promotion, 223–24, 230, 235,
        237
    individualism, 234
    information provision, 224
    Internet, 228–29
    Japan, 194, 229–30, 234, 235, 236
    latent function, 225–27
    lifestyle formation, 225
    lines of inquiry, 237–39

Advertisement *(continued)*
    localization approach, 226–27
    manifest function, 224
    media literacy analysis, 243–44,
        245–46, 247
    metonymy, 111
    microcasting strategy, 228–29
    modernity, 230, 234
    Moldova, 197
    neologisms, 236–37
    neologistic image, 237
    ownership patterns, 227–28
    political function, 142, 223–24
    product identification, 224
    production elements, 111, 235–37
    profit motivation, 227–28
    regulatory systems, 152
    Russia, 205, 206, 237
    sexuality, 234
    South Africa, 217
    Soviet Union, 227
    standardization approach, 225–27
    symbolic representations, 236
    terrorism impact, 31
    Thailand, 226, 235, 237
    translation, 235–37
    transnational media conglomerates, 31,
        227–28
    United States, 67, 223, 224–28, 230,
        231–33*t*, 234, 235–37
    Western culture values, 224–27,
        231–33*t*
    Western culture worldview, 230
    word choice, 235–37
Advertising Standards Authority (Great
    Britain), 65

273

Cultural context *(continued)*
cultural sensibility, 65–66
editing, 99
film, 67–68, 69, 70, 73, 77
Internet, 71, 72–73
lines of inquiry, 78–79
media literacy analysis, 251–53
media reflection
attitudes, 66, 68–69
cultural script, 68
ideology, 69–73
imperialism, 69–73
mythic reality, 68
myths, 67–69
popular culture, 66–73
preoccupations, 67
values, 66–67
music, 66, 69
radio, 66
stereotypes, 76–77
television, 68, 69, 70, 72, 76, 77
Western culture impact
advertisement, 224–27, 231–33*t*
attitudes, 68–69
class conflict, 72–73
gender conflict, 71
generational conflict, 70–71
urban-rural conflict, 71–72
Western culture values, 224–27,
231–33*t*
Western culture worldview
achievement, 75
advertisement, 230
consumerism, 74, 230
cumulative message, 69–70
embedded messages, 73–74
globalization, 74
individualism, 75–76
latent message, 73–76
modernity, 74–75
progress, 74
Cultural goods, 39
Cultural hybridity, 29
Cultural imperialism
defined, 69
India, 182–83

Cultural imperialism *(continued)*
Western culture
impact of, 68–69, 70–73
worldview, 69–73
Cultural myths
defined, 67
media influence, 68–69
media reinforcement, 68
mythic reality, 68
narrative elements, 84–85
popular culture, 67–69
Cultural preoccupations
connotative image, 109
defined, 67
genre, 87–88
media influence, 68–69
media reinforcement, 68
popular culture, 67
Cultural script, 68
Cultural sensibility
defined, 65
editing, 103–4
media impact, 65–66
media literacy analysis,
250–51
message interpretation, 65
translation, 107–8
Cultural Survival, 73
Cultural taboos
Egypt, 174, 177
Japan, 193–94
Russia, 211
Cultural universals, 225–26
Cultural values
media influence, 68–69
media reinforcement, 68
narrative elements, 85–86
popular culture, 66–67
See also Cultural context
Cumulative message
advertisement, 230
defined, 8
media literacy approach, 8–9
narrative elements, 83–84
Western culture worldview,
69–70